ɪna

In the shadow of history

MANCHESTER
1824

Manchester University Press

In the shadow of history

Sinn Féin, 1926–70

AGNÈS MAILLOT

Manchester University Press

Published by Manchester University Press
Altrincham Street, Manchester M1 7JA, UK
www.manchesteruniversitypress.co.uk

British Library Cataloguing-in-Publication Data is available

ISBN 978 0 7190 8489 8 hardback
ISBN 978 1 5261 5295 4 paperback

First published by Manchester University Press in hardback 2015

This edition published 2021

Typeset by Koinonia, Manchester

To Bairbre

Contents

Note on referencing

As this book relies heavily on primary sources, it was decided to implement a referencing system that would be clear and accurate without being cumbersome for the reader.

All the newspaper articles quoted were found on the Irish Times Digital Archives and the Irish Newspaper Archives websites. The most often quoted are the *Irish Times, Irish Independent, Irish Press* and *Sunday Independent*, all abbreviated in the text as *IT, II, IP* and *SI*, followed by the date of the article in day/month/year format. The same system was adopted for *An Phoblacht (AP)* and *United Irishman (UI)* followed by month and year of publication. The names of less frequently used newspapers and magazines are given in full.

The National Archives files come from three different sources: the Four Courts, the Department of the Taoiseach and the Department of Justice.

The files from the Four Courts relate to the documents gathered for the hearing of the Sinn Féin Funds Case (Funds Case) in 1948, which can be sub-divided into three categories: the Sinn Féin Standing Committee minute books, referenced by date (SC, day/month/year); the testimonies of those called to the witness stand, referenced with the name of witness – for example (De Valera, Witness Statement, 1948, page number); and all the other documents, such as letters, minutes of other meetings, extracts of newspaper articles, which are to be found in the files; the nature of the document is specified within the body of the text and referenced in specific terms – for example (letter from Kathleen Lynn to de Valera, 07/11/22, Funds Case, 1948).

The files from the Department of the Taoiseach include all the official documents that were used in preparation of the drafting of the Sinn Féin Funds Bill (1947) (memos, consultation with other departments, Dáil debates), as well as newspaper reports and the final text of the decision of the High Court. These files are the Sinn Féin Funds: Control and Disposal of (1941), Disposal of Certain Sums of the Old Sinn Féin Organisation (1946), Sinn Féin Funds

Disposal (six different files ranging from 1941 to 1956). For the purpose of clarity, the nature of the document quoted has been specified followed by the date –for example (Memo from Wyse Power to de Valera, 12/11/41, Dept of Taoiseach, file number). The different archive files used are all listed in the bibliography.

The files from the Department of Justice include Garda reports from officers on surveillance duty at several Sinn Féin public meetings, Ard Fheiseanna, and other events organised by the party. These files, which range from 1923 to 1950, also contain Sinn Féin internal documents such as minutes and agendas, copies of newsletters, financial accounts, etc. The nature of the document used is clearly indicated in the text and referenced as (Garda report, day/month/year).

The UCD Archives hold the Mary MacSwiney papers, which are a collection of documents of various nature, ranging from her personal correspondence with political and religious leaders to memos and documents, covering the period of her political engagement from 1914 to her death in 1941. These have been referenced as (UCD, MacSwiney, date).

Finally, the Sean O'Mahony papers, held in the National Library of Ireland, contain a rich body of documents of different types, such as newsletters, memos, newspaper articles, although they are for the most part concerned with other Republican organisations (Republican prisoners, Clann na Poblachta, the IRA) rather than with Sinn Féin itself. They are referenced as (nature and date of document, NLI, O'Mahony Papers, file number).

Introduction

When the Republican movement's ranks were on the verge of a split in 1969, future Provisional leaders Seán Mac Stiofáin and Ruairí Ó Brádaigh visited veteran Republican Tom Maguire, the only surviving member of the 1921 Second Dáil, to enlist his support for the forthcoming walkout. This initiative mirrored that taken by the IRA in 1938 when the then chief of staff, Seán Russell, consulted with the seven surviving members of the Second Dáil in order to get their approval for the pending IRA campaign in Britain. Maguire sided with the Provisionals, as he felt that the convention of the IRA, which had decided on the end of abstentionism, 'had neither the right nor the authority to pass such a resolution' (Bowyer Bell, 1983, 367).

Some months later, in May 1970, a lengthy feature article appeared in the columns of the Provisional Republican paper, *An Phoblacht*, describing the life and political engagement of 'one of Ireland's greatest women', Mary MacSwiney, who was also a member of the Second Dáil. The article praised her contribution to Irish political life: 'she was an outstanding woman of the Irish resistance movement because within herself she combined the forces of intellectual superiority and an inability to compromise national principles' (*An Phoblacht*, May 1970).

These two incidents are interrelated insofar as they show the attachment and the loyalty that leaders and members of the Republican organisation kept, throughout the years, to that nebulous but fundamentally symbolic body known to them as the Second Dáil. Composed of those Sinn Féin TDs elected in 1921 who sided with the anti-Treaty faction, it remained unflinchingly faithful to the aims of Republicanism as embodied by Sinn Féin after its split with de Valera and the formation of Fianna Fáil.[1] They reveal the profound significance that the party ascribed to its own history and to the men and women whom they considered the defenders of Republicanism.[2]

The history of the Second Dáil is inextricably linked to that of the fourth Sinn Féin, which came into existence after Éamon de Valera and his followers left the party in 1926 and formed Fianna Fáil, and came to an end in 1970 with the split between Officials and Provisionals. However important this party and its legacy might have been to its successors, its contribution to the history of the Free State (1922–37), Éire (1937–49) and the Republic of Ireland has been largely sidelined by historians and politicians alike. Evidently, the party's involvement in the political life of post-Treaty Ireland was, until the 1950s, quite unremarkable. Therefore it is only briefly mentioned in historical works that deal with this period. While the books scrutinising the history of the IRA contain references to Sinn Féin (English, Bowyer Bell or Coogan being among the most prominent), those on the political parties that claimed the Republican heritage focused on well-established organisations such as Fianna Fáil or, to a lesser extent, Clann na Poblachta. When the history of that period is studied through the lens of socialism, Sinn Féin is simply dismissed. In their study on socialism in the twentieth century, Rumpf and Hepburn barely dedicated a page to Sinn Féin post-1926, considering that 'the history of the party need be carried no further in a work of this nature. A great national movement had become a political curiosity, in which condition it has been preserved until today' (Rumpf and Hepburn, 1977, 89). Eoin Ó Broin, himself a Sinn Féin activist who authored a study on Republicanism and socialism, dismissed this particular period of the history of his party in the following manner: 'Sinn Féin receded into political obscurity, arguing over issues such as the legitimacy of its members taking state pensions. Sinn Féin ceased to be a functioning political party and had become a small association of like-minded people, disconnected from the cut and thrust of politics whether mainstream or marginal' (Ó Broin, 2009, 195–6). Ó Broin's analysis focuses on what he terms 'left Republicanism', which encompasses groups as varied as Republican Congress, Clann na Poblachta or the Workers' Party. Evidently the fourth Sinn Féin does not fit into the definition he gives of the chosen expression, which 'connotes all those Republican activists, intellectuals and organisations who during the course of the twentieth century attempted, with varying degrees of success and failure, to integrate a left-wing politics in the most plural sense of the terms with traditional Republican demands for full national independence and popular political sovereignty' (Ó Broin, 2009, 3).

To date, only two studies deal with Sinn Féin's history from 1905 through to 2005: Brian Feeney's *Sinn Féin: A Hundred Turbulent Years* (2002) and Kevin Rafter's *Sinn Féin 1905–2005: In the Shadow of Gunmen* (2005). However, they only dedicate small sections to the era of the fourth Sinn Féin. Rafter narrates the eclipse of Sinn Féin and gives a brief account of the 1948 Funds Case, with a lengthy biography of the main protagonist of those years, Margaret Buckley. Feeney paints a broad picture of the 'lean years', as he describes them, and pays closer attention to the 1950s and the relationship of the party with the IRA, dedicating a specific chapter to the period following the Border Campaign (1962–69). While these works are extremely useful when looking holistically at the history of the party, neither is based on the archival material explored in the present study. In general, Republicanism between 1926 and 1970 is usually studied through the lens of the IRA or the numerous offshoots that it generated throughout the 1930s and 1940s. Sinn Féin from 1926 becomes a footnote in most history books, which mention its rapid decline from 1926 onwards and its revival in the early 1950s, being eclipsed first and foremost by Fianna Fáil, but also, by the IRA. Consequently, the predominant narrative on Republicanism, until the end of the Second World War, has been that of the IRA.

Nevertheless, Sinn Féin did not disappear altogether from the political scene after 1926. It was undoubtedly overshadowed by more powerful political forces, but although it operated in very restricted circumstances over long periods of time, its final objectives, the end of partition and the establishment of the Republic proclaimed in 1916, always found sufficiently passionate advocates to keep it alive throughout those years. It retained a level of activity and support, albeit minimal, and saw itself as the guardian of Republicanism in Ireland. Its journey was a lonely one, as it was shunned by its former allies, including the IRA, until the late 1940s, when there was a resurgence of activity, and therefore interest, in the party. It vehemently opposed the Second Dáil's move in 1938 to make the IRA the repository of the Irish Republic. In fact, the relations between the two branches of Irish Republicanism were at best tense, if not antagonistic, throughout most of the period of the existence of the Free State.

Tracing the history of a party that was, for most of the period, out of the limelight, either because its activities were limited or because it did not arouse much interest in the press, is a challenging task for several reasons. Indeed, the question of the relevance of the history of such a small, almost invisible political formation must be raised. Arguably, if this story has not yet been written, it could be because it is of little historical significance, or because what could be said about such a small party has already been said. However, there are a number of compelling reasons for such a study to be carried out, in light of the fact that the present Sinn Féin, which is the first Nationalist force in Northern Ireland and is poised to become a coalition partner in the next government of the Republic, saw itself for decades as the descendant of a long line of previous emanations of Sinn Féin. While its rhetoric and tactics have undoubtedly changed beyond recognition, its legacy can contribute to explaining the reluctance expressed many times by politicians in the Republic to consider a close relationship with the party. From 1921, Sinn Féin refused to accept the institutions in place, as it deemed them illegitimate, in spite of the fact that they had been accepted by the majority. However, one of its most glaring failures was its incapacity to put forward a social and political alternative to the status quo. The fact that the fourth Sinn Féin operated for most of the period of its existence in complete isolation from the rest of the political world enabled it to develop a vision of Irish society which was out of synch with the socio-economic developments of the context in which it operated. This was yet another legacy from which the party had to emancipate itself. Furthermore, this was a party so deeply convinced of holding the truth that it never questioned neither the legitimacy nor the efficiency of armed action or of abstentionism, two tactics that became enshrined as core principles. Clinging to the past was the key to all its political choices. This was not helped, in the Free State years, by the state's tendency to 'recall its revolutionary origins in the Easter Rising, launched by a militant vanguard in the absence of what we would now call a revolutionary mandate' (McBride, 2011, 692). Finally, throughout the period under study, Sinn Féin was seen as a potential threat by the authorities and treated as such, which raises the question of the ability of the successive governments to address an opposition of that nature, as well as the main political parties' own relationship to their past and to memory in general.

One difficulty that embarking on such a study presents is that the documents available are, for the most part, primary sources, which raises the issue of their objectivity and their adequacy as the main corpus for an academic study. Indeed, most of the existing sources on the history of the party during those years are to be found in archival material and newspaper reports. Articles published during the period concerned show that, in spite of falling numbers and activities, there is an occasional interest in what remains of Sinn Féin at times such as commemorations and Ard Fheiseanna (annual conferences). Other sources of information include the UCD Archives which hold the Mary MacSwiney papers, containing not only some of the documents and statements released by the members of the Second Dáil until the early 1940s, but also her personal letters and notes. These provide an invaluable insight into the emotional and personal engagement of some individuals within the party; as there were so few representatives in that period, that dimension is far from irrelevant. Most importantly, it is the Sinn Féin Funds Case that constitutes the backbone of this study from 1926 to 1948. Indeed, had Margaret Buckley, president of Sinn Féin from 1937 to

1950, not sued the Irish state in an attempt to recover the funds that had been lodged by the Sinn Féin treasurers in 1922 in the Free State Courts, there would hardly be any trace of the activities of the party. All the documents that were gathered as evidence for the court hearings are held in the National Archives in Dublin, and represent over 2,000 pages which were submitted by the plaintiffs' and the defendants' lawyers, so that the court could decide whether there was continuity between the second Sinn Féin (1917–21), which originally set up the funds in question, the third Sinn Féin (1922–26) and the fourth Sinn Féin (from 1926 onwards). As High Court judge Kingsmill Moore put it:

> we have to decide whether there was a break in the organisation (1922–23). Mr de Valera has not claimed that his cessation formed a break. Have you not got to prove for each year, the following things, in order to show continuity: that you kept up an Ard Fheis [annual conference] the necessary steps to constitute an Ard Comhairle [executive committee], and a Standing Committee, that the Ard Comhairle met with proper delegates, summoned the Ard Fheis, and so on? (Sceilg, Witness Statement, 1948)

Sinn Féin was confident that the continuity which it was necessary to show in order to obtain the funds would be evidenced by the fact that the party had never ceased to exist, had not altered its constitution and aims, and had maintained regular meetings and operational structures. Therefore it submitted to the court all the evidence at its disposal: the minutes of all Standing Committee meetings between 1921 and 1948, as well as documents such as the Constitution drafted by the Second Dáil in 1929 and subsequently endorsed by Sinn Féin, and some correspondence between the party, the Second Dáil and the Army Council of the IRA. These written records then fed the questioning and counter-interrogation to which former presidents and officials of the party were subjected, the transcripts of which also represent a unique interpretation of the history of the tumultuous years of the independence period.

The Funds Case provides an interesting insight into how the main political actors of the time construed their own history. Indeed, when de Valera sought to short-circuit the outcome of the case by putting forward a piece of legislation to the Dáil, he did so in a cautious manner, inviting all the cabinet departments and opposition leaders to comment on what should be done with the funds. These documents also constitute a rich body of data as they include memos from and to the government, transcripts of court hearings and witnesses' testimonies. Together with the various Garda reports that were commissioned throughout those two decades in order to maintain a level of surveillance on Republican activity, all held in the National Archives, they provide valuable information not only on Sinn Féin, but on the manner in which it was viewed by the successive government officials and political leaders who, for the most part, had actively shaped its destiny in the revolutionary period. It must be stressed, however, that these documents only shed light on the operations of Sinn Féin south of the border, and therefore, this dimension will be the main focus of the study.

So far, these primary sources remain underused by historians and researchers alike. Through them, the history of Sinn Féin can be reconstituted week after week, and an untold narrative emerges: that of a party that was kept alive, in spite of its abysmally low support and its arguably self-destructive, righteous approach to politics. To say that Sinn Féin played an important role in those years would be overstating the case. But to disregard the party altogether would be to miss out on the light its existence sheds on fundamental issues such as the manner in which the state dealt with dissidence and subversion. The relentless rooting of its actions and strategies in the past was possibly one of the reasons why the party would become, at times, an irksome presence within the Free State. As the years went by, the institutions were not only strengthened, but adapted to changing circumstances, and some leaders increasingly took the view that forgetting was, much along the lines of what French thinker Ernest Renan had advocated some fifty years before, a necessary virtue for nation-building: 'Forgetting, I would even go so far as to say historical error, is a crucial factor in the creation of a nation, which is why progress in historical studies often constitutes a danger for [the principle of] nationality. Indeed, historical inquiry brings to light deeds of violence which took place at the origin of all political formations, even of those whose consequences have been altogether beneficial' (Renan, 1882, 3). De Valera himself, in a letter to Mary MacSwiney in June 1936, just weeks after the IRA had been declared an illegal organisation, wrote: 'I had refrained from replying to your previous letter because to reply to it in full would have meant engaging in a futile controversy on matters of past history at a time when the problems of the present and the future claim all my attention' (UCD, MacSwiney, 23/06/36).

By its very existence, Sinn Féin represented an alternative vision to that developed by the new state. As such, its discourse was undermined by the new leaders and sometimes even censored. The party put forward a competing memory, insofar as it availed of the same symbols and the same 'lieux de mémoire', to use Pierre Nora's expression (Nora, 1997), as those of the state, therefore further muddying the waters. The annual Bodenstown pilgrimage and 1916 were prime examples of this, and became, at different times, the sites of conflicting interpretations between the state and those who remained outside of the institutions.

Indeed, it was difficult to find a consensus around the meaning to attribute to pre-revolutionary Nationalism as it 'could not be detached from the unresolved conflict of the measure of independence secured in 1922'; 1916 also presented difficulties; while it could have 'offered a credible focus for reconciliation' it was instead celebrated 'with competitive enthusiasm by all factions descended from revolutionary Sinn Féin' (Fitzpatrick, 2001, 188–95). The state and its representatives often clashed with Republicans, pointing to an interesting fault-line, not so much regarding the significance that each ascribed to the events as the manner in which those events would be reinterpreted in the shaping of the political culture of a nation. The twentieth anniversary of the Rising in 1936 provides an interesting case study of the complex role of memory and will therefore be further developed.

The narrative that Sinn Féin put forward after 1926 was that of an unfinished revolution, the Free State representing a betrayal of the goals which the nation as a whole had shared and for which Republicans had fought. The vision which Cumann na nGaedheal, and then Fianna Fáil, developed was that of a successful endeavour to validate the status quo that had been reached by the Treaty, enabling leaders to maintain the social and political order that the new institutions afforded them. The new state representatives justified the introduction of successive emergency legislation by the need to defend it against internal dangers. The letters exchanged between Mary MacSwiney and de Valera in 1936 epitomised this dichotomy. The former was convinced that 'our resistance to you is as just and lawful as was your and our resistance to them. The Free State has not become sacrosanct because Fianna Fáil has taken it over, and it is just as true today as it was in 1922' (UCD, MacSwiney, 22/05/36).

There were other reasons why Sinn Féin became an unwelcome feature within the Irish state's political life in its early years, but these did not have as much to do with ideology as they had with tactics. What the party aspired to was rather conservative, seeped in Christian and monocultural identities, and certainly did not seek to overthrow the social order as such, but rather to dismantle the Free State and to put an end to the partition of Ireland with the establishment of a Republic. Its social and economic vision did not in any way challenge the dominant ethos of the Free State; if anything it was more conservative. One of its main characteristics, until 1962, was its insistence on the need to cherish and promote 'Christian values', this being made very explicit in the 1929 Constitution proposed by Sinn Féin, but also in later policies that were published in the 1950s. This was one more glaring contradiction in which the party found itself, but which was not identified as such: by seeking to overthrow the state and its institutions, by supporting an illegal armed faction and by promoting the setting up of alternative institutions, it claimed a revolutionary streak. But it remained profoundly conservative. The Republic to which Sinn Féin aspired, had it been established, would have made very little difference to the lives of most people. Therefore, it was not so much its revolutionary potential as its subversive discourse that the state combated, although Republicans did not seem to take the full measure of how unacceptable their position was and did not even seek to explore further the challenge that they were seen to pose.

The study of Sinn Féin throughout the years of the Free State shows a constant preoccupation with denouncing the legal apparatus put in place to ward off opposition, although the fact that the different pieces of legislation were rarely, if ever, directed at Sinn Féin was an indication of the innocuity of the party. Indeed, in the late 1920s and early 1930s, one of the main perceived threats was that of communism, which was identified with the IRA and its offshoots such as Saor Éire or Republican Congress, a view that was echoed by Sinn Féin and which revealed its estrangement from a sizeable faction of the Republican family.

The party that emerged after 1926 was purist, conservative and narrow-minded. When asked what had become of Sinn Féin after 1926, former President John O'Kelly, who also went by the name of Sceilg,[3] stated in 1948 that it was first and foremost an 'educational organisation' (Sceilg, Witness Statement, 1948, 4). But it was more than that; its very existence raised questions about the foundations upon which the Irish state had been constituted, such as the legitimacy of armed resistance, or the nature of the relationship between the executive and the legislature which came to the fore in 1947.[4] Nevertheless, to quote a much-used formula by IRA activist Peadar O'Donnell, 'those who were left with Sinn Féin formed, in 1926, a really right-wing group of cranks' (McInerney, 1974, 114). Indeed, to the man who was to be the architect of the IRA's left-wing orientation for the years to come, the composite group that constituted Sinn Féin for the next two decades had every attribute of a conservative, Catholic body. Some, such as Mary MacSwiney or Brian O'Higgins, were devout Catholics. MacSwiney's correspondence with the church authorities and the Papal nuncio throughout the late 1920s and early 1930s reveals a religious zeal, but also a formidable faith in her Republican cause, which put her at odds, on more than one occasion, with the Catholic hierarchy whom she did not hesitate to criticise for their condemnation of Republicanism. O'Higgins's total identification to his religion[5] sometimes led him to quarrel with his colleagues within the party, most notably, and ironically, Fr Michael O'Flanagan, whose commitment to the cause was rooted in the conviction that social justice was an essential ingredient to the Nationalist agenda. This would lead him to condemn the First World War for being a war of the ruling classes and later to defend the Spanish Republic in 1936. Sinn Féin's personnel was diverse, and included those whose Nationalism was essentially cultural, such as Sceilg who was president of the Gaelic League from 1919 to 1923 and who took a particular interest in the Irish language.[6] It was also relatively gender-balanced, as revealed by the list of the members of the Standing Committee throughout the years, showing a stronger presence of women than was the case in other parties, a phenomenon undoubtedly due to the fact that all women TDs voted against the Treaty (Garvin, 1996, 96). These women, some of whom such as Caitlín Brugha were widows of historical figures, had all played their part in the revolutionary period; Kathleen Lynn had fought in the ranks of the Irish Citizen Army and was then elected to the Dáil in 1923. But the figure who dominated the 1937–48 period was that of Margaret Buckley, who presided over a party on the verge of extinction but played a central part in the Sinn Féin Funds Case. 'In a way, Margaret Buckley and her colleagues in Sinn Féin kept alive a political brand name that could be handed on to other Republicans' (Rafter, 2005, 74). Overall, what united these Republicans was a 'secular religion' rather than a political theory (Garvin, 1996, 144), the profound belief in the alienable right of the Irish nation, of which they were the repository, and of which the embodiment was the Republic.

The party that de Valera left in 1926 soon became crippled by its adherence to inalienable principles, which prevented it from taking part in the political life of the country. The 1926 split certainly represented a traumatic experience for those who decided to stay within Sinn Féin, as reflected in the sometimes bitter and acrimonious tone of the leaders. They considered themselves the guardians of the ideals of 1916 – and of the Republic which included the whole island – and their approach to social and economic issues became increasingly conservative. The party's relationship with the IRA became strained throughout the inter-war years, and the role played by the remaining members of the Second Dáil, the institution to which Sinn Féin looked for legitimacy, further contributed to the isolation of a party that was already operating, by the mid-1930s, on the margins of the system.

In 1948, during the first convention held since the Second World War, the IRA decided to resurrect the moribund Sinn Féin, with a limited role, that of assisting the IRA. Sinn Féin therefore became the 'political wing' of the movement. The shift in policies, with the fight against partition being the main, if not the sole, priority, was accompanied by the publication of a *National Unity and Independ-*

ence Programme in 1954, which could be seen as the first attempt in many years to articulate a policy. The early 1950s saw a revival of militarism, with an increasing number of splinter groups. This led to a decision by the IRA to wage a military border campaign. In this context, Sinn Féin used a tactic that would later become the cornerstone of the National H-Block-Armagh committee electoral strategy during the 1981 hunger strike, that of the nomination of prisoners as candidates for general elections, and which led to the tactic coined by Sinn Féin's director of publicity Danny Morrison in 1981 of the 'armalite and the ballot box'. The initial successes of the 1955 and 1957 elections on both sides of the border were reversed in 1959 and 1961. These elections provide a good case study for the analysis of the limits of such a strategy.

The failure of the Border Campaign, leading to the reappraisal of strategies and ideology, led to a profound change in leadership in the IRA and Sinn Féin. This signalled the start of a soul-searching within both organisations, initiated by a commission set up by new IRA chief of staff Cathal Goulding, to examine the causes of the failed campaign. The new political thinking emanated in part from within the Wolfe Tone Clubs, which attempted the merging of Republicanism and Marxism. It also advocated an end to Sinn Féin's isolationist stance, with the creation of tentative links with trade unions and other political parties. The recommendations of Goulding's commission in 1966 heralded a new departure and triggered simmering discontent within the Republican movement. Parallel to these developments, Sinn Féin kept an active role in Northern Ireland, mainly through the Republican Clubs, created in order to circumvent the ban on the party. Sinn Féin's involvement in the Civil Rights movement remains a source of speculation. Did it contribute to its creation? Did it infiltrate it? Or did it simply witness its development and support its objectives to eventually realise it had potential for its own cause?

The history of the fourth Sinn Féin came to an end with the 1970 split between Officials and Provisionals, opening a new page in the fortunes of a party which had substantially morphed during its forty-five years of existence. Ironically for an organisation which had, for most of the period, been almost entirely based in and led from Dublin, it was the situation in Northern Ireland which struck this composite formation its fatal blow. Its ideological and strategic journey constitutes one of the legacies of the period of independence and as such, its narrative represents an integral part of the political and social fabric of contemporary Irish society.

Notes

1 Mary MacSwiney defined that body in the following manner: 'The present members of Dáil Éireann are those who took their oath to the Republic in the Second Dáil in August 1921 and have faithfully kept that oath. At different periods deputies have forsaken their allegiance, but though greatly reduced in numbers Dáil Éireann and its faithful members will continue to maintain and guard the Republic pending the moment when it will receive International recognition and its government be able to function freely' (UCD, MacSwiney, 10/08/27).

2 For reasons of convenience, the term Republicanism as used throughout this book refers to those who rejected the institutions and worked on the fringes of the system. However, it is not meant to exclude those parties and individuals who belong to the Republican tradition and who have upheld the ideal of the Republic.

3 John O'Kelly, whose Irish name was Seán Ó Ceallaigh, used the pen-name Sceilg in reference to the island of Sceilg Mhichíl in County Kerry where he was originally from.

4 See Chapter 3, 'The Funds Case'.

5 O'Higgins was a prolific writer. Many of his books had a religious content, such as *The Little Book of the Blessed Virgin*, *The Little Book of the Blessed Eucharist* and *The Little Book of the Sacred Heart*, published between 1936 and 1952, along with a number of other writings on Republicanism and the Easter Rising.

6 For a detailed biography of Sceilg, see Murphy, 2005.

1

Pragmatism versus principles, 1923–32

We have no prospect to offer but the old unrequited service of a deathless cause.
(John J. O'Kelly, 1928)

The short-lived third Sinn Féin

The Sinn Féin party which emerged out of the bitter divisions generated by the 1921 Treaty was, from the outset, a party in crisis. Its leaders nevertheless still believed in its potential to rally the majority of the people around the ideal of the Republic. What this actually meant was not developed, then or subsequently, and this lack of vision would come back to haunt later generations of Republicans, who relied on the adage that the Republic, per se, was the best option for Ireland. The lack of external references, the incapacity of the leaders to identify what they actually meant, was a double-edged weapon, as it would enable the more pragmatic tendency within the movement to adapt to the circumstances in which they found themselves, and it would impede the most fundamentalist from moving away from their narrow positions.

In October 1922, de Valera was still convinced that the future for the country rested in Sinn Féin as 'the only common ground on which Nationalist Irishmen and women can meet. It is an existing organisation, and an all-Ireland organisation. It had a glorious record for four years and was known all over the world. Its aims and objects are exactly in line with the Republican ideal. We should have no interest in killing it' (Letter from de Valera to Kathleen Lynn, 31/10/22, Funds Case, Vol. 1, 1948). De Valera's appraisal of the role that Sinn Féin could play, much like his successors', was predicated on the potential unifying force that the party had been, much more than on a specific vision of what lay ahead for the country. However, less than four years later, he and his followers left that party to found their own organisation, as they deemed the existing Sinn Féin no longer viable as an alternative.

The bitterness of the 1926 split, which gave birth to the fourth Sinn Féin and Fianna Fáil, is rooted, in great part, in the U-turn that de Valera and his supporters made in such a short interval. Undoubtedly, there were objective reasons for this radical change of perspective, not least the failure of the party to find its place in the early years of the Free State and to give credibility to the alternative that it put forward. Logically, the accusations of betrayal levied against the advocates of the abandonment of abstentionism in 1926 echoed the acrimonious tone which prevailed in the correspondence of the pro- and anti-Treaty factions, as the latter could not envisage working within the institutions they so vehemently condemned. Moreover, for those who rejected the Treaty, as much as for those who upheld abstentionism as an essential principle, Sinn Féin was more than just a party. It was a philosophy, a way of thinking. In essence, its aims were not just political and economic, they were moral, as they sought to improve the human condition not just from a societal but from an individual perspective. Therefore, in 1922, de Valera talked of his opponents having 'departed from the spirit of Sinn Féin', and seeking to 'let the organisation die' (Letter from de Valera to Kathleen Lynn, 31/10/22, Funds Case, Vol. 1, 1948). Years later, while giving his testimony in 1948 at the Sinn Féin Funds Case, de Valera was asked by the judge: 'You regarded the Sinn Féin organisation as one which could embody people of different views or of any politics but who might share a broad ultimate groundwork of opinion?', to which he replied: 'Yes. My anxiety was to keep Sinn Féin as big as possible, an all-embracing national organisation, alive. I do not think it was likely but it was possible' (Funds Case, de Valera, 1948, B8–9).

That possibility did not materialise, and the project was probably doomed to failure, as the main cementing principle for this group, the defence of the Republic, was devoid of long-term vision. The third Sinn Féin soon stagnated and failed to live up to the aspirations it so wished to put into effect. Even though evidence showed that it was still a viable party both in terms of support and finances (Ó Beacháin, 2009, 9), seen for instance in the fact that it had secured forty-four seats in the August 1923 general election,[1] its capacity to interact with the new political realities soon became a cause for concern for some of its leaders. The task of reorganising the party after 1922 was a momentous one, and a committee was therefore nominated, calling on 'all members or former members of Sinn Féin who adhere to its Republican object to resume their active support' (Sinn Féin Reorganising Committee, 04/07/23). One of the first initiatives of this body was to launch a daily newspaper, *Sinn Féin*, which became within a month a weekly paper, this being an indication of the gap between the ambitions of the party and its actual capacities. In its first editorial, de Valera reaffirmed the aims of Sinn Féin: 'Our purpose is to link all Irishmen in a brotherhood of love and mutual service. We mean to make Ireland one, Ireland free, Ireland prosperous, Ireland Irish' (*Sinn Féin*, 13/08/23).

Both at leadership and grass-root levels, fundamental aspects of the party's politics were being questioned. Its lack of visibility, and the fact that it remained at the periphery of Irish public life, were increasingly attributed to abstentionism. Therefore, the tactic that had proven so effective less than a decade before was now being scrutinised. Nevertheless, it was at the core of Republican identity. To sit in the parliament of a state the legitimacy of which Sinn Féin did not recognise was seen by those who were most attached to that strategy as nothing short of treason. To some members of Sinn Féin, no concession to the Free State (and sitting in its parliament was a major one, in their view) could be contemplated, under any circumstances. Moreover, the oath that had to be sworn to the British monarch was a further obstacle to their potential participation in the newly established institutions, as it was seen as the perpetuation of British control over Irish affairs.[2]

Sinn Féin's position was becoming inextricable. It sought to rally the majority of Irish public opinion to its ideals and objectives, namely the establishment of the 1916 Republic and the end of British rule in Ireland. The focus on the end of partition was to come later. In the early years of the Irish Free State, there seemed to be a level of consensus on the fact that partition, which was condemned by all sides, was not a priority as such. As English states, 'One thing that the Irish nationalist debate on the 1921 Treaty was emphatically not about was the partitioning of the island into two states: only a tiny fraction of the Treaty debate in the Dáil concerned partition, and pro- and anti-Treatyite attitudes were not, in fact, all that differing on the north' (English, 2007, 313).

However ambitious its objectives, the party did not have the means to implement any of them. It wished to demonstrate that the Free State was unworkable, and therefore maintained parallel structures such as the Second Dáil, which Republicans still viewed as the only legitimate incarnation of the government of the Republic. It reversed the roles, seeing itself as being in a 'position of a sovereign state suffering under invasion and a state of rebellion' (*Sinn Féin*, 20/10/23).[3] The very contradiction of such a statement, as it emanated from those who were attempting to instigate the rebellion, was not seen as problematic, as they adopted a rhetoric that would enable them to ignore the democratic mandate of the institutions they were seeking to overthrow. Moreover, the irony that the very Republic that was described as sovereign had been proclaimed by a rebellion was not identified either. But this did not help to further achieve the party's objectives, as its attempts to counter the newly established institutions were soon to be thwarted. It certainly wasn't lacking in initiative, as shown by the setting up of a Sinn Féin university and, with the progressive release of the prisoners,[4] of an unemployment agency to help Republicans find employment. But the party did not have the financial or organisational means of its ambitious programme and neither of these initiatives delivered any visible results (Pyne, 1969, 37). The dilemma which Sinn Féin soon faced was whether it should remain intransigent and politically unadulterated, or whether it should accept compromise which could in turn lead to a possible breakthrough in Irish politics. Some of the most prominent leaders were already convinced that the latter was the only viable option: 'Lemass, who was more of a pragmatist than most of the Sinn Féin leaders, realised that, unless radical changes were made, the organisation would continue to decline until eventually it would be reduced to the status of a minor party with no hope of ever forming a real government' (Pyne, 1969, 44).

When the Boundary Commission was established in 1924, under Article 12 of the Treaty, to determine, 'so far as may be compatible with economic and geographic conditions, the boundaries between Northern Ireland and the rest of Ireland' (Anglo-Irish Treaty, 1921), the internal turmoil in which Sinn Féin found itself was further aggravated. The proceedings and their outcome highlighted how ineffectual and impotent the party had become. It had stated from the very start its opposition to the very principle of such a body, with de Valera explaining in August 1924 that the Treaty had 'settled' nothing, rather had 'unsettled' a lot, and claiming that his party had no interest in the Commission. The position of the so-called Republican Cabinet[5] was simple: it was 'willing to give Ulster a Parliament for its own local affairs, with such a large measure of autonomy as was consistent with the unity of the Irish state; and they would gladly have given such a Parliament to Munster, Leinster and Connaught, for decentralisation of government was positive as far as it was consistent with the economy' (*Irish Times* (*IT*), 25/08/24).[6]

De Valera re-stated his party's view on the issue at a public meeting in Carlow in October 1924:

> Our position was that we neither could nor would, and neither can nor will, ever make a treaty, except for the whole of this island. We will never, under any circumstances whatsoever, see the sovereignty of this island contracted by a single inch. That is our policy. We will not consent to the mutilation of this country, whether the portion proposed to be cut off be six counties, or four counties, or a single city. (*IT*, 06/10/24)

To further strengthen its position, Sinn Féin put forward a number of candidates to the October 1924 Westminster elections in the newly formed Northern Irish state, in order to ensure 'that the people of the North-East shall be given an opportunity of proving their adhesion to the principles of Irish unity and Irish independence, and their detestation of the opposite principles of partition and subjection' (*IT*, 13/10/24). Clearly, the party's failure to fully acknowledge the reality of Unionism itself would become one of the main flaws of its appraisal of partition. Although it had succeeded in obtaining just above 20 per cent of the vote in the first general election to take place in the new state of Northern Ireland in May 1921, its absence in the November 1922 and December 1923 Westminster general elections heralded its eclipse from the political life of the north-east. This was one of the most glaring contradictions that the party would not be able to address or overcome in the following decades. Its refusal, or perhaps even incapacity, to address the *raison d'être* of Unionism, and its aspirations to establish a republic for the whole of Ireland, were based on the taken-for-granted geographical, insular nature of the nation, as shown in the tract circulated for the 1918 elections, asking voters to 'Look at the map – God has made Ireland one' (Sinn Féin, 1918). The following year, Laurence Ginnell, TD, who had been appointed by the party for the drafting of Ireland's case, made this clear in his submission to the Peace Conference: 'Ireland is historically entitled to independence as one of the primary sovereign states of Christendom' (Ginnell, 1919, 7). Therefore, the vision of the nation that Republicans put forward had the attributes, according to Garvin, of 'ethnic nationalism' (Garvin, 1996, 143), as opposed to the more 'civic' vision contained in the 1916 Declaration, as Kearney argues: 'Ethno religious nationalism thus replaced the civic ideals of Pearse and Connolly. Nation-building in both North and South almost inevitably took a sectarian turn' (Kearney, 2007, 35).

Sinn Féin inroads into the politics of Northern Ireland were short-lived. Its electoral ambitions were thwarted with the 1924 elections where, having put forward eight candidates, it only succeeded in seeing two honourable scores: one in Armagh with 28.83 per cent of the first preference vote and another with 15.75 per cent. The remaining six candidates were well below the 10 per cent mark, three of them losing their deposits.[7] This was all the more humiliating as all of these candidates bar one were unopposed in the Nationalist camp. Furthermore, the two seats that had been gained by Nationalists in the previous year, who had obtained 53.7 per cent of the vote, were lost in 1924. Sinn Féin's vote totalled 13.2 per cent, which meant that the two Unionist candidates were elected with a redundant majority.

Another general election was held in April 1925 within Northern Ireland, but this time for the internal parliament, or House of Commons, which had fifty-two seats. In May 1921, Sinn Féin had put forward twenty candidates, six of whom had been elected: four who would side with the pro-Treaty forces (Michael Collins, Seán Milroy, Eoin McNeill and Arthur Griffith) and two against (Éamon de Valera and Sean O'Mahony). It was perhaps to be expected, then, that the divisions that split the Republicans in the south would have a direct impact on the party's performance in the north. Sinn Féin's record proved the weakness of its position, as although it did succeed in retaining, under a 'Republican' anti-Treaty ticket, two of the six seats it had secured in the 1921 election, its share of the vote dropped to 5.2 per cent, representing a loss of 15.2 per cent. The remaining four seats were taken over by Nationalist candidates. By the following general election in 1929, Sinn Féin disappeared from the electoral map and possibly from the political life of Northern Ireland altogether.[8]

In the Free State, a number of by-elections were due to take place in the spring of 1925, following the resignation of nine Cumann na nGaedheal TDs over the handling by the government of the army mutiny. The crisis had been in part generated by the decision of the government to reduce the army's numbers to 20,000 from 49,000 men (Keogh, 2005, 19). Those opposed to such measures sent an ultimatum to the government demanding the suspension of army demobilisation and the removal of the Army Council, headed by Minister for Defence, Richard Mulcahy.[9] Sinn Féin entered the by-elections with high hopes, predicting that they would show how the 'flowing tide' was with the Republic. However, the results were disappointing, if not alarming. Of the nine seats contested, only two were won by Sinn Féin, the remaining seven going to Cumann na nGaedheal. Clearly, the Republican message and the abstentionist position which Sinn Féin candidates represented no longer held much attraction for the Irish electorate, on either side of the border.

The Boundary Commission sat throughout 1925. Its very existence was opposed, for reasons diametrically different from those of Republicans, by the Unionists who were uncomfortable with the idea of such a commission, claiming that the question had been settled with the Government of Ireland Act 1920.[10] In fact, they refused to designate a nominee, prompting the British government to appoint Joseph Robert Fisher, editor of the *Northern Whig*,[11] to represent Northern Ireland. Some reports stated that the Free State was claiming the cities of Derry, Enniskillen and Newry, which, if agreed by the Commission, would, according to Unionist MP Malcolm Macnaghten, 'destroy the economic life of the province' (*IT*, 02/10/25). Other rumours suggested that parts of Donegal could be attached to Northern Ireland, which seemed to greatly worry the farmers of the region (*IT*, 18/11/25). This was probably based on a report leaked to British newspaper *The Morning Post* on 7 November 1925, which prompted Eoin McNeill, Minister for Education and representative of the Free State on the Commission, to resign his position some two weeks later. However, after much discussion and debate, a tripartite agreement was reached on 3 December 1925, ruling that the boundary between the Free State and Northern Ireland was to remain unchanged. Those who had hoped, as had Collins, that the Boundary Commission 'would save Tyrone and Fermanagh, parts of Derry, Armagh and Down' (quoted in Rankin, 2006, 9) were disappointed:[12] Northern Ireland was constituted of Ulster less three counties, Cavan, Monaghan and Donegal. The land annuities were still owed to Britain[13] and the Free State took responsibility for the cost of the damage caused during the 1919–22 period, a clause which would be opposed, in particular, by the Labour Party (Staunton, 1996, 44).[14] After several days of heated debate, the Bill was passed by the Dáil by seventy votes to twenty with fourteen abstentions (Kennedy, 2000, 18).

The ratification of this agreement accelerated internal developments within Sinn Féin. De Valera remained, publicly at least, defiant: 'Today 44 elected members, representing over one-third of the people, are carefully excluded from voice or vote. Were they not excluded […], were these articles to be submitted to an assembly of all representatives of the people, they would be rejected' (Macardle, 1951, 894). However, in spite of this rhetoric, the episode highlighted the impotence of the party and its self-imposed isolation, and probably gave its leader 'the escape route he sought into constitutional politics. He could now argue that only the absence of a 'Republican presence in the Dáil had allowed Cosgrave[15] to push through his London agreement with Craig[16] and Baldwin' (Lee, 1989, 151). There were other indications pointing to the obsolescence of the abstentionist policy. As an article in the *Irish Times* put it, 'in view of the boundary agreement, it is probable that now they [Nationalist members] will decide that the interests of their constituents demand their presence in the Commons. The fact is that the policy of abstention was a huge mistake' (*IT*, 02/01/26). Among the ten abstentionist representatives in the Northern Ireland Assembly, two were Sinn Féin representatives, one being de Valera who had been elected in County Down.

Other, more pragmatic considerations were being looked at within Sinn Féin, primarily the fact that the party was declining at an alarming rate. Reports suggested that the number of branches had fallen from over 700 in 1924 to 380 in 1925 (Pyne, 1969, 42). It was also acknowledged that in parts of the country, the organisation only had a nominal existence, not to mention the fact that the party was seriously in debt, contracted during the elections of the previous years. A special finance drive had been launched in the autumn of 1925, but did not get the expected results. Its main financial source, the US, was also drying up. This, added to the fact that nearly half of the party's branches had not paid their affiliation fees in full, might also have been an indication of the lack of support from the grassroots or, at least, lack of motivation (*Irish Independent* (*II*), 15/01/26). Sinn Féin was facing serious difficulties, as shown by the County Dublin Sinn Féin convention's unanimous decision not to contest a by-election in January 1926, as no funds were available and no prospect of raising any was in sight. Moreover, it was feared that the very choice of a candidate would precipitate divisions (Sinn Féin Standing Committee (SC), 30/01/26).

As early as July 1925, an internal report handed to the Ard Chomhairle signalled the general apathy and lack of interest in the party. A motion was put to the vote at the November 1925 Ard Fheis by the Cahirciveen cumann (local branch) stating that 'owing to insidious rumours that Republicans will enter the Free State Parliament we call on Sinn Féin to get a definitive statement from the Government that they will adhere to the policy of Cathal Brugha, Erskine Childers and their fellow martyrs and enter only an Irish-Republican Parliament for all-Ireland' (*II*, 25/03/48, in Funds Case, 1948). A section of Sinn Féin was looking to short-circuit the debate before it had even taken place. After a lengthy discussion, an amended motion was adopted: 'It is agreed that no subject is barred from the whole organisation or part of it with the exception of acceptance of allegiance to a foreign king and the partition of Ireland; and if at any time a change of policy is proposed the Ard Fheis must be summoned to deal with such proposal' (*II*, 25/03/48). Thus, the issues of abstentionism and of the oath were now seen as distinct.

The extraordinary Ard Fheis

In January 1926, an Ard Chomhairle meeting was convened to discuss the party's finances. Although the proceedings were private, what transpired from the decisions taken was an indication of the problems that Republicans were facing. A £10 levy was imposed on every Comhairle Ceantair (area council) for headquarters' purposes; all cumainn (local branches) were urged to send in their affiliation fees at once. The question of the old Sinn Féin funds, which was to resurface in the 1940s, was raised. This involved the monies from the 1917–21 period that had been impounded in the Free State Courts since the beginning of 1924. The Gaelic League had suggested using the funds in the service of the Irish language, but this was rejected by the Ard Chomhairle, who instead gave the Standing Committee full powers to deal with the issue (*II*, 13/01/26).[17]

However, the most pressing problem that needed to be addressed was that of the rising discontent and disillusionment of the main and most emblematic leader, Éamon de Valera, concerning the party over which he was presiding. On 6 January 1926, in a speech delivered in Rathmines, Dublin, in front of Sinn Féin delegates, he announced that he was prepared to enter 'any representation of the Irish people' (*II*, 7/01/26) if the oath were to be abolished. The controversy generated by such a statement led to the organising of an extraordinary Ard Fheis in March of the same year, whose very convening did not appear to be consensual. O'Kelly stated in 1948 that 'the organisation did not desire that extraordinary Ard Fheis at all, Mr de Valera sent out that motion without the authority of the Standing Committee. Almost the entire officer board opposed de Valera's motion' (Sceilg, Witness Statement, 1948, 76). Again, this echoed the criticisms that had been voiced in 1922, when some members of the party had accused their adversaries of not fully respecting the rules and attempting, for instance, to forcibly close down the Harcourt Street Headquarters and shut down the party altogether.

On the occasion of the extraordinary Ard Fheis, de Valera's motion, 'That once the admission oaths of the 26 counties' and 6 counties' Assemblies are removed, it becomes a question not of principle but of policy whether or not Republican representatives should attend these Assemblies' (*An Phoblacht* (*AP*), 19/02/26), was debated. When testifying during the Sinn Féin Funds Case some twenty-two years later, de Valera gave a very nebulous explanation for the wording of this resolution: 'The importance of the word "principle" was that we would not get a majority on the principles but on a matter of policy we could, but if declared by the Ard Fheis to be a matter of policy everybody would be inclined to accept it. I knew there would be an objection as this was a matter of principle, that a minority would not be prepared to accept a majority vote on it' (de Valera, Witness Statement, 1948, 25). De Valera's proposal represented a watershed in Republican thinking, as the prospect of recognising the legitimacy of both parliaments would have been unimaginable only a few months previously. What this heralded was the acceptance, albeit indirectly, of the status quo and of partition, although the arguments elaborated for and against abstentionism at the Ard Fheis focused, in great part, on the former rather than on the latter. Indeed, de Valera's motion contained other clauses, which stipulated that entry to the parliament would be effective as of the next general election, and that those elected representatives would defend 'the ideal of an Ireland self-sustained and self-supporting economically' (*Meath Chronicle*, 20/02/26).

The above motion was not put forward in the name of the party but in that of de Valera, which was yet another indication of the willingness of the president to distance himself from the organisation. In the view of some of the most hard-line Republicans, what its wording implied was tantamount to betraying the very core beliefs of the party. One such representative was Fr O'Flanagan, whose Republican commitment to the Republican ideal had jeopardised his career in the priesthood.[18] He suggested an amendment to de Valera's resolution which read: 'That it is incompatible with the fundamental principles of Sinn Féin as it is injurious to the honour of Ireland to send representatives to any usurping legislature set up by English law in Ireland' (*AP*, 19/02/26).

While both sides were fine-tuning their arguments and trying to win the hearts and minds of the delegates for their respective resolutions, the party decided to test its support, putting forward Art O'Connor, who had been elected to Dáil Éireannn in 1919 and again in 1921 but defeated in 1922, as the Sinn Féin candidate for the Leix Offaly[19] by-election, so that 'the people of that constituency might be afforded an opportunity of reaffirming their loyalty to the ideal of the Irish Republic – Ireland free and undivided – and of pronouncing judgement upon the policy of those who recently agreed to the partition of our country and betrayed their fellow countrymen of the North-East' (*II*, 26/01/26). However, the issue of abstentionism was present during the campaign, and not only within Sinn Féin ranks. During an electoral meeting in Portlaoise, Cumann na nGaedheal leader William Cosgrave did not hesitate to ridicule his opponent's stance: 'How many of you would employ a labourer who made it a condition of his contract that he will never handle a tool? Yet that is the proposal that Mr O'Connor and his famous friends ask you to accept' (*Kilkenny People*, 06/02/26). De Valera threw his energies into the campaign, attending a number of meetings in support of O'Connor, the 'real farmers' man' as he came to call him (*Kilkenny People*, 13/02/26). The result was insufficient to gain O'Connor the seat, but the two candidates' first preference votes were close (40.3 per cent compared to 37.4 per cent), leaving the third, the Labour Party candidate, in a position of arbiter. However, over one third of his votes were not transferable, and although the overall transfer was beneficial to O'Connor, his opponent was elected with a margin of some 800 votes. O'Connor attempted to minimise the blow that this result actually meant for his party by pointing out that Sinn Féin had increased its share of the vote by approximately 4,000 since the previous election (*II*, 22/02/26). However, this was going to prove insufficient to salvage the unity of the party. De Valera had already made up his mind as to what the future held for an intransigent abstentionist party:

> The question at issue is whether with a view to massing the people of Ireland against the oath of allegiance, which is a national humiliation and a barrier to unified, national action, it could be promised officially on behalf of the organisation at any time that if the oath were removed, the members would sit with the other representatives of the people in the Free State assembly, regarding the assembly frankly as a non sovereign, subordinate twenty-six county institution, but one which in fact was in a position to control the lives of a large section of our people. (*II*, 15/01/26)

Twenty-seven resolutions in total had been put forward for discussion at the extraordinary Ard Fheis of March 1926. Some, such as that of the County Cavan Bailieborough Sinn Féin cumann, proposed an addendum to de Valera's motion, which read: 'I shall never give allegiance nor willing obedience to any authority other than an authority exclusively responsible to, and elected by, the free will and consent of a majority of the Irish people resident within the four provinces of Ireland' (*Anglo-Celt*, 06/03/26). Obviously, what those against the removal of the abstentionist policy feared most and were probably, with hindsight, justified in fearing, was that such a fundamental change would drive elected representatives to sit in the Dáil, whether the oath was removed or not. Indeed, some members within the party did not see this as an indefinite obstacle preventing them from taking their seats (*Sunday Independent* (*SI*), 07/03/26). The change that was proposed had thus more far-reaching implications than it seemed at first sight, as it was also an admission of the defeat of what Sinn Féin had fought for. For those supporting the end of abstentionism, sitting in the Dáil had become an acceptable course of action, in fact, the only valid course of action. In a letter to the *Dundalk Examiner*, P. J. O'Loughlin, county councillor for Loughrea, stressed that the duty of Republicans was to fight the presence of the British by all and every means, and that therefore the very concept of abstentionism had become counter-productive and inefficient:

> If a man takes possession of my house I will never get him out by stopping outside and putting out my tongue at him every time he appears at the window or the door. Let me enter the house by any and every means, and if I cannot rule it, well, let me make it so hot for him that I will at least prevent him ruling, and so break up the house and the usurper, and if I cannot rule at least I will prevent either an alien or a traitor from doing so. (*Dundalk Examiner*, 09/03/26)

In 1948, de Valera insisted, when testifying in the High Court in the Sinn Féin Funds Case, on making his position clear regarding abstentionism. Interestingly, he used arguments then that had not been developed at the time. One was that entering the Free State parliament was a way to avoid resorting to violence: 'We were abstaining from entering the Parliament. That blocked the peaceful method by which we were hoping to attain our objectives. It was a critical situation because it meant that we would be driven back to force' (de Valera, Witness Statement, 1948, C3). Indeed, there were signs of restlessness within the IRA, or at least among some of its members. At the 1925 convention, what transpired from some of the resolutions presented was a feeling of frustration on the part of some brigades to what they considered the inactivity of their organisation. 'The present policy of passive resistance is destroying the spirit and discipline of our army', stated one such resolution from the Dublin brigade (Garda report, 21/05/25). However, this threat of violence seemed to be quite contained, as the resolution was only considered, not adopted, by the convention, and was referred to the Army Council for consideration. Discontent was certainly real but whether this was the main reason for the change of policy was not stated at the time.

On 9 March 1926, O'Flanagan's amendment was carried by a majority of five votes (223 to 218), showing the extent to which this issue was dividing the party at its very core. This gave rise to a peculiar situation, as when it then became a motion against de Valera's own motion, it was defeated by a margin of two votes, making de Valera's proposal the valid one. However, in light of the result, de Valera tendered his resignation as Sinn Féin president the following morning, explaining that the vote could only be interpreted as going against his policy. Of the fifty-seven remaining members of the Second Dáil, twenty-two followed de Valera and his supporters and left Sinn Féin.

It is probable that de Valera was looking for a way out in the long term, as neither he nor his allies put up a fight to retain control of the party. Indeed, the result of the vote was extremely close and his own motion had been carried. But perhaps being associated with the party that bore the name Sinn Féin was no longer viewed as an asset, rather a liability in political terms, as it was now a static and rigid organisation incapable of representing a credible opposition. Moreover, there were indications that a new, Republican party would, if it were willing to participate actively in the political life of the country, win over a considerable section of public opinion. An editorial in the *Meath Chronicle* explained that 'If [de Valera] does [create his own party] he will gather to his support a great number of people who would not otherwise support his candidates – those who are not satisfied with the record of the present government'. Moreover, the prospect of a new Republican party was welcomed as a way to avoid what the newspaper called opposition on 'vocational lines' (i.e. the Farmer's Party) or 'class lines' (the Labour Party) (*Meath Chronicle*, 20/03/26). Others believed a conspiracy was at work which sought to divide the Republican forces in order to weaken them. 'The enemy has, undoubtedly, been very busy for some time past. His policy is not always easy to follow. Sometimes he would seem inclined to root up the Republican organisations one after the other; other times he would seem gladder that internal friction would occur among Republicans, but whatever his method the enemy has certainly been proceeding very cleverly', stated John O'Kelly at a meeting of the Second Dáil in December 1926 (Minutes of Dáil Éireann, 18–19 December 1926, Garda report, n.d.).

The split

The party nonetheless still hoped that a split could be avoided and issued a statement to that effect: 'the division within our ranks is a division of Republicans who are unanimous on this fundamental issue – that in no circumstances can any Republican take an oath of allegiance to an alien king, or assent to the partition of our country' (*II*, 12/03/26). Mary MacSwiney – TD of the Second Dáil and sister of dead hunger striker and former mayor of Cork, Terence MacSwiney – who was to become one of the most passionate voices in defence of purist Republicanism, took over the temporary chair of Sinn Féin. She paid tribute to its former president, talking about the 'deep love and gratitude which each member feels for the man who was described by one delegate as the greatest Irishman for a century' (*II*, 12/03/26). The interpretation of the outcome of the Ard Fheis and the consequences it would have were, however, difficult to call in the short term. The fact that the abstentionist position had been retained did not mean that those who supported this policy had won the day and had the upper hand, as the *Irish Independent* suggested (*II*, 13/03/26). Indeed, an editorial from the *Connacht Tribune* left no doubt as to what public opinion would think about the dispute. 'What the Irish people feel and think – let there be no mistake – is that the people elected to represent them in an Irish Parliament should find some means of fulfilling their responsibility. Until the Republican Party applies itself frankly to doing this, little interest will be aroused by its proceedings' (*Connacht Tribune*, 13/03/26).

The very word 'split' conjured up some painful memories, as future Sinn Féin president O'Kelly subsequently remembered: 'The whole of the atmosphere of that Ard Fheis was the fear of a split, on account of the split that had taken place in 1921–22' (Sceilg, Witness Statement, 1948, 78). In order to fully explore an alternative to this scenario, a committee was appointed by each side which held three joint meetings. Some, such as O'Flanagan, seemed intent on avoiding, at all cost, a division and the creation of a new political formation. He even went as far as 'raising the question of Miss MacSwiney's conduct of affairs since the President's resignation at the Ard Fheis. He declared that Miss MacSwiney had acted in such a manner as to facilitate one section of the organisation in creating a division, and establishing a rival organisation' (SC, 22/03/26). MacSwiney retorted that O'Flanagan was prepared to allow those who supported de Valera's policy to 'advocate that policy publicly through the Sinn Féin organisation', when 'this question was not put to the Standing Committee for decision' (SC, 22/03/26). Before the discussion could generate a rift among those who were already weakened by the Ard Fheis decision, Art O'Connor managed to have the following resolution passed: 'That the Standing Committee is satisfied with the senior Vice President's conduct of affairs since the resignation of the President' (SC, 22/03/26).[20] This short exchange was indicative both of the bitterness that existed within the ranks of Sinn Féin and of the personal dimension that the political debate would inevitably take, given the close proximity that the members of the Standing Committee and Executive had been sharing for a number of years. The relationship between former allies would be partly founded on personal resentment, mostly, in the years to come, directed at de Valera. Unsurprisingly, the outcome of the discussions between the two parties was that the unity of Sinn Féin could not be preserved, and that consensus on the proposal of entering the Free State parliament if the oath was removed was not possible. Sinn Féin reserved the right to decide whether cooperation with a newly formed organisation could be considered (SC, 27/03/26). Ten members of the Ard Chomhairle tendered their resignation, which was accepted by the Standing Committee (*AP*, 10/04/26). The leadership of Sinn Féin, and subsequently the presidency of the Republic that existed, at least virtually, in the eyes of the most radical Republicans, was taken over by Art O'Connor.

For some, de Valera and his supporters were showing political realism, for others they were betraying the 1916 Republic to which Sinn Féin had sworn an oath. For those in favour of abstentionism, de Valera's position was a step backwards, amounting to an acceptance of a situation similar to that which had preceded the Civil War. Nevertheless, the fundamental issue was raised by de Valera's supporters in different terms. What had Republicans achieved during and after the Civil War? Their leader's position was undoubtedly more visionary than that of his adversaries, insofar as it meant, implicitly, the acceptance of the defeat of a rigid Republican stance. The future Fianna Fáil leaders did not necessarily renounce their Republican ideals, but sought to give a new impetus to their policies. The question, framed in a different light, was the following: should the fight against partition and the effects of the Treaty be carried out inside the political system or outside?

Among those who refused to follow de Valera, some came to conclusions that were far from being dichotomic, such as IRA member Peadar O'Donnell:

> Many Republicans who had been through the Civil War asked angrily: 'Why was this not done before? Why, in fact, resist the Treaty at all if de Valera was prepared to go into the Free State parliament at that stage? [...] This was to miss the real difference in politics, tactics and strategy which a defeat forces on a leader. (McInerney, 1974, 101)

Overall, however, the analysis of most of those Republicans who opposed de Valera was far more limited, as it was essentially based around the issues of abstentionism and the oath. They did not seem to take the measure of the problems of cohesion that the party was experiencing. Therefore, for Mary MacSwiney, de Valera was making a serious error of judgement. In a letter addressed to 'some friends' in the United States, she exposed her point of view, which considerably lacked long-term political vision and realism:

> But while disappointed, we are going ahead. We believe that this new policy will be a failure. That the oath will not be removed until the country is ready to 'scrap' the Treaty. That oath is the one barrier the present junta have against political extinction, and they will cling to it. When those who are following the new departure find that out, most of them will come back [...] The country will finalise realise the fact that 'No compromise' is the only sane policy in Ireland. (Cronin, 1972, 143)

Republicans soon had to face reality. Not only did Mary MacSwiney's predictions not come to pass, but the 1926 split had serious consequences for Sinn Féin as a political party. The very foundations of the division explain the progressive decline of the party as a political machine. Evidently, the split had not broken up the membership in even numbers. Even if de Valera had not secured the majority that he needed to end abstentionism, his departure meant the loss not only of a significant level of support but of prestigious and apt leaders. As early as April 1926, reports suggested how popular the new direction taken by de Valera was. In Roscommon, the whole Sinn Féin Comhairle Ceantair was formally dissolved, with delegates stating that their areas were in favour of de Valera's policy (*II*, 29/04/26). Evidently, this new departure was quickly gathering momentum 'in striking disproportion to the support de Valera obtained at the recent Congress', explained an editorial of the *Sunday Independent* (*SI*, 16/05/26). There was also some indication that locally, the depleting of Sinn Féin's ranks was creating serious problems. The Killarney Sinn Féin Club attempted to call on both leaderships to reconsider their positions, but clearly blamed the leadership of Sinn Féin for the situation: 'we feel that headquarters are thoroughly responsible for this national calamity' (*II*, 22/05/26). To further compound things, the party was struggling with an impossible financial situation, as shown by the decision taken by the Standing Committee in April 1926: the premises that housed Sinn Féin headquarters were now too large, and too expensive, for the party to retain. Therefore, it was decided to downsize the offices from the two rooms on the first floor which cost £260 a year to a more modest one room on the first floor, for £80 a year. The saving amounted to £180, not including, as noted in the minutes, the caretaker fee which would go down from ten to five pence a week (SC, 06/04/26). Moreover, some austerity measures were introduced, such as the 'temporary deductions' in some officials' salaries and the scaling down of the number of typists to one (SC, 06/04/26). The small sums that Sinn Féin was preoccupied with saving were a clear indication of the extent to which the situation had become desperate.

Despite these alarming signals, the Sinn Féin leadership continued to adhere to the same discourse, the same principles, as if almost paralysed by the recent split. It did not seem to acknowledge the extent to which it had been affected by the division, but continued to show misguided optimism, hoping to raise the number of clubs affiliated from 163 in April 1926 to as many as 1,000 in the following months (SC, 06/04/26). At the end of May 1926, it urged all elected representatives in the Free State and Northern parliaments to resign their seats if prepared to enter those parliaments, 'as they no longer represent the organisation which nominated them and secured their election' (*II*, 26/05/26). Sinn Féin's resolution generated some anger among Republicans, who accused the Ard Chomhairle of not respecting the will of the Ard Fheis and of creating friction among Republicans. De Valera made it clear the following day that he would not resign his seat, as his proposals were to be put before the people at the elections, and no sooner (*II*, 27/05/26). The main challenge facing his followers was indeed that of explaining why the battle over the oath was so fundamental. As Gerry Boland[21] stated, since they had failed to break the Treaty along the whole front, it had to be attacked at its weakest link: the oath (*II*, 21/06/26). The seeds for an even more bitter division between the two factions of Republicanism were therefore being planted.

On 15 May 1926, de Valera founded Fianna Fáil, to which the label 'Republican Party' was added at the suggestion of Seán Lemass.[22] The new party's main objectives included reunification and economic self-sufficiency. The arrival of Fianna Fáil on the political scene heralded a considerable change, as it presented a credible alternative and a challenge to the party in government, something which the third Sinn Féin had never succeeded in doing.

Re-defining Republicanism

'Post-civil war Republicans were thus divided into three broad groups: negotiable Republicans, absolute Republicans and social Republicans' (O'Neill, 2008, 20), the first being Fianna Fáil, the second Sinn Féin and the Second Dáil, and the third, a sizeable faction of the IRA, those who opted for a radical, Marxist analysis of the struggle that lay ahead of them.

The split within the Sinn Féin ranks had consequences for other organisations which were, at the time, part of a nebulous grouping of Republican bodies. Cumann na mBan, the women's military organisation founded in 1914,[23] sided with the abstentionist section of the party, as did na Fianna Éireann.[24] Other smaller groupings, which were nonetheless influential as they had either a symbolic or financial role to play, were the National Graves Association[25] or the Wolfe Tone Committee, in charge of annual commemorations; none openly sided with either faction. Interestingly, none of these smaller groups identified, at the time, with de Valera. The Second Dáil, finally, which gathered those fifty-seven deputies who had stood against the Treaty prior to the Civil War, saw its status dramatically altered, as it only represented those who were willingly staying outside the political arena. Therefore, it was considerably weakened by the Sinn Féin split. This new situation was acknowledged by the members of that body. A meeting during which proceedings were recorded by the Gardaí was called to decide on the future of the Second Dáil, one of the first realities being that it was 'absolutely impossible for [us] to restrict ourselves to carrying on with the quorum of twenty' (Garda report, 10/12/27), since that rule had been established when there were 128 members 'or thereabouts', according to the report. Thus, the rules had to be amended to take account of the new situation. This was, however, but a detail in the more complex situation in which this virtual body found itself. The first issue that was identified was the lack of support of the IRA, which had decided, the previous year, to withdraw its allegiance from the so-called 'Government of the Republic'.

Therefore, concluded Art O'Connor, 'As a government we are left without the physical force to carry out any orders of Decrees we might be seeking to enforce with the strong hand, and with the departure of Fianna Fáil from the Dáil as a moral force we are greatly weakened' (Garda report, 10/12/27). However, he saw the role of the Dáil as ensuring unity among the various Republican organisations, which were at the time, in his view, 'doubting the sincerity of members of the other Organisations'. But clearly, the focus of the proceedings was on the future of the Dáil and on its status. Some argued that it was not accurate to call it the Second Dáil, which referred to the full Dáil elected in 1921. Therefore, in Michael Collivet's view,[26] 'the people had taken away its authority, which may come back in different ways'. Essentially he was refuting the legitimacy of the Second Dáil on the grounds that it was no longer a democratic representation of the people. This argument was immediately countered by Mary MacSwiney, for whom the Second Dáil was 'the symbol of a very important fact and that is, that a people have no right to surrender their independence at the ballot boxes – if you allow this, you are raising a situation in which you are appealing to the majority and they will always take the line of least resistance. The majority will always go after the easiest thing' (Garda report, 10/12/27). The lack of democratic convictions of those who claimed to be the only true government of the Republic was never questioned in subsequent years, and the fact that a majority of the people had opted for the Treaty was never seen as sufficient reason for accepting the status quo. As Garvin argues, 'from the point of view of the moderate Republicans under de Valera and also that of the fundamentalist Republicans under Liam Lynch and other IRA chieftains, the voters were slavish and intimidated into wanting peace at any price' (Garvin, 1981, 126).

Moreover, the inflexible position of those who refused to grant legitimacy to the new institutions carried strong implications for their personal and professional lives, as President Art O'Connor was soon to find out. His announcement that he would work as a lawyer in the Free State Courts caused a level of uneasiness among his colleagues. Indeed, logic dictated that he refrain from doing so. As Seán Buckley[27] pointed out, this decision was inconsistent with his political position, as O'Connor would have to appeal to the Free State constitution and to the Free State laws. Seán MacSwiney[28] added: 'an ordinary volunteer could not recognise the court, and you would be the head of the Republic acknowledging it every day. That is how it would look to the man in the street' (Garda report, 10/12/27). Art O'Connor tendered his resignation as President of the Second Dáil, and although he would continue, for a time, to be a member of Sinn Féin, he eventually resigned from that position a year later. The party had adopted the same rigid principles regarding the institutions of the Free State, deciding at the 1926 Ard Fheis that no member of the organisation could use the courts on either side of the border for civil action if settlement by a Republican arbitration had not been attempted first (*II*, 01/11/26).

The main organisation within Republican circles which was to represent a major challenge for Sinn Féin over the next two decades was the IRA, who had refused, as early as 1925, to take sides in the debate that was dividing the party. It justified its position by explaining that it was preferable for a 'revolutionary army' not to take part in a partisan fight, as it could run the risk of dividing its own ranks along similar lines:

> An Executive was elected, the Executive in turn appointed the Army Council. The decision was taken to ensure that the split which was about to take place in the political movement would not in any way extend to the IRA [...] it was bad for a revolutionary army like the IRA to be under the control of a semi-constitutional party. (*AP*, 01/10/25)

Undoubtedly, a split within the ranks of the IRA would have further weakened the entire Republican forces. Such was the thinking of the Army Council which, at a meeting on 14–15 November 1925, decided to modify the status of the organisation by putting an end to its allegiance to the Second Dáil: 'That the Supreme Council of the IRA shall remain vested solely and absolutely in the Army Executive and that under no circumstances shall the Army be subject to any political party whatsoever until such time as a properly constituted government be established and functioning' (Garda report, 16/11/25).

However, there is no doubt that de Valera's decision to enter the Free State parliament was problematic for the armed organisation as well. At its 1925 convention, one of the resolutions 'considered at length by the convention but [on which] no decision was taken', according to the Gardaí, read: 'that if at any time any officer serving in Óglaigh na hÉireann states publicly or in Council that members of the Irish Republic enter the Free State Parliament as by British Law established he be immediately suspended pending court-martial' (Garda report, 21/05/25). From then on, the IRA would function as an independent body. Such a decision represented a major blow for the political emanation of the Republic, as it meant that in the view of the armed organisation, the Second Dáil was not a 'properly constituted government', and therefore was not seen as legitimate. More particularly, this position was to further compound Sinn Féin's isolation. Yet the distancing between both organisations was seen by some as an opportunity for the IRA to pursue a different agenda to that which the party had set until then. *An Phoblacht* editor Peadar O'Donnell thus adopted a much more pragmatic position:

At once, the delegates misinterpreted de Valera's radical plan for militant but constitutional means as surrender and assumed that this was the reason for O'Donnell's proposal to break with Sinn Féin. But O'Donnell's reason for the break was to make the IRA into a Socialist and political organisation that would lead the Republican Movement forward. (McInerney, 1974, 112–13)

With the split, the IRA was faced with a serious dilemma. On the one hand, it saw itself as having played the role of a revolutionary army for a number of years and was therefore prone to observe a degree of mistrust towards the constitutional choice made by Fianna Fáil. On the other hand, the emergence of this party had left the Republican movement bereft of its most prestigious names. A measure of pragmatism was necessary if it did not want to be dragged into the downward spiral in which Sinn Féin was already caught.

The future of Sinn Féin was closely linked to that of the IRA. The party now had to rely on the columns of *An Phoblacht*, which had replaced *Sinn Féin* in June 1925, to convey its messages and policies, as it no longer had a newspaper of its own. This clearly became an issue some weeks after the split. The Republican publication was under the control of an advisory board, which had been set up alongside Cumann na Poblachta in 1922 as a rallying organisation for those who opposed the Treaty. After the 1926 split, it had become an autonomous entity, although the Sinn Féin Standing Committee was reassured by Count Plunkett, who sat on the advisory board, that it would 'be run on purely nationalist or separatist lines and not for party purposes' (SC, 31/05/26). In the first few months, the newspaper refused to take sides, and published advertisements for Fianna Fáil alongside Mary MacSwiney's articles in defence of Sinn Féin's position. But the IRA had effectively taken control of the paper in April 1926 (Ó Drisceoil, 2001, 44). The relationship between the representatives of Sinn Féin and the editor of *An Phoblacht* were to become antagonistic, if not confrontational. Indeed, in an editorial devoted to the reorganisation of Sinn Féin, O'Donnell bluntly stated that:

> Sinn Féin is facing the problem of reorganising itself. Republicans are seeking to come closer. People who have been described as Fianna Fáil because they worked in the election, or as reactionaries because they preferred a local trade-union official to abstentionism or Fianna Fáil, are now unattached, almost astray. (*AP*, 22/10/27)

Mary MacSwiney replied in the following issue of *An Phoblacht*: 'That is the weakness of Peadar O'Donnell. He wants to replace Sinn Féin by a loose organisation whose beliefs are even more nebulous than those of the bluffers of 1921' (*AP*, 29/10/27). O'Donnell concluded the debate by writing: 'If Sinn

Féin will reorganise itself and tune in to the present need, then Sinn Féin will have become again an organisation with a creed, not a committee with rule books and typewriters' (*AP*, 29/10/27). O'Donnell was not specific as to what Sinn Féin should be, but the controversy that he provoked, perhaps wittingly, showed the extent to which Sinn Féin leaders were blinded by their principles and saw any attempt to reform the party as a threat to its moral and political integrity.

The IRA took on the role of mediator between the two rival Republican organisations, trying to ensure that they retained some level of cooperation. Sinn Féin was approached, in September 1926, both by the IRA and by Cumann na mBan to contribute to the setting up of a new association, with branches throughout the country. Its membership was to be opened to all organisations which were considered anti-imperialist bodies, such as the GAA, Fianna Fáil and Labour. However, Sinn Féin categorically refused to take part in such an endeavour, deeming that there was 'no need for forming any such organisation, as the fighting of imperialist propaganda was part of the programme for cumainn' (SC, 10/09/26). For a time, the IRA seemed to hesitate as to which Republican party to support. It attempted to retain an amicable relationship with Sinn Féin, sending a delegation to the 1927 Ard Fheis, comprising chief of staff Moss Twomey, Seán MacBride, George Plunkett, Peadar O'Donnell and Seán MacSwiney, although, according to police reports, 'these men did not participate in the debates and were there purely as representatives of the army' (Garda report, 05/12/27). However, it was unclear what the IRA actually expected its relationship with Sinn Féin to be. Some members of the party suspected the IRA of trying to seize control of the executive committee and other posts of importance in the party structures; this manoeuvre was welcome by some such as Kathleen Lynn who considered that this would strengthen the party, and viewed with suspicion by others (Garda report, 05/12/27).

The test of the ballot boxes

Notwithstanding the setback that the formation of a rival political organisation represented, Sinn Féin leaders toured the country after the split, organising meeting after meeting, repeating the same message over and over. Attendance at those meetings compared poorly with that of Fianna Fáil's rallies, according to newspaper reports (*II*, 23/08/26). But Sinn Féin's explanation for the loss of enthusiasm that even the most dogmatic leaders could not ignore was simple: it was the split in Republican ranks, imputable mainly to de Valera, that had created the apathy 'which prevented people from crossing the road now to hear the leaders of any party' (*II*, 23/08/26). 'Had the present cleavage not taken place in the Republican ranks, and basing my argument on the large increase in Republican votes at the last by-elections and analysing these figures under PR, I was of the opinion that Sinn Féin would probably have won out at the next general election', stated a letter to the editor of the *Irish Independent* (*II*, 24/08/26). The party put forward a strategy to end partition in a speech delivered in Dublin, that of convincing the 'Northern elements' that their best interests were linked up with the rest of the country, and that partition was 'commercial folly' (*II*, 21/09/26), again showing a poor understanding and a lack of interest in the reasons why those 'Northern elements' had opted for partition in the first place.[29]

The battle for the hearts and minds soon had a specific objective, as it became focused on the general elections announced for June 1927. The political climate was tense, as shown by the enactment, two years earlier, of the Treasonable Offences Act (1925) 'which permanently criminalised rebellion' (Knirck, 2014, 69). It defined any attempted 'act of war', including attempting to overthrow the government by arms or any other violent means, as treason and therefore punishable in the same manner as murder. Clause 5 was directed explicitly at those who still refused to grant legitimacy to the new state:

> Every person who takes part in any proceedings of any assembly or body (other than the Oireachtas or either House thereof) which claims, purports, proposes, or attempts to take upon itself, or does take upon itself, all or any of the powers and functions of the Oireachtas or of either House thereof shall be guilty of a misdemeanour and shall be liable on conviction thereof to a fine not exceeding five hundred pounds or, at the discretion of the Court, to imprisonment with or without hard labour for any term not exceeding two years or to both such fine and such imprisonment.[30]

This piece of legislation was aimed directly against Republicans (O'Halpin, 1999, 59–65). It gave vast powers of detention and suspended *habeas corpus*. The death penalty could be applied to those who waged a war against the state.

The electoral campaign also made obvious the problems with which Sinn Féin was confronted, particularly regarding its relationship with the IRA. The army's headquarters had put their negotiating skills to the test when they sought to bring about a rapprochement between the two parties, around a common programme. On both sides, intransigence prevailed. Sinn Féin's preconditions to any negotiation were draconian:

- A guarantee they will not enter a foreign-controlled parliament with or without the oath.
- The Government of the Republic is the only lawful government
- If there is a Republican majority, the representatives of all Ireland shall be summoned. (SC, 02/04/27)

Obviously, these conditions were turned down by Fianna Fáil, as they would have contradicted, had they been accepted, the very reasons which had led them to part ways with Sinn Féin. Predictably, the results of the June 1927 elections heralded the end of Sinn Féin as the dominant Republican party, and its replacement by Fianna Fáil, with five of the fifteen former abstentionist candidates being elected, against forty-four for the latter. Moreover, some of the party's biggest names were eliminated with dismally low scores.[31]

The issue of the oath became a concrete one on the day following the elections. The doors of Dáil Éireann remained closed to those elected representatives who refused to accomplish that formality. In spite of the fact that the government party, Cumann na nGaedheal, had failed to obtain a majority (forty-seven seats) and now had to contend with a serious opposition within the Dáil, Cosgrave was able to form a new government, in which Kevin O'Higgins cumulated the functions of Vice-President, Minister for Justice and Minister for External Affairs.[32] While Fianna Fáil remained outside the parliament, the majority party was able to govern. The situation was profoundly modified following the assassination of Kevin O'Higgins on 10 July 1927, as he walked from his home to the church in the Booterstown southern suburb of Dublin. For the authorities, this confirmed their own vulnerability and the necessity to defend the state against further threats and attacks. Cosgrave declared in the Dáil that '[i]t is the political assassination of a pillar of the State. It is the fruit of the steady, persistent attack against the State and its fundamental institutions' (*Dáil Debates*, 12/07/27). The IRA denied responsibility, and it was later established that the murder had been committed by three men who were supporters of the IRA but were not acting on orders from their hierarchy.[33] A Sinn Féin councillor, L. Raul, subsequently explained that '[i]f Republicans had shot Kevin O'Higgins they would have said so. They never denied any shooting that they ever did' (*IT*, 25/05/28). However, while the government 'assumed that [while] this organisation [the IRA] as a whole did not plot and carry out the assassination of Mr. O'Higgins, there is very little doubt that some section of it did', and therefore, 'this revolutionary organisation is a menace to the peace and security of the people, and to the lives and liberties of the people, and steps must be taken to break it up and to make its continued existence impossible or at least difficult' (*Dáil Debates*, 26/07/27).

This political assassination had long-lasting effects, not only for Sinn Féin itself but for the future of the country. The government moved swiftly by introducing a new Public Safety Act, more drastic than the previous one introduced in 1923. It made illegal any organisation which called for the destruction of the state or supported armed action. President Cosgrave, in his introduction to the Bill in the Dáil, mainly spoke of the danger that the IRA still represented in the country, alleging that the organisation intended to shoot any Fianna Fáil TDs who took their seats in the Dáil. The IRA quickly moved to contradict such statements, deeming them 'absolutely untrue' and a 'contemptible attempt to stampede people into sanctioning this new coercion' (*IT*, 29/07/27). The Bill provided for a special tribunal with the power to inflict the death penalty or life imprisonment on those found guilty of possession of firearms. Interestingly, the draconian measures contained in the Act did not result in a wave of arrests and convictions, which raises a question about the actual purpose of the legislation. Indeed, when de Valera asked, almost a year after the Bill had been introduced, how many arrests and convictions had been made as a consequence of the Bill, the Minister for Justice replied that 'Four persons were arrested under the provisions of the Public Safety Act, 1927. There are no persons at present being detained under that Act. No person was convicted under that Act of any offence' (*Dáil Debates*, 24/05/28). Thus it could be argued that the objective of such measures were not so much to strike at the heart of dissidence but rather to show the government's resolve and its zero tolerance regarding subversion.[34]

Politically, a further blow was inflicted upon Sinn Féin, as within this legislation, an amendment to the electoral law was introduced on 20 July 1927, making it compulsory for all candidates to state their intention to take their seat if elected and to swear the oath to the Crown within two months of the election (*Dáil Debates*, 20/07/27). As Cosgrave stated in the Dáil to justify this new piece of legislation:

> The majority of the people of this country have declared in unmistakable terms that they desire to work out their destinies peacefully under the Constitution's liberties and parliamentary institutions which they enjoy. This they cannot do if a minority is to be permitted to play fast and loose with the basic principles of democratic government in their application if they are allowed to persevere in their effort to bring Parliamentary institutions into disrepute. (*IT* 29/07/27)

The aim of the Bill was obviously to reinforce the legitimacy of the institutions of the Free State as well as to ensure that politics were played out within the confines of these institutions, and not outside. What the new state seemed to fear most was the existence of forces which operated outside of its control and which could become difficult to contain. This legislation mainly targeted Fianna Fáil as the biggest party operating on the margins of the system, but not all deputies within the Dáil were in agreement as to its purpose. Captain Redmond of the newly formed National League Party 'entirely disagreed with the Minister when he said that the action of the Fianna Fáil party would inevitably lead to violence. The removal of the means of expression of public opinion, which the bill sadly amounted to, was the removal of the only safety valve against violence' (*IT* 29/07/27). However, the Bill was passed by a redundant fifty to twenty-five votes.[35]

This Bill put Fianna Fáil into a delicate situation. It now had to take a clear position on the issue while not seeming to contradict the principled stance that had been held until then, as the party had been strongly campaigning to show that the exclusion of its TDs from the Dáil was not legal. Different routes were considered for the removal of the oath, such as a petition to be signed by 75,000 people (*IT*, 02/07/27) and a referendum. A writ was filed in the High Court seeking the expulsion of TDs as well as the election of the Ceann Comhairle, to be annulled, as he had been elected in their absence (*IT*, 09/07/27). However, some members of the parliamentary party dissented from this position, such as Patrick Belton who stated that he would take his seat; the party quickly moved to expel him (*IT*, 26/07/27). This direct challenge to Fianna Fáil's official stance, together with the dead-end in which abstentionism put the party, meant that a decision had to be taken regarding its future participation in parliamentary politics. The party was keenly aware of the potentially damaging consequences that a U-turn could have within its own ranks; but a far more real danger was that of being sidelined. The language used by the leaders regarding the oath began to alter slightly, being described in early August as a 'distasteful formality' (*IT*, 09/08/27). De Valera's use of the expression 'empty formula' was to pave the way for the party's entry to the Dáil,[36] as it came to the conclusion that it could be taken 'without becoming involved, or without involving, their nation, in obligations of loyalty to the English Crown' (*IT*, 11/08/27). The issue of the oath was a catalyst for the Republican aspiration. Indeed, the motion that had been put at the 1925 Ard Fheis, before the split, allowed for a discussion on the possibility of entering Dáil Éireann but not on swearing allegiance to a foreign monarch. Therefore, this was a Rubicon that no Republican could cross. De Valera insisted, more than twenty years later when testifying during the Sinn Féin Funds Case, that 'no such oath was taken. It is a matter capable of judicial determination with the witnesses and documents available that no such oath was taken either by me or, so far as I know, by any member of Fianna Fáil [...] No such oath was taken. This is a historical fact, and I am on Oath' (de Valera, Witness Statement, 1948, C1).

The entrance of Fianna Fáil to the Dáil was to alter considerably the balance of power that had prevailed until then, and which had enabled Cumann na nGaedheal to govern. The party's position was threatened from the very day the Fianna Fáil deputies tabled a motion of no confidence, which, if narrowly defeated, indicated that the Cosgrave government had very little room to manoeuvre. In October 1927, new elections were held. Fianna Fáil won fifty-seven seats, tailing Cumann na nGaedheal by five seats only.

Political vacuum

Sinn Féin, being unable to even nominate candidates in light of the new legislation, was forced into a position of onlooker in the elections. While the new electoral law had indirectly served Fianna Fáil's interests by obliging it to get involved in constitutional politics, it reinforced Sinn Féin's isolation. Its financial situation was so dire that even had it been legally able to do so, it could not have put forward any candidates, not having the funds to finance an electoral campaign, as was made clear in the short-lived Sinn Féin newspaper *Saoirse Freedom*: 'The financial position of the organisation makes it impossible to effectively contest an election and the indecent haste with which this election is being forced leaves us no time for an appeal to friends of the Republican Movement' (*Saoirse Freedom*, September 1927).

This downward spiral rapidly transformed Sinn Féin into a ghost-like, bureaucratic organisation, more interested in respecting rigid rules than in addressing actual problems. Its decline was rapid and alarming. There were obvious signs that it had been considerably affected by the split and that the leaders were not willing to take the measure of how critical the situation had become. Financially, the party was on the verge of bankruptcy. In November 1926, president Art O'Connor wrote to an American correspondent, J. Hearn, mentioning the total amount available to the party: £40 (Cronin, 1972, 123). Another dramatic consequence of the split was the loss of support. Attendance at the 1927 Ard Fheis declined even further compared to the previous year, the number of delegates having now dropped to 150 according to police reports (Garda report, 15/12/27), representing a loss of almost half of its support in a year, and of 90 per cent since the pre-split years. The total number of affiliated cumainn had also decreased, falling from 232 in 1926 to 87 in 1927. In his report, the honorary secretary even warned that 'the strength of actual member-ship of the cumainn is, we have reason to believe, much worse than even the small number of affiliated cumainn would appear to represent', due to three factors: emigration, the split and the 'loss of national spirit' among the Irish people (Garda report, 15/12/27). Another issue that the party would soon have to face was the fact that it was increasingly becoming a Dublin-based organisa-tion: out of the seventy-seven cumainn in Ireland, forty-five were in Leinster, of which twenty-seven were in Dublin and region, with only one cumann in Northern Ireland (Garda report, 15/12/27).[37] The loss of support that the party was suffering could also be measured in the dwindling numbers attending its regular commemorations. Marches were organised throughout the country in 1928 to celebrate the Easter Rising, but according to the *Irish Times*, although 'a great many women and girls took part, it did not seem to be as large as that of last year, and there was a paucity of bands'. Interestingly, Sinn Féin's name was not even mentioned in the newspaper report, which attributed the organisation of most events to 'the extreme Republican Party' (*IT*, 09/04/28).

At the 1927 Ard Fheis, the question of funds was discussed. The amount at the disposal of the party was, according to some accounts, £90. The party was nevertheless ready to use all and every means to remedy the situation. It was therefore suggested to secure the monies initially advanced as election deposits to members of the party prior to the split, some of these being now members of Fianna Fáil. Seán T. O'Kelly[38] was decided upon as a 'test case', whereby he would be asked to return the money and summoned to a 'Republican court' for this matter. In the event of his refusing such a course of action, the IRA would then seize property at his house for the equivalent amount to what he was deemed to owe the party. That such proposals did not generate any criti-cism or debate among the delegates was an indication of the lengths to which the party was ready to go to retrieve what it considered as its rightful property (Garda report, 15/12/27), but testifies to the authoritarian streak that Sinn Féin displayed as well as its contempt for the rule of law.

The party's dogmatic stance on Republicanism led it to take decisions which were meant to protect its principles but which divorced it further from its original aims. The price to pay for the defence of its position was the dropping of some of its core work, most notably that of the defence of prisoners. The 1929 Ard Fheis, for instance, put forward a resolution for Sinn Féin to 'give its whole-hearted support to any committee working for the release of political prisoners', but the Standing Committee decided that 'Cumainn and Comhairle cannot be represented on committees where there is a danger of people using prisoners' platforms to further their own and political parties' aims' (SC, 02/01/30). It clearly defined the conditions for the prisoners' committees to have Sinn Féin support: the organisations had to ensure that their membership was not open to political parties, in particular Fianna Fáil, and that speakers should be carefully selected so as not to promote causes other than that of Republicanism (SC, 14/02/01). Likewise, when the Standing Committee was notified that the Roger Casement cumann in London had signed a petition for the release of Francis Breen and Patrick Gavin,[39] it deemed the action 'contrary to the principles of the organisation which has always tried to secure the release of Republican prisoners as a matter of right, and has never identified itself with a petition to any British government urging the release of prisoners as an act of clemency or otherwise' (SC, 10/09/30).

Cooperation with other groups was equally problematic, and was only considered by the Standing Committee if there was a guarantee that it involved no party or individual associated with a party sitting in the Dáil. The 1926 Ard Fheis had reaffirmed that Sinn Féin would enter into no pact for the general election, although the possibility of an 'understanding' between the two Republican parties regarding the elimination of rivalry was considered (*II*, 02/11/26). This understanding, nevertheless, never materialised. On the contrary, as the weeks and months went by, the relationship between the two Republican parties further deteriorated. While both had managed to attend the Wolfe Tone annual commemoration in 1927 together, with Art O'Connor delivering the oration, the funeral of Austin Stack in May 1929 epitomised the gap that existed between former allies. Although de Valera and other members of Fianna Fáil attended the event, they had not been specifically invited by the committee in charge of the organisation of the funeral and were, according to the report in the *Irish Times*, 'well towards the end of the procession', having been merged within the group of 'Public bodies and other organisations' (*IT*, 02/05/29).

The following year, Seán MacBride, honorary secretary of the Irish section of the League Against Imperialism and for National Independence, invited the cooperation of Sinn Féin in the organisation of a public meeting on 10 November 1930, 'to protest against imperial displays associated with Armistice Day'. Two members of Sinn Féin were announced as speakers on the posters advertising the event. The Standing Committee urged them not to take part in such meetings as they would have to share a platform with 'members of the usurping Free State who not only had abandoned the Republic but had also sworn an oath to the Head of the British Empire' (SC, 07/11/30). A year later, it was revealed that a member of the Dublin Rathmines cumann, Helen Moloney, had actually taken part in the meeting and shared a platform with speakers who had sworn an oath; she was expelled by her cumann, by four votes to two, as she refused to pledge that she would abide by the so-called Bogus unity rule (SC, 16/10/31), which was enshrined in the rules of the party and forbade membership to anyone who 'associated for any purpose whatsoever with what can only be a bogus unity with those who have signed, and not renounced, an Oath of allegiance to the Head of the British Empire' (*Scheme of Organisation, Rules, etc.*, Garda report, 05/10/31).

The proactive, innovative party of the early 1920s had now become a quasi extinct political formation. It had been reduced to a narrow organisation characterised by an extreme ideological purism which was not supported by any political programme. The rule for any member of Sinn Féin seemed to consist in following, word for word, the ideas and principles which the party had elaborated in its more glorious years, but which evidently had lost currency after 1926. The rigour that characterised the party was manifested at all levels, and those who did not strictly adhere to the principles had no place in the movement. Art O'Connor, who had already stepped down as president of the Second Dáil, was also forced to resign from the party when he announced his intention to practise as a lawyer in the Free State tribunals, in 1927, as such a move was deemed contrary to the principles of the party and represented a betrayal of the Republican tribunals which were still in existence, albeit only virtually.

Rejection of the Free State logically entailed that members of Sinn Féin could no longer take part in parliamentary elections, and they were therefore prohibited from voting, other than in those elections held for the purpose of electing candidates to Dáil Éireann. The code of discipline that Sinn Féin imposed on its members was strict and denied them any free choice and will. The ranks of the party were divided between those who felt that it should withdraw from electoral contests altogether, including local elections, and those who feared that this would not only further isolate them but play into the hands of their adversaries. The Thomas Ashe cumann in Mayo therefore put forward a motion that 'in order to prevent Sinn Féiners becoming adherents of the Fianna Fáil policy by working and voting for them at elections. Sinn Féin should not allow further elections either parliamentary or local government to go uncontested' (Garda report, 19/11/28). Some were therefore obviously aware that if the party was too intransigent, the grassroots would soon feel isolated from the leadership as there was little for them to do in terms of even local involvement.

Sinn Féin's isolation was compounded by the fact that it had no press organ which could adequately, in its view, convey its message. For a while, it published *Saoirse Freedom: The Organ of Intransigent Republicanism*. But some two years after coming into existence, in November 1928, the paper disappeared, primarily for financial reasons. It therefore had to rely on other Republican publications to convey its message. Sinn Féin's relationship with *An Phoblacht* was equally tumultuous, as revealed by the existence of a correspondence between the general secretary of the party and the newspaper editor regarding the 'hostile attitude of the paper in reporting the Ard Fheis'. Nevertheless, at the 1930 Ard Fheis discussions were held over the viability and desirability of a press organ. The motion that the Standing Committee should 'explore the possibility of a monthly paper and appoint a committee' was voted upon, with Sceilg and Brian O'Higgins asked to look into it. Mary MacSwiney suggested buying *Saoirse na hÉireann* (SC, 12/12/30), a newsletter independently published by a member of the Standing Committee. However, in view of the financial and organisational difficulties the party was experiencing, none of these initiatives came to fruition.

The Sinn Féin leaders' rhetoric became increasingly inward-looking and judgemental. They could not hide their contempt for their opponents, especially de Valera, who gradually came to be seen as the main cause for the break-up of the party. Therefore, O'Flanagan explained that the 'root cause of the disaster to Republicanism was the national worship of unity', de Valera being 'the supreme worshiper of unity which created a split in the country' (*IT*, 16/10/26). They developed a discourse which was largely disconnected from pragmatic considerations, being mainly founded on a rhetoric of suffering and martyrdom, with obvious religious overtones. At the 1926 Ard Fheis, Mary MacSwiney did acknowledge the degradation of her party, as shown by the attendance which had dropped from 1,000 delegates the previous year to a mere 200. However, instead of articulating a proactive strategy to counter this decline, she insisted on the suffering that her organisation was experiencing and the burden that was theirs to shoulder. In her view, the IRA's decision the previous year to withdraw its support from the Second Dáil had been 'heart-burning'. Art O'Connor added that although material forces were against them, work – trust in God and themselves – would bring them success (*IT*, 16/10/26). Two years later, O'Kelly made similar remarks at his party's annual convention, explaining that:

> To avoid the public dissension which would give joy to the enemies of the Republic we have borne in silence a good deal of misrepresentation at home and abroad, for the past couple of years. If I break that silence now it is because our forbearance hitherto has only emboldened the seceders from our organisation to

misrepresent us more and more and join with England's obedient instruments in challenging the whole status of the Government of the Republic and its constitutional arm. (*II*, 19/11/28)

Sinn Féin's vision of the future of the country was apocalyptic and might have deterred even the most loyal Republican sympathisers. Turning a blind eye to the glaring loss of popularity and relevance that they were facing, Mary MacSwiney warned that Irish people were being brought back to a state of slavery and cowardice, while Art O'Connor talked of apathy, which in his eyes was nothing less than national heresy and laziness (*II*, 29/06/26). The image of Ireland enslaved was taken up by another speaker, Brian O'Higgins (member of the Second Dáil and future president of the party), who, at a public meeting in Cavan, questioned the manhood of Ireland, the country being content to be held in slavery by England, and predicted the end of Ireland nationally and its eternal damnation (*Meath Chronicle*, 14/08/26). This choice of register was also indicative of a very rigid Catholic ethos, showing how closely related, in the leaders' views, the credos of Catholicism and Republicanism were. Anyone who diverged from the strict Republican path was seen as a heretic or apostate.

The leaders attempted to tackle some concrete social issues. Sceilg, in an effort to highlight the injustice to which Ireland had been subjected for centuries, estimated that England owed Ireland £2 billion, as it had been robbing Ireland for 750 years. He concluded that it was 'the right of the hungry child to take whatever came next to him' and added that he did not care whether he would be regarded as a communist for preaching that policy (*II*, 14/07/26). Brian O'Higgins's understanding of communism was quite rudimentary, greatly tainted with his devout Catholicism: labelling it 'Eastern materialism', he deemed it was to be condemned at all cost, as '[m]en who deny God, who are traitors to God, will be false to every person and everything less than God – to all things on earth and in heaven. That is a simple truth about which there can be no argument' (*II*, 14/04/30). This confusion between religion and politics led to some curious and unusual developments within the party. In 1931, for instance, the Ard Fheis proceedings were overshadowed by the dispute which opposed staunch Republican Fr O'Flanagan to the then president Brian O'Higgins. Ironically, it was the former's criticism of the church that brought on this debate. Fr O'Flanagan had talked of the Pope as the enemy of Irish Republicanism and Irish independence, which in his view was nothing new as the Pope's predecessors had also been opponents of the independence of Ireland.[40] O'Higgins retorted that the 'Pope, as the Vicar on earth of the King of Peace and the King of Love, could not be the enemy of any country on earth' (Garda report,

05/10/31), and stated that he could not share a platform with someone who uttered such profanities. O'Flanagan refused to back down and reiterated his statement on the Pope, at which point O'Higgins declared that he would in future 'refuse in public and in private to be associated with O'Flanagan' (Garda report, 05/10/31). He then turned to the delegates but the matter was dropped, according to the Garda on duty.

This rhetoric was but a symptom of the fragile, paradoxical position in which the party found itself. While incapable, from a political and financial point of view, of putting forward an alternative, Sinn Féin nevertheless stubbornly continued on a path that would prove self-destructive. Mary MacSwiney was partially aware of this problem: 'One of the present difficulties of Sinn Féin lies in the fact that to those outside Sinn Féin, at home and abroad, these people [Fianna Fáil] are accepted as Republicans' (*Saoirse Freedom*, August 1927). In his 1928 Ard Fheis speech, the president of Sinn Féin, O'Kelly, explained the decline of Sinn Féin in the following terms:

> If prestige has fallen, it is because repeated defections have somewhat shattered public confidence in the Republican movement. If our numbers seem alternated, it is because of the bad example lately set by making politics a profession instead of regarding patriotic service as a labour of love; because to counter that tendency, we have no prospect to offer but the old unrequited service of a deathless cause. (O'Kelly, 1928)

Therefore, while accusing the other parties of being clientelist, if not opportunistic, he indirectly referred to the lack of relevance of his own organisation, which was incapable of making inroads into the political life of the country and of creating its own image. Sinn Féin, cut off from a possible base, refusing any compromise, was fast becoming an elitist organisation which was exclusively concerned with issues of principles and not with the social or economic realities of the country.

From 1928 onwards, Sinn Féin became a forgotten institution, a circle of faithful who brandished the flag of traditional Republicanism. Some attempts were made to address the decline of the party, such as the re-establishment of a Sinn Féin section in Tralee, with Austin Stack stating that they would do 'their best to restore their movement to the powerful position it had occupied a few years back' (*IT*, 12/11/28). At a meeting in January 1929, Brian O'Higgins suggested that in order to raise the badly needed funds 'to carry on the fight', each member should sacrifice some luxury for a week for their country's sake' (SC, 21/01/29), which again showed the religious dimension that was ascribed to the Republican cause. But this was to little avail. At the 1929 Ard Fheis, the total number of affiliated branches stood at seventy-two, one more than the previous year, but still abysmally low. More worryingly still, there was only one section for Northern Ireland, which heralded the eclipse of Sinn Féin from Northern Ireland (Garda report, 10/12/29).

Mary MacSwiney attempted to reinvigorate the Republican project by drafting, in 1929, a 'Constitution of the Republic'. Among its provisions were 'Free university for the capable; pensions, health insurance, unemployment compensation, and national housing schemes, subdivision of big ranches, nationalisation of transport, shipping and banks' (Sinn Féin Constitution, 1929, in Funds Case, 1948). This apparently progressive social agenda was heavily influenced by a traditional and conservative view of social relations, which were to be guided by Christian principles: 'No provision shall be made for godless schools, no legislation which is definitely anti-Catholic should be provided for'. The confessional aspects of the proposals were in contradiction with the ideals of the 1916 Declaration of which the party and the Second Dáil saw themselves as being the representatives. Sinn Féin nevertheless enthusiastically endorsed the document, and at its 1930 Ard Fheis, urged all cumainn 'at home and abroad, to discuss it clause by clause, at their regular meetings, to take steps to arouse the widest possible interest in it, so that the citizens may be generally familiar with its provisions and suggest such amendations as may be calculated to make it a more efficient instrument when the time comes to put it into operation' (SC, 28/11/30). However, it is doubtful whether this document was discussed beyond the walls of the Sinn Féin headquarters. No mention of it is to be found in any newspaper report, and even *An Phoblacht* dealt both Sinn Féin and the Second Dáil a sharp blow by refusing to publish it, justifying its decision in the following manner: 'We do not admit the claim of surviving members of the Second Dáil that they constitute the Government of the Republic' (quoted in Fallon, 1986, 151).

The efforts of the leadership to explain the dwindling of their numbers were, at best, wishful thinking, considerably lacking in political vision. Brian O'Higgins, launching his party's latest initiative to keep in touch with potential members – the organising of Irish language classes in the party's headquarters – explained the situation as follows: 'We who are keeping the idea of Sinn Féin to the fore, look forward with hope to the day when the people of Ireland will grasp the truth and the commonsense of the Sinn Féin idea, and go forward by the light of it to the complete independence of the country' (*Irish Press* (*IP*), 07/10/31). Clearly O'Higgins gave a messianic dimension to his party, whose role was therefore to enlighten the Irish people who had been led astray and get them back on the straight and narrow.

The political choices of the IRA

The IRA also faced issues of internal cohesion. Since 1925, it had been, so to speak, independent. The question of the role that it should play was all the more pressing. Some advocated that it confine its activities to the military, but the risk of isolation was great. Indeed, Fianna Fáil, since it had joined the Dáil, had started to embrace constitutionalism and Seán Lemass's description of Fianna Fáil as a 'slightly constitutional party' in 1928 (Fanning, 1983a, 99) left little doubt as to the position that the party would come to adopt on the fundamental issue of armed struggle. Others such as Peadar O'Donnell opted for a greater involvement in bread-and-butter issues. During the 1929 IRA convention, he proposed the creation of a radical political formation, Saor Éire, the main objective of which was to achieve 'an independent revolutionary leadership for the working class and working farmers aiming at the overthrow in Ireland of British imperialism and its ally, Irish capitalism' (Coogan, 1966, 257). A majority of the delegates rejected the proposal, considering it too radical. The IRA annual convention approved instead the creation of Comhairle na Poblachta, the Central Council of the Republic. This organisation included members of Sinn Féin, Cumann na mBan, and independent Republicans, which was 'presented by the Sinn Féin leaders as being essentially a call on all Republicans to unite in order the more successfully to forward their common aims' (Coughlan, 1977, 264). However, it was short lived, as the only element that seemed to unite this group was their opposition to the Cosgrave government, and it was dissolved shortly after its creation.

While Ireland was suffering from an economic depression, with rates of unemployment estimated between 70,000 and 100,000, the IRA, or at least some of its members, were moving towards an increasingly radical political direction. O'Donnell had advocated since 1926 the non-payment of land annuities, which represented £3.13 million per annum (Lee, 1989, 110), calling for a campaign of civil disobedience and resistance (Ó Drisceoil, 2001, 45). This was subsequently discussed at the Sinn Féin Ard Fheis of November 1928, when several resolutions in support of the non-payment of land annuities had been put forward (Garda report, 19/11/28). In June 1929, the Irish Defence Corps was founded by trade unionists and Dublin-based IRA volunteers. On 7 July, the convention of this movement, which was attended by influential members of the IRA such as Frank Ryan, renamed it the Irish Labour Defence League. This organisation had, according to Fianna Fáil TD Éamonn Cooney, 'as its object the raising of funds to provide legal assistance to working men and women who may be charged, or even arrested without charge, during the course of economic struggles to prevent wages being lowered, or other such objects; [that] the organisation also undertakes the succour of the innocent dependents of such workers' (*Dáil Debates*, 13/03/30). However, it was considered by the Minister for Justice to be a front for the IRA and, as such, was the target of several security raids. Meanwhile, O'Donnell founded, on 13 March 1930, the Revolutionary Workers Party in which some IRA members took part. It published its own newspaper, *The Workers' Voice*, which was banned in 1931, along with a number of political organisations.

Faced with the growing radicalisation of its own members, the IRA attempted to define its position on economic issues, and particularly on land rents. On 1 February 1931, the Army Council officially authorised the formation of Saor Éire, proposed by Peadar O'Donnell, Frank Ryan and George Gilmore. On 28 September of that year, the first national convention was held, organised by Seán MacBride, during which its Standing Committee was elected from within the ranks of Cumann na mBan and the IRA. Given that in its view the Labour Party had dropped 'all pretence to being a party of the working class and had deserted the trade union basis', it aimed to achieve '[a]n Irish Republic based on the possession and administration by the working farmers and wage earners of the land, and instruments of production, distribution and exchange, and [that] the cleaning of Ireland from British imperialism involves the abolition of the inhuman and degrading social system'. It also sought to bring about cooperation between urban and rural workers in order to mobilise the Irish people behind a revolutionary government (*IT*, 28/09/31). However, O'Donnell was to say later that 'Saor Éire was not so revolutionary as it seemed to be. It was academic really, and constituted, in effect, an alibi enabling [the IRA] to slide out of doing something practical to implement its aims' (quoted in McInerney, 1974, 116).

Sinn Féin, which had been adamant that nothing should compromise its Republican dogma, left itself out – or was left out – of any new political organisation. It refused to support the land rent campaign. According to the deputies of the Second Dáil, 'such agitation leads to politics and politics lead to the snake pit of the Free State' (McInerney, 1974, 122). Similarly, it rejected any collaboration with Saor Éire, as it 'deprecated any attempts to promote class distinction and class warfare' (Bowyer Bell, 1983, 89). However, Sinn Féin had good reasons to want to keep its distances with the new political organisation, if the reports of the Gardaí were to be believed. Indeed, from the discussions held at the 1931 Ard Fheis, it appeared that the IRA had no intention of giving allegiance to the Sinn Féin organisation, but that they had set up a 'quasi political' organisation, the executive of which was formed of the most highly placed members. But more importantly, as far as Sinn Féin was concerned, the Gardaí estimated that 'It would appear that "Saor Éire" is intended to replace Sinn Féin although the latter body will not admit to the fact' (Garda report, 05/10/31).

The Garda assessment of the situation was probably inaccurate, as it is improbable that the IRA had much interest in Sinn Féin and had no control over its existence. Nevertheless, there is no doubt that what Saor Éire stood for was repugnant to most Sinn Féin leaders, who were perpetuating a solid belief, already present in Arthur Griffith's position, that any notion of class struggle and any political approach which was not exclusively centred on the national question should be rejected, as this was seen as divisive and weakening for the movement. Brian O'Higgins therefore sought to distance his party from Saor Éire. He was reported as saying, according to the Garda report, that Sinn Féin was 'neither communistic nor anti-Christian, that it had no connection with a number of the banned organisations and that he was not sympathetic with the principles of the majority of these banned organisations' (Garda report, 31/10/31).

Subversion and the state

The IRA had been involved in a number of incidents since 1926, although it was 'never engaged in an armed campaign' for the duration of the decade 1926–36 (Hanley, 2002, 71). A member of the Gardaí was killed in November 1926 in a raid on a barracks, and a superintendent was murdered in 1931.[41] Obviously, the armed organisation was closely monitored by the authorities. An issue of *An Phoblacht* was seized by members of the Criminal Investigation Department (CID), as it was seen as 'treasonable', 'containing matters which amounted to the encouragement of the murder of jurors who carried out their duties' (*IT*, 01/03/29). Even Sinn Féin was considered to pose a threat to the state's security. Regular raids were carried out on the party's headquarters, the purpose and findings of which were questioned by members of Fianna Fáil in the Dáil. According to the Minister for Justice Fitzgerald-Kenney, however, the 'persons who frequented these offices were responsible for various anti-State activities and for the intimidation of jurors, and for incitement to assassination of various persons' (*IT*, 25/04/29). The raids continued throughout the late 1920s, the CID searching and arresting members of Sinn Féin on a number of occasions (*IT*, 10/12/29).

At the 1930 Ard Fheis, John O'Kelly outlined the difficult conditions under which his party was operating, mainly due to repeated interference through raids on the offices, making it all the more difficult to keep in touch with the branches throughout the country. Moreover, according to him, members were continuously under the 'forceful attention of England's hirelings, both native and imported; and meetings broken up, detentions for hours, sometimes days' (*IT*, 01/12/30). While it is possible that these assessments were exaggerated for propaganda reasons, there is no doubt that Sinn Féin remained the object of surveillance on the part of the state, even if what the authorities hoped to achieve was unclear. Sinn Féin was far from representing a danger to the stability of the state. Ideologically it held views which were quite similar to those advocated by the government, in its traditional Catholic ethos and its rabid anti-communism. Numerically it was so weak that it could not be seriously considered a threat. A close reading of the Standing Committee minutes for those years shows that nothing the party did was illegal, and that its workings, if anything, were tedious but certainly not subversive. Sinn Féin's sole purpose in those years was to act as a constant reminder not only of the origins of the state, but also of the unaccomplished work that most TDs and ministers had pledged to do prior to 1922, and of the contradictions that the new state had had to accept.

In an effort to suppress any opposition which was seen to threaten the very foundation of the state, the government took some rash measures to try and prevent the assembly of so-called seditious groups. In 1931, for instance, the annual Bodenstown commemoration[42] was targeted, with all special trains previously booked banned by the Minister of Defence in order to prevent any illegal assembly. The message was clear: only one army would be allowed in the country, and that was the army established and maintained by law. This led to a vigorous debate in the Dáil, as Fianna Fáil TDs questioned the appropriateness of the measures taken. But the minister was adamant that no subversive opposition that threatened the very foundation of the state was tolerable: 'was it dishonourable, or was it dishonouring the nation to accept the State as set up? Would it not be more dishonourable to have a spirit in the country permitting men to urge individuals to upset the State by force?' (*IT*, 25/06/31).

There is no doubt, however, that for the last half of the decade and until the Second World War, Sinn Féin would still be seen as a potentially disruptive force worthy of the attention of the security forces. Its meetings were all attended by Gardaí, who then reported to their hierarchy as to where they took place, the numbers that had attended and what had been said. However, what emerges from those reports contradicts the very purpose of that surveillance. Firstly, these meetings were peaceful, the reports generally concluding with a note stating that there was nothing to report, that the proceedings were orderly and that there was no traffic disruption. The danger of one of those meetings developing into some sort of disruptive threat seemed quite unlikely. Secondly, attendance at these meetings varied greatly, depending on their location. Public meetings held outdoors could gather up to 1,000 people, those organised within indoor premises varied between 70 and 200, hardly a sufficient number of people to seriously challenge the state. Finally, although it could be argued that the content of the speeches was seditious in nature, in that it demanded 'the complete independence and separation from the British Empire' (Garda report, 31/10/31), no specific action was recommended to achieve this objective.

Surveillance of the party entailed identification of its members and as the organisation's numbers were quite low, this made the task of the police officers relatively easy. A list of attendance at meetings of the Standing Committee between 15 December 1927 and 11 September 1928 put the total number of such meetings at thirty-two (Garda report, n.d.). The information contained was extremely precise. All participants were identified nominally, with their roles being specified (TD, councillor, treasurer) as well as the number of times that individuals had attended the meeting. This list shows the extent to which the security surveillance was taken seriously. A note on Mary MacSwiney, for instance, explained that 'she had attended two weekly meetings and a special meeting. Gobnait Ní Bhrudair and Daithí Ceannt each attended one weekly and one special meeting. And Sean O'Shea attended a special meeting' (Garda report, n.d.).

The report on the 1929 Ard Fheis detailed the names of all Sinn Féin delegates, with the cumainn to which they were affiliated, as well as the names of the visitors to the convention. Some individuals were obviously more relevant than others. A note at the end of the report remarked: 'it should be noted that Eamon Enright who acted as Vice President to the proceedings is subject of file C.S. 964/25. He is an employee of the Electricity Supply Board' (Garda report, 10/12/29).

The prime objective of this surveillance was not, obviously, crowd control, but political control. Therefore the reports contained a summary of what was said by the speakers, which in turn gives an indication of the type of rhetoric developed by Sinn Féin leaders. Most reports remarked on the fact that the leaders tended to review the history of the previous ten years, which became a mantra, a legitimisation of the very existence of the party. The Garda surveillance was also meant to assess the relevance and the influence of the party. When reporting at the 1931 Sinn Féin Ard Fheis, for instance, the detective present at the proceedings described the presidential speech delivered by Sceilg as 'not so virulent as in previous years'. The 1931 Ard Fheis was described as 'arousing no public interest, and nothing calling for police interference occurred' (Garda report, 05/10/31).

The reason behind this surveillance was made clear in a memo addressed to the Department of Justice Garda Commissioner on 23 January 1929. Reporting on a meeting of Sinn Féin TDs which 'aped the proceedings of An Dáil', the report stated: 'This may be very amusing at this stage, but when such an assembly begins interfering in vital matters, "authorising" acts of violence, boycotts, etc., it may have serious effects. A good many of those present certainly have the intention of setting up a pretended government, and if this is tolerated the repercussions are too obvious to need be emphasised' (Garda report, 23/01/29). But the report also pointed to the anecdotal character of the event insofar as 'no public interest was taken in the proceedings', thereby undermining the potential threat that this meeting posed.

However, the perception that there was an imminent danger of a revolutionary force disrupting and perhaps even derailing the institutions was real. As O. Grattan Esmonde, Cumann na nGaedheal TD, said: 'I think I am not exaggerating when I say that, as far as the danger of disturbance is concerned, the situation today is more serious than at any time since the civil war of nine years ago' (*IP*, 12/10/31). Eoin O'Duffy introduced the project on the Free State Constitution (amendment 7), which became law on 17 October 1931. Under these measures, a five-member military tribunal was set up to deal with political crimes, and empowered to impose the death penalty. The government could ban some organisations and the police were given wide powers of arrest and detention.

One of the main targets of this legislation was Saor Éire, which was made illegal and denounced as communist. The government had been indirectly aided by the statement of the Catholic Church which vehemently condemned Saor Éire: 'The two organisations [Saor Éire and the IRA], whether separated or in alliance, are sinful and irreligious and no Catholic can lawfully be a member of them' (Bowyer Bell, 1983, 88). The Minister of Justice was in no doubt that the organisation had been infiltrated by Russian elements, and to support this view, he claimed that ten communists had gone to Russia in 1927 and that Peadar O'Donnell himself had been sent to the Lenin College in Moscow to study the techniques of revolution, a claim which O'Donnell himself denied, stating that he had never set foot in the Soviet Union. But the minister concluded: 'I myself do not see how it is possible for this country to endure, as it has endured – for this country to be in the future what it has been in the past, a really Catholic country – if it is going to permeated by force of arms with doctrines of that nature' (*IT*, 15/10/31). He explained that in abnormal circumstances when the state is threatened by force, the normal law was not enough, therefore justifying the banning of the main Republican or socialist organisations.[43] Some days later, Saor Éire was also declared an unlawful association in Northern Ireland (2 November 1931). But whether the situation called for such extreme measures was open to question. Seán Lemass remarked that 'although government had stretched the few threads of evidence almost to breaking point they did not prove the case' (that there was a widespread conspiracy in the country to overthrow the state and bring about social revolution) (*IT*, 23/10/31). As Fanning observed, 'it was their [Cumann na hGaedheal's] inability to trump Fianna Fáil's green card which made them take refuge in the red scare' (Fanning, 1983a, 102).

Only Sinn Féin escaped these draconian measures: 'The organisation that is getting arms and money and becoming active in the country realises that Miss MacSwiney's party is finished, and that Mr de Valera has failed to break up the Dáil from inside. For these reasons Saor Éire was set up, whose intention is to establish a republic on the lines of the Russian Republic' (*IT*, 12/10/31). Sinn Féin had become, in six years, quite an innocuous party, engaged in a struggle that saw itself as subversive but which, seemingly, was no longer considered as such and only represented a name, a mere memory in the contemporary history of the country.

Notes

1 Ó Beacháin (2009, 389) notes that 'Sinn Féin increased its representation from forty four seats to forty eight during this period, and succeeded in augmenting its share of the popular vote'. Indeed, its vote increased by 5.6 per cent, as opposed to 0.5 per cent for Cumann na Gaedheal.

2 Article 4 of the Anglo-Irish Treaty required the following of all members of the Dáil: 'I [name] do solemnly swear true faith and allegiance to the Constitution of the Irish Free State as by law established, and that I will be faithful to H.M. King George V, his heirs and successors by law in virtue of the common citizenship of Ireland with Great Britain and her adherence to and membership of the group of nations forming the British Commonwealth of Nations'.

3 Sceilg explained when giving evidence in the Funds Case that firstly, the Third Dáil 'was not attended by more than half, and second, I would say that the Second Dáil never handed over as was decided it should hand over' (Sceilg, Witness Statement, 1948, 64).

4 De Valera, along with some 2,000 others, was then imprisoned. He was the last detainee to be released, in July 1924.

5 Sinn Féin considered itself the only repository of legitimate institutions in Ireland, and therefore saw the cabinet formed after the 1923 elections as the only valid one.

6 Interestingly, this idea was developed decades later, in 1973, by Provisional Sinn Féin, which put forward a detailed programme, Éire Nua, based on the concept of a federal Ireland divided into the four historical provinces, much in the line of what Sinn Féin had already envisioned in 1925.

7 All the following results have been taken from ElectionsIreland.org.

8 The next time that Sinn Féin was to put forward a candidate in Northern Ireland was in 1955 in the Mid-Ulster by-election.

9 For a detailed account of the 1924 Army mutiny, see the works of M. G. Valiulis (1983, 1985, 1992).

10 Indeed, the Government of Ireland Act clearly stated that 'For the purposes of this act, Northern Ireland shall consist of the parliamentary constituencies of Antrim, Armagh, Down, Fermanagh, Londonderry and Tyrone, and the parliamentary boroughs of Belfast and Londonderry, and Southern Ireland shall consist of so much of Ireland as is not comprised within the said parliamentary counties and boroughs'. www.legislation.gov.uk/ukpga/1920/67/pdfs/ukpga_19200067_en.pdf.

11 Daily newspaper published in Belfast from 1824 to 1963.

12 A four-county secession had been envisaged in 1914 at the Buckingham Palace Conference when partition had been discussed. One of the concessions made by Unionists was that six counties would be excluded permanently from Home Rule unless they expressed the wish, on a county-by-county basis, to accept it, which would have meant, given the Catholic–Protestant ratios in counties Fermanagh-Tyrone, that Northern Ireland would have ultimately consisted of four counties only. See Ward, 1993.

13 The Free State had agreed in 1923 to collect annuities from tenants. This arrangement was renewed in 1926. See Ó Drisceoil, 2011, 42.

14 The extent of the Free State's debt was colossal according to the Irish delegation, as it amounted to almost £2 billion, to which was added the cost of the Civil War (Staunton, 1996, 44).

15 William T. Cosgrave was president of the Executive Council of the Free State (Prime Minister) Cumann na nGaedheal, 1922–32.

16 James Craig was Prime Minister of Northern Ireland, 1921–1940.

17 The issue of those funds was to resurface periodically throughout the next two decades, but was only tackled in the early 1940s when the then Sinn Féin leadership decided to claim them through the courts. See Chapter 3.

18 Fr O'Flanagan stands out in Republican and Catholic history for the role he played both as a politician and a man of the church. His radical stances on social issues – he was chosen to recite the invocation at the first meeting of the newly proclaimed Dáil Éireann in January 1919 – lost him his position within the church, in spite of the popular support he clearly enjoyed – see 'A Remonstrance addressed to the Most Rev. Dr. Coyne, Bishop of Elphin and signed by almost every man, woman and child in the parish of Crossna' [against the suspension of Fr Michael O'Flanagan], National Library. Fr O'Flanagan rejected the Treaty in 1921 and later refused to follow de Valera. He was suspended from office in 1927, and later expelled from Sinn Féin in 1936 for having taken part in a radio documentary in 1936. See RTÉ, 1973.

19 This constituency changed its name to Laoighis-Offaly in 1961 and has been known since 2007 as Laois Offaly.

20 O'Flanagan and MacSwiney's relationship was a stormy one. At the 1927 Ard Fheis,

O'Flanagan accused her of being there to spy on behalf of Fianna Fáil. 'This incident left a very chilling effect on the proceedings', according to the Garda superintendent who attended the debates (Garda report, 15/12/27).

21 Brother of Harry Boland, a personal friend to both de Valera and Collins, who was killed during the Civil War. Gerry Boland followed de Valera in 1926 and held several ministerial posts under Fianna Fáil-led governments until 1954.

22 Seán Lemass was a close ally of de Valera, with whom he formed Fianna Fáil, and in whose governments he served as Minister for Industry and Commerce and during the Second World War as Minister for Supplies. He succeeded de Valera as Taoiseach in 1959 and remained in this post until 1966.

23 Cumann na mBan was founded in 1914 as an affiliate organisation of the Irish Volunteers which was prepared to take up arms if necessary. Its members fought in the 1916 Rising as part of the Army of the Republic. See McCarthy, Cal, 2007.

24 Na Fianna Éireann was a Republican youth organisation founded by Bulmer Hobson and Countess Markievicz in 1909. It took part in all the main events of the Irish revolutionary period and sided in 1921 with the anti-Treaty side. Its allegiance to the Republic led it to continue siding with those who refused the oath.

25 Formed in 1926 as the continuation of the '98 Memorial Committee', itself founded in 1898 to mark the burial places of the United Irishmen. See www.nga.ie/history.php.

26 Michael P. Collivet had been elected in 1918 and again in 1921. Although he disagreed with de Valera on the issue of abstentionism, he did not remain within Sinn Féin or the Second Dáil and left political life shortly after the split.

27 Séan Buckley had been elected to the Dáil in 1923, so, technically, he was not a member of the Second Dáil. He lost his seat in the 1927 election. He joined Fianna Fáil and was elected TD in 1938, a seat he retained until 1954.

28 Séan MacSwiney, elected TD in 1921, lost his seat in 1922. He was the brother of hunger striker Terence MacSwiney and of Mary MacSwiney.

29 This position was to be that of the future generations of Republicans, who, until quite late in the twentieth century, refused to see that partition had been a choice, whether well or badly informed, and not simply a whim that the British had granted. By not taking into account the reasons behind this specific political and economic choice, Republicans tended to put forward analyses and solutions that were both unconvincing and poorly informed.

30 Full text available at: www.irishstatutebook.ie/1925/en/act/pub/0018/sec0007.html.

31 Brian O'Higgins received a mere 3.55 per cent in Clare, Mary MacSwiney (Cork) 7.80 per cent, Seán Buckley (Cork West) 3.78 per cent, Kathleen Lynn (Dublin County) 2.75 per cent, Charles Murphy (Dublin South) 4.18 per cent, Art O'Connor (Kildare South) 5.11 per cent, Seán Farrell (Leitrim Sligo) 6.94 per cent, Conor O'Byrne (Longford Meath), 4.67 per cent, Count George Plunkett (Roscommon) 5.06 per cent. The party retained support in some areas: Austin Stack was elected in Kerry, Joe Madden in Mayo North and Cathal Brugha's wife Caitlín in Waterford. The Cork East candidate, elected Sinn Féin candidate Oscar Traynor, topped the poll and moved the following year to Fianna Fáil, on whose ticket he was elected ten times, between 1932 and 1957.

32 O'Higgins is described by Prager as 'not a beloved figure in Irish politics, but he was immensely respected for his dedication, his brilliance, and his all-consuming concern for the survival of the nation' (Prager, 1986, 167).

33 According to T. P. Coogan, it was later revealed that one of the three men was a member of Fianna Fáil (Coogan, 1966, 160).

34 Prager argues that the objective behind the introduction of the different bills was political order, which would be achieved 'through suppression of Republican opposition and development of effective institutions' (Prager, 1986, 169).

35 The result could have been forty-nine to twenty-six votes, had not one deputy, Michael Heffernan of the Farmers' Party, not mistakenly voted for instead of against the Bill. But by the time he realised that he had 'inadvertently voted in the wrong lobby. [I] wished to vote against the Bill, whereas [I] accidentally voted for it', he was told by the Ceann Comhairle that it was too late to change the overall vote (*Dáil Debates*, 04/08/27).

36 For a full account of the manner in which Fianna Fáil circumvented the obstacle, see Ó Beacháin, 2010b, 376–94.

37 This trend was confirmed during the following years. In 1929, the total number of affiliated cumainn was seventy-one, with thirty for Leinster, ten for Munster, fifteen for Connacht, four for Ulster, seven for Scotland and seven for England (Garda report, 10/12/29).

38 Fianna Fáil TD who was appointed vice-president of the Executive Council in 1932 and who subsequently became President of Ireland in 1945.

39 The two men, who had been sentenced in 1925 to penal servitude for a raid on a bank in Manchester in 1922, were eventually released in December 1930 (*IT*, 27/12/30).

40 This was not the first time that O'Flanagan criticised the Vatican. In a meeting on 12 September 1929, he contended that the rule of Rome was even worse than the English influence, explaining that 'there was an intrigue between England and Rome with regard to the appointment of Bishops in Ireland so that any patriotic priest would not be appointed Bishop' (Garda report, 12/09/29).

41 For a detailed account of IRA activities throughout that decade, see Hanley, 2002, 71–92.

42 An annual ceremony for the commemoration of the death of Theobald Wolfe Tone, buried in the cemetery of this small County Kildare village.

43 The organisations banned were: Saor Éire, IRA, Fianna Éireann, Cumann na mBan, Friends of Soviet Russia, the Irish Labour Defence League, the Workers' Defence Corps, the Women Prisoners' Defence League, the Workers' Revolutionary Party, the Irish Tribute League, the Irish Working Farmers' Committee and the Workers' Research Bureau.

2

Oblivion, 1932–45

Sinn Féin's part for the moment is to hold the fort for the Republic.

(Mary MacSwiney, 1932)

The 1930s were characterised among Republicans by the tensions that dominated the relationships between the different groups. Sinn Féin's role and visibility were increasingly limited, and its rigid stance and principles made it a difficult organisation with which to cooperate. Nevertheless, although its contribution to the major political debates of the period was minimal, it retained a level of activity that warranted both a level of surveillance by the security forces and some attempts by the IRA to establish a working relationship. Through the minutes of the fortnightly Standing Committee meetings, the story that emerges is one of confusion, bitterness and lack of direction among the various Republican organisations. The fact that the personnel of all of these was at times interchangeable (Mary MacSwiney, for instance, was a member of Dáil Éireann, Sinn Féin and Cumann na mBan until she resigned from the two latter organisations) made it all the more difficult to distinguish between the different positions taken by each organisation.

What does transpire from this decade, however, is the difficulty that these groups faced when dealing with their recent past and their relative decline after the revolutionary period of 1916–22, particularly Sinn Féin and the IRA. Both had experienced success and popularity; both were considerably diminished in size and influence by the emergence of the Free State. The fact that they lived in such close proximity with those who ran the institutions, with whom they shared a common and recent past, compounded the difficulties they faced in terms of finding their place and their role in the new political climate. This is quite obvious when studying the trajectory of the IRA from 1932 to 1938, a period during which it seemed to hesitate as to the path to take and ended up investing in diverse but eventually failed political initiatives.

A close study of Sinn Féin during that period shows that the party is quite distinct to the one which surfaced after the Second World War, one which was subservient to the IRA. The links between the two organisations was complex from the very moment that the IRA decided in 1925 not to take a stance in the upcoming split; but once the honeymoon period between the IRA and Fianna Fáil was over, the IRA made several attempts to enlist the support of its former ally, not always successfully, in its various endeavours to find its place in the new political environment. Eventually, it was the Second Dáil that the IRA turned to, perhaps as a result of the intransigent stance taken by Sinn Féin throughout the period. The decade nevertheless demonstrated to the IRA that it could not operate on its own, that it needed a political force, whatever shape this might take, and the experience proved that Sinn Féin was indeed the best possible choice.

Fianna Fáil in power

The 1932 general election was fought in the context of an economic and political crisis. As Ó Gráda suggests, 'at a time of rising unemployment and economic nationalism, Cumann na nGaedheal's policies were sure to lose votes. By the early 1930s the party was viewed by more and more voters as the party of complacency and privilege, and Éamon de Valera's Fianna Fáil as the representatives of the "plain people"' (Ó Gráda, 1997, 5). Those unemployed could not avail themselves of state relief, as the Unemployment Assistance Act only came into being under the Fianna Fáil government, in 1933.[1] Therefore, only one third of the unemployed benefited from some form of insurance, making the remaining two thirds reliant on what could have been termed as public works schemes or poor relief systems.[2]

The drop in popularity of the Cumann na nGaedheal government further increased when it decided to take a libel case against Fianna Fáil's daily paper, the *Irish Press*,[3] in the military court, a move which was viewed by many as an attempt to stifle free press (O'Brien, 2001, 39). Fianna Fáil, for its part, centred its campaign on social and economic issues, promising more social expenditure and more self-reliance: 'Fianna Fáil explicitly appropriated Griffith's economic policy, spiced with de Valera's own social policy, which he presented as the essence of 1916 social doctrine' (Lee, 1989, 170). It therefore resorted to simple but effective slogans, making unemployment the number one preoccupation, and presenting Ireland's resources as being infinite yet in need of being protected: 'The protection of industries means more money in Ireland and more money in Ireland means more employment and more employment means more buyers and more buyers means more buying of Irish goods and more buying of Irish goods means money in Ireland and why should it ever stop?'[4]

The 1932 election was a fundamental turning point in the short history of the Irish Free State, as this was the first time that the democratic institutions would be put to the test.[5] There had indeed been other elections in the previous decade, but only one, in 1927, in which Fianna Fáil had taken part as a non-abstentionist party, only months after having entered the Dáil, and thus not yet being in a position to be a serious contender to the party in power. Cumann na nGaedheal was aware that this election would be more difficult to win than the previous ones, and opted for a campaign strategy the aim of which was to discredit its most potent challenger, Fianna Fáil. De Valera and his party were presented as a danger to the stability of the new state, but also to social order and to democracy in general. They were portrayed as 'un-Irish and un-Catholic', posing a threat to what the country stood for. The main argument used to support this view was the connection, or alleged connection, that Fianna Fáil maintained with the IRA. Indeed, the IRA was actively campaigning to oust the Cosgrave government. As O'Donnell clearly put it in an article published by *An Phoblacht*, the aim of the organisation was to 'put Cosgrave out', thus opting to support the most acceptable party by openly calling on readers to vote for de Valera; the final objective did remain 'to break the connection with England, the never-failing source of all our ills' (Oglaigh na hÉireann, 1933b).[6] For Cumann na nGaedheal, the conclusion was clear: 'The so-called IRA of the present day is a conspiracy against the people and its programme is murder. It wants Fianna Fáil in power because Fianna Fáil is afraid of it. If a Fianna Fáil Government once took office, future elections would be won not by argument and persuasion but by naked terrorism. Fianna Fáil needs your vote to put it into power. It would not need your vote to keep it in power. The gun-bullies would do that.'[7]

However, the IRA's decision to support Fianna Fáil brought to light the difficulties facing the various groups within the Republican camp. On the one hand, the attempt by some IRA leaders to regroup the Republican forces into a united front had been unsuccessful, and since 1931, the organisation was illegal, as were Saor Éire and Cumann na mBan. Sinn Féin, for its part, was in no position to put forward a candidate, as it was mandatory to take the oath, making any abstentionist strategy impossible. In any event, its financial situation did not allow the party to consider putting together an electoral campaign, however modest. Mary MacSwiney's assessment of what was at stake summed up the extent to which her party was out of touch with the political environment. In her words, 'Sinn Féin's part for the moment is to hold the fort for the Republic, to help to educate the people, especially the youth of the country on the futility, as well as inanity, of compromises on national principles, to be, together with the other loyal Republican organisations, Cumann na mBan, the IRA and the youthful Fianna Éireann, the rallying point for the reawakening spirit of the *Gael*' (MacSwiney, 1932). Sinn Féin was therefore not prepared to face the fact that the IRA was actively engaging with the electoral process outside of the realm of the so-called Republic.

In February 1932, Fianna Fáil became the majority party of the Free State, with seventy-two seats against fifty-seven for Cumann na nGaedheal. The Labour Party obtained seven seats, while three went to the Farmers' Party and the remaining fourteen to independent candidates (McCarthy, 2006, 511). De Valera formed a government, but he had to count on the support of the Labour TDs as Fianna Fáil lacked an overall majority. These results inevitably altered the IRA's position. The *raison d'*être of an army that operated in parallel to the system was now questioned by the very victory of the candidate that it had supported. However, the structures of the organisation remained unchanged: as long as the Free State was in place and the Republic had not been proclaimed, the existence of the IRA was justified in the eyes of its members. This would, in due time, raise fundamental issues for the government, as the existence of an armed group would become, quite soon, simply unacceptable.

Furthermore, the IRA leaders did not seem to agree on the role of the Republican army in this new environment. For O'Donnell:

> With de Valera in power in 1932, mainly through IRA support, the Army had the chance of its life in being the social vanguard for land, work, homes, security, economic growth, unity with the North. But instead of confronting de Valera with the social questions the IRA insanely took issue with him on its right to be an army, its right to use the gun and the bomb, the right to drill in the corner of some field. (McInerney, 1974, 134)

O'Donnell's analysis according to which Fianna Fáil owed its electoral victory to the support of the IRA was problematic, as there were clearly many other fundamental factors that influenced the vote for de Valera's party. What did emerge from the first few months of the new government was that the measures that it took matched, at least partly, some of the most fundamental Republican expectations. On 10 March, the Free State Executive Council freed twenty men who had been detained under the various pieces of legislation including the Constitution Amendment Act. A few days later, on 18 March 1932, the ban that had made the IRA illegal was lifted, giving the organisation the opportunity to stage a march in support of the recently freed prisoners, but during which some words of caution were also uttered: 'We must admit, amidst our rejoicing, that while the days of coercion have passed for a time, the task we have set ourselves to achieve has not yet been achieved', said MacBride in his speech to the crowds assembled in College Green (*IT*, 19/03/32). In May, the Removal of Oath Bill was introduced in order to amend the Constitution of the Free State. The Dáil voted for the law which was rejected by the Senate, who wanted the British and Irish governments to agree beforehand on the removal of clause 4 of the 1921 Treaty on this point; it was implemented the following year, on 3 May 1933.

In July 1932, the government withheld the payment of the land annuities to Britain,[8] retaining it in the Irish Exchequer, thereby starting the economic war (Ó Drisceoil, 2011, 44). This could have been seen by those who had been involved in Saor Éire as a victory, as they had been campaigning, under the leadership of Peadar O'Donnell, for this very objective.[9] It was also a sign that the newly elected government would put up some resistance to the British government, which in effect considered this initiative as a violation of the 1925 financial agreement, and imposed custom taxes of 20 per cent on all cattle and agricultural produce (Ó Gráda, 1997, 6). Ireland imposed in turn customs charges on all British imported products. The value of Ireland's agricultural exports fell by more than a half in six years, generating difficulties for the economy as a whole, as 91 per cent of Irish exports were bound for the UK market (Lee, 1989, 187). Nevertheless the impact of the economic war is difficult to ascertain: 'the course of the Irish economy in the 1930s was dominated by three factors – the Economic War, the protectionist policy and the impact of the Great depression. It would be difficult to distinguish the separate effects of these factors, nor would be altogether appropriate to do so given that they were to some degree interdependent' (Giblin et al., 1988).[10]

Another measure which met Republican expectations was the passing of the Army Pensions Act of 1932 which extended the eligibility to pension rights of former combatants. This was a marked change from the legislation in place until then, which only granted this right to those who had served during the Civil War 'in the National Forces or the Defences forces of Saorstát Éireann' and had 'rendered military service in Óglaigh na hÉireann or in the Irish Volunteers or in the Irish Citizen Army or in Fianna Éireann or in the Hibernian Rifles' during the week of the Easter Rising (Military Service Pensions Act, 1924), therefore excluding from the provisions those who had fought against the Treaty in the Civil War. The 1932 Act redefined military service, which could be of two natures, either pre-truce (between 1 April 1916 and 11 July 1921) or post-truce (from 12 July 1921 to 30 September 1923). Interestingly, it also introduced a clause concerning those who had been engaged in military service at those dates and had subsequently suffered during detention as a result of a hunger strike or while attempting to evade capture or arrest, until 30 September 1924.[11] Overall, this Act concerned a substantial number of people and was bound to have an effect on IRA members.[12]

With Fianna Fáil in power, the relationship between Sinn Féin, the IRA and the new party in government was inevitably to undergo a profound transformation. On the one hand, it would prove increasingly difficult for the state representatives to accept, or even tolerate, the presence within their midst of an organisation which did not acknowledge the legitimacy of the institutions and which was prepared to take up arms to defend its cause. As a result, the Fianna Fáil Executive Council ended up resorting to the same type of rhetoric and legal instruments as its Cumann na nGaedheal predecessors. On the other hand, the presence of Sinn Féin, as discreet as it may have been, was meant as a nagging reminder of the fact that Fianna Fáil had fallen short of its aspirations. Although Sinn Féin did not represent a serious contender for de Valera's party, its negative and self-righteous discourse could have proven, at least, irksome to the newly elected government. The 1930s was a difficult decade for the former allies of Fianna Fáil, which turned out to be, possibly, a more formidable adversary than Cumann na nGaedheal in the previous years. However, the relationship between the IRA and Fianna Fáil remained cordial throughout the first year of the latter's term of office. The IRA now being a legal organisation was free to organise social events, one of which, for instance, was a céilí held in Dublin, attended by 800 people according to the *Irish Press*. The guest list was indicative of this new – albeit ephemeral – atmosphere of *entente* between Republicans, as aside from all the known IRA leaders, the céilí was also attended by Fianna Fáil TD James Lynch and the Gaelic League general secretary and the GAA secretary (*IP*, 31/10/32), showing that for a time, the IRA had once again become a somewhat respectable organisation.

At the end of 1932, de Valera announced that new elections would be held on 24 January 1933. This was done in the hope of consolidating Fianna Fáil's position, and as the opposition was divided, with the creation of a new party, the National Centre Party, the timing seemed appropriate. The IRA was hesitant as to the approach to take, but decided once more to support Fianna Fáil, albeit more reluctantly than the previous year:

> Our support for Fianna Fáil is not because of their ideas. Indeed we realise the Fianna Fáil administration intends to pursue a dangerous policy of negotiations on issues that are non-judiciable – the unity and independence of this country and its freedom from all foreign domination whatsoever. [...] We are supporting

Fianna Fáil because it is a way of driving out of public life a party which has sold itself to the British Empire. (*Manifesto to the Irish People*, Óglaigh na hÉireann, 1933b)

However, the position of the IRA was clearly made difficult by the fact that this time, it was asking its supporters and members to vote for a party whose record, after ten months in office, they repudiated: IRA prisoners still in jail, negotiations on issues that were 'non-negotiable', payment of compensation to Royal Irish Constabulary (RIC) pensioners, and payment of land annuities (*IT*, 10/01/33). But in order to ensure the victory of Fianna Fáil, the organisation went as far as lifting the restriction preventing its members from taking part in the elections, which had been imposed in 1925.

Sinn Féin was equally critical of Fianna Fáil's record, and perhaps even more so, because it foresaw that the IRA's support for Fianna Fáil would lead, in the longer term, to an untenable position. But its reasons for refusing to engage with this particular election were more principled than pragmatic:

The election of a year ago was not a free election and the result of it did not repre-sent the true will of the Irish people who would, if given a free choice, declare for complete independence today, as they did in 1918. In last year's election, as in every election since the Treaty of surrender and dishonour, the threat of war was held over the heads of the electorate. One party raised the cry of 'War by the Communists'. The other party carried the cry of 'War by the Freemasons' throughout the twenty-six counties, and the bewildered people were stampeded into the polling booths through fear of one bogey or the other. That both cries were false and misleading has been proved very clearly since. (*IT*, 14/01/33)

With seventy-seven seats, de Valera's party now had an absolute majority. Cumann na nGaedheal only gained forty-eight seats and the National Centre Party eleven, with Labour obtaining eight and others nine (McCarthy, 2006, 511). However, there was now a more forceful opposition with the presence of the Army Comrades Association (ACA), founded in 1932 by T. O'Higgins, brother of Kevin O'Higgins. It was fiercely opposed to the IRA, which it considered a communist organisation and whose aim it saw as being 'to force a Bolshevist government on the people, to smash the tenant rights of the farmer, to confiscate property rightly belonging to the individual, and to reduce this country to a state of chaos and anarchy such as exists in Russia and Mexico today' (*II*, 20/01/33). The ACA was led from July of that year by Eoin O'Duffy, who had been dismissed from his position of commissioner of the Garda Síochána, de Valera estimating that he could not entirely trust someone who had overtly campaigned against him (Cronin in Feldman et al., 2008, 190).[13] The members of this organisation adopted in April of that year a uniform, the blue shirts, which were reminiscent of the brown and black shirts on the European continent. It also resorted to the fascist salute at meetings (*IP*, 05/09/33), as part of the movement's overall fascistic liturgical element (Cronin, 1995, 314). On 20 July, the organisation was renamed 'National Guards' and merged with Cumann na nGaedheal and the National Centre Party to form the party of the New Ireland, Fine Gael. O'Duffy remained at its head until September 1934. The IRA and the Blueshirts were involved on more than one occasion in violent clashes, one of which took place after some IRA volunteers, including Civil War veteran Dan Keating, had planned an ambush in an attempt to assassinate Eoin O'Duffy, in 1933. Keating was subsequently arrested for taking part in the riots that opposed the two organisations and was imprisoned for six months. Interestingly, however, the IRA's opposition to that particular group was not so much rooted in the rejection of fascism per se as in the conviction that it went against Irish Republican aspirations: 'Our opposition to the Fascists is not because they wear blue shirts, because we believe that the wearing of any particular garment counts for nothing. In common with the great mass of Republican Ireland, we are opposed to them because they stand for the domination of Ireland by British imperialism; because they stand for the connection with England and with the British empire and for the subjugation of the mass of the Irish people to imperialism' (*IP*, 05/02/34).

Much like in the previous election, the IRA's assessment of the victory of Fianna Fáil was ambivalent, and left little doubt as to the distance that the organisation would necessarily take with Fianna Fáil. 'The Volunteers are pledged to achieve complete independence – a Republic politically and economically free from foreign domination. This task still remains for us. Our aim will not be realised until the system which has arisen out of the conquest, and exists in alliance with British imperialism, is destroyed at its roots and until those who run it are decisively routed' (*IP*, 03/02/33). The issue of the presence of the IRA was going to become increasingly problematic, however, and it would soon have to face the fact that its very existence was objectionable and that the very government that it had called on the electorate to vote for had every intention of strengthening the institutions of the Free State and, inevitably, weakening the IRA. This was nowhere more evident than in the realm of military affairs, the responsibility of which, in the eyes of the IRA, rested solely with the 'Army of the Republic'. Therefore, the announcement of the recruitment of a reserve force for the Free State was a further step in the realisation that the IRA's own status and existence were at stake: 'The Free State Army was organised to overthrow the Republic and to uphold the Treaty', said the organisation, and therefore was a potential adversary to which no one being loyal to their 'oath to the Republic' could join (*IP*, 08/11/33). Moreover, the IRA was increasingly divided as to the political route on which it should embark, as some of its members were showing signs of impatience at the organisation's failure to commit to a social agenda.

That the IRA had no intention of exiting the scene now that Fianna Fáil's position had been reinforced was made clear almost immediately with the publication, in March, of a pamphlet entitled *Governmental Policy and Constitution of Óglaigh na h-Éireann* (Óglaigh na hÉireann, 1933a), which partly sought to counter the representation that the IRA was a 'secret society' whereas 'there was never any secrecy as to its aims and objects, nor as to the control of the organisation'. The first part of the document consisted of a Constitution and governmental programme which laid down the IRA's vision on the future of Ireland. Undoubtedly influenced by the left-wing ideas of those who were advocating a Marxist approach, it held that the state should promote the 'cooperative organisation of the agricultural industry', albeit on a voluntary basis. This was a way of nationalising the agricultural sector, as those who remained outside the cooperative movement would not be 'entitled to share in the State credits and facilities'. Regarding the industry, it would become 'the property of the community'. The distribution of products was also to be carried out on a cooperative basis. The document supported the nationalising of transport and making the insurance sector a state monopoly. Individuals were to be encouraged and assisted by the state to become owners of their own homes but the building of houses for sale or rent would be declared illegal after a certain agreed date. The second part of the document was dedicated to the Constitution of the organisation itself. Its objectives were unchanged (establishment of the Republic, of a lawful government, securing civil and religious liberty and promotion of the Irish language).

What was more interesting in the stated objectives was what was not there: the reunification of Ireland. Aside from the reference to religious freedom, which could have been indirectly meant to address the question of partition, not one section of the document mentioned this issue. It did however reiterate that the means to achieve the overall aims was, first and foremost, 'force of arms', as well as 'organising, training and equipping the manhood of Ireland as an efficient military force'. The document described in detail the internal operation of the organisation, its hierarchy, ranging from the General Army convention, 'supreme army authority', relayed by the Army Council when the general convention was not in session. Finally, all new volunteers had to sign the following oath: 'I .... promise that I will promote the objects of Óglaigh na h-Éireann to the best of my knowledge and ability, and that I will obey all orders and regulations issued to me by the Army Authority, and by my superior officers' (Óglaigh na hÉireann, 1933a).

In light of this document, the reasons that the IRA had put forward to justify its support of Fianna Fáil showed the lack of long-term vision of the organisation. There was little doubt that Fianna Fáil would fall short of the IRA's aspirations, as no more than its predecessor did it have the political means to declare a Republic in the immediate future, however strong this aspiration might have been. More importantly, the stance that the new government would take on armed action had been made clear by de Valera, who had stated, on the issue of partition: 'we can only protest. There is no effective step that we can take to abolish the boundary. Force is out of the question' (Bowman, 1982, 112). Such was, in a few words, the message that was conveyed to G. Gilmore and S. Russell during the meetings they held with the new government representatives (Bowyer Bell, 1983, 100). Therefore, the IRA's support for the use of force was bound to become a major problem. The choice of the 'most acceptable candidate', which had motivated the IRA's position, only served an immediate objective, that of ousting the Cosgrave government in 1932 and of ensuring it was not elected to government in 1933.

Holding the fort

None of this held much sway with Sinn Féin, which continued to denounce the Free State and its institutions as a usurpation of the legitimate ones established in 1919. At the 1932 Ard Fheis, the president, Brian O'Higgins, explained: 'We are the die-hards, the wild Irishry of today. We swore an oath of allegiance to the Republic of Ireland proclaimed in 1916, established in 1919, and never since disestablished. [... the Dáil is] an English-made institution, it is usurpation, it is a living sign of British imperialism and the removal of its degrading oath does not make it a whit less distasteful to us' (*AP*, 10/10/32). As a consequence, in a rhetoric which reversed the roles and which had become a feature of Sinn Féin's discourse, those in government were 'guilty of rebellion against the Republic'.

Notwithstanding the lack of relevance of this rhetoric to the reality of the political debate within the Irish Free State at the time, such statements were fundamentally aimed at undermining the very legitimacy of the institutions and those who ran them, using a discourse that was similar to that of the representatives of the state. In an attempt to embarrass the new Fianna Fáil government, O'Higgins thus quoted a decree, signed on 17 November 1922 by then Sinn Féin president Éamon de Valera, which cancelled the resolution of 7 January 1922 approving the Treaty:

> That decree has never since been revoked or rescinded: the legality or binding force of it has never been questioned by loyal citizens of the Republic of Ireland. If it means anything it means that the 'Free State' Government and Parliament and subordinate institutions are illegal assemblies, and that membership of them is a denial of the sovereignty of the Republic of Ireland, and that no citizen of the Republic can help them in any way without committing an unlawful act. (*IT*, 10/10/32)

The visit of the Prince of Wales for the inauguration of the Northern Ireland parliament buildings in Stormont, on 16 November 1932, provided Sinn Féin with an opportunity to engage more actively with political activism and embark on a campaign that would, for a time, give the party a level of visibility. According to a speech delivered in Dublin by Liam Gilmore, honorary secretary of Sinn Féin, the visit constituted 'a deliberate attempt to perpetuate partition'. The speaker warned his audience against buying a poppy as it was 'nothing but an Imperialist emblem' (*IT*, 7/11/32). Nationalist councillor Collins in Belfast deemed it ill-becoming on the part of any member of the Royal family to lend himself to what he considered a 'travesty' (*IT*, 19/10/32), while the Newry urban district council rejected by nine votes to five the proposal by Unionist councillors to present an address of welcome to the Prince on the grounds that 'a Catholic who would take part in any address of the sort would have no respect for his religion' (*IT*, 26/10/32). Nevertheless, the fact that some companies, as well as several city councils such as Belfast or Coleraine, decided to give their workers a day off with full pay on that occasion showed the enthusiasm which the visit was generating in Unionist circles (*IT*, 02/11/32). The Nationalist representatives in the Northern parliament, for their part, issued a statement condemning partition as 'a national evil, disastrous to the six counties and injurious to the twenty-six' (*IT*, 07/11/32).

In an initiative unprecedented since the 1926 split, Sinn Féin put the following resolution to the vote of several local county councils: 'That we resent the visit to Ireland of a representative of the British Crown, in the person of the Prince of Wales, as a deliberate attempt to perpetuate the partition of this country, and to misrepresent its people to the outside world as being loyal to an Empire they hate for its countless crimes against themselves and against other victims of its greed and cruelty all over the world' (*IP*, 07/11/32). The reaction to this motion in the councils where it was tabled showed how deeply divided opinions were on the issue of partition. On one side of the argument were those who expressed their fear that adopting such a motion would bring recent divisions to the fore, and deemed it better to bury the past and avoid opening up old wounds. One councillor explained: 'I fully object to that resolution coming from a body which, for all intents and purposes, does not exist and does not represent the views or the opinion of any considerable portion of the Irish people. I don't live by hatred. I have no hatred against any Englishman' (James Coburn, TD, independent, Louth, quoted in *IP*, 08/11/32). The Athy urban council chairman argued: 'I do not think we should interfere in any way because we have already partition and that is sufficient. I think the Council should have some common sense' (*IT*, 08/11/32). Wexford council considered Sinn Féin's resolution 'out of order'. In Dún Laoghaire, the vote was evenly divided between those who felt that it was an insult to the Prince of Wales and, in the words of the chairman of the council, it 'tended to revive bitterness and vindictiveness', and others who considered that this visit was calculated to perpetuate the partition of Ireland, pointing out that if the parliament of Northern Ireland were the parliament of all Ulster, it would not be a Protestant parliament; 'the Catholics and Nationalists would have a majority and the North could then unite with the South' (*IT*, 08/11/32). Other councils adopted the motion, such as Limerick or Tuam, while Cork corporation decided to amend it and passed a motion stating 'that they protest against partition' deeming that as a council they had no power to prevent such a visit, this being a matter for the Dáil (*IP*, 16/11/32).

Although this episode could have shown the party that its ultimate objective still held a degree of sympathy among some elected representatives, Sinn Féin did not capitalise on it. It was a one-off initiative and as soon as the visit was over, the party reverted to its more traditional activities such as commemorations and public meetings, which attracted little public attention. This was due, in the eyes of O'Flanagan, to the fact that all national newspapers were 'party organs' and were therefore not inclined to report anything that had to do with Republican activities (Garda report, 24/09/33). The Gardaí, on the other hand, who dutifully reported on all meetings, attributed the low attendance at such meetings (estimated at an average of 200) to the fact that the crowds did not engage with the issues: 'the attendance was rather poor and apart from sections of the IRA from Galway City and surrounding area little interest appeared to be taken in what the speakers had to say' (Garda report, 09/12/33).

The main principle that guided Sinn Féin's rhetoric and action was that any interaction with the Free State was unacceptable. This concerned all spheres of activity, from elections to professional commitments. It was seen as a contradiction of the very essence of Sinn Féin that its members could also be part of any organisation that stemmed from the institutions in place. However, Sinn Féin's rejection of the Free State was at its most virulent when it came to electoral policies, as it was 'opposed, not to any particular party in the partition Assemblies in Dublin and Belfast but to those institutions themselves. Sinn Féin cannot, even by implication, ask or advise citizens to help or vote for any candidate, no matter what his professions or promises may be' (*II*, 01/01/32).[14] The logical conclusion of this analysis was, in the view of the die-hard Republicans, that Sinn Féin members should abstain from voting in any Free State election. This was a follow-up to the 1927 decision to forbid any member to vote in parliamentary elections 'other than those held for electing candidates to Dáil Éireann' (SC, 15/04/32).[15] The fact that this stance, in practice, disenfranchised its own members, as the odds of the holding of a Dáil Éireann election were quite minimal, was not raised in the discussions. Loyalty to the pre-Treaty institutions was deemed paramount to any other political consideration. The Standing Committee embarked on the process of identifying whether anyone had crossed the party line, revealing an authoritarian streak that underpinned many of the party's decisions. It first sought to verify 'whether it is true that members of Dáil Éireann voted in the recent Free State elections' and if this were the case, their names were required (SC, 09/05/32). This 'offence', as the party labelled it, was committed by two members of Sinn Féin, one of whom was Seán Breathnach, a member of the Cork cumann, who admitted at the 1933 Ard Fheis to having voted for a Fianna Fáil candidate. He was suspended from his cumann for six months, having refused to commit himself to not voting again. He was eventually expelled by the Standing Committee on 16 April 1934, and the decision was confirmed a month later, in spite of a letter from the cumann judging the sentence too harsh (SC, 13/04/34).

This position had important repercussions for the party, further depopulating it at all levels. Some members resigned on the grounds that the president was accepting a salary from a 'usurping government' (SC, 26/10/34). Mary MacSwiney also left the party because, according to Sinn Féin, 'the Ard Fheis, by a vote, sanctioned the acceptance of members of the Standing Committee and officer board, as well as all other members, of salaries and pensions from what she considered to be an usurping British government in this country'. Her resolution opposing this motion having been defeated, she resigned (SC, 23/12/34). As a result of this drift, the function organised to commemorate the anniversary of the creation of Dáil Éireann in January 1935 was attended by none of the remaining Second Dáil TDs. Even the dead paid the price of the party's intransigence. Thus, when the Roger Casement cumann in London asked for

Sinn Féin's support in its campaign to bring back his remains to Dublin, Sinn Féin bluntly replied that it 'could not join in any representation made to the enemy government of England' (SC, 26/04/35).

Unsurprisingly, the Sinn Féin headquarters report of activities from November 1933 to June 1934, read out at the September 1934 Standing Committee meeting, was brief, and corresponded more to the undertakings of a small cultural association than to those of a political party: '15 lectures delivered at headquarters, whist drives every Sunday night, Wolfe Tone week collection, drawing of prizes and turkey drive held at Christmas and participation at Easter commemoration' (SC, 08/09/34). The only political initiative taken that year was to allow the local Galway cumann to put forward two candidates for local elections, 'only on the condition that they go forward on a straight abstentionist policy' (SC, 17/05/34). But the decision was rescinded, by five votes to four, at the following Standing Committee meeting, as the motion put forward by Sceilg and seconded by Buckley – 'that Galway Comhairle be given permission to nominate candidates on the condition that they go in solely to use the county councils as a Republican platform and thwart rather than facilitate its work' – was defeated. The by-election in Galway announced after the death of the sitting TD Martin McDonogh (Cumann na nGaedheal) presented a new challenge for the organisation. Although in principle not opposed to elections per se, the objective was to ensure that this would be an election to Dáil Éireann, 'so that the candidate, if successful, could represent Galway in the Government of the Republic' (SC, 31/05/35). The IRA was eager to present a candidate to challenge the Fianna Fáil government (Hanley, 2002, 130–2), and Sinn Féin reluctantly agreed to the holding of a convention to nominate a joint, abstentionist candidate. A conference was arranged between the Army Council and the Standing Committee to determine whether there were enough grounds for cooperation. Although it was viewed as desirable, the process was still fraught with difficulties, as the estrangement of both organisations was deep. In the end, when Count Plunkett decided not to go forward as a candidate, no Republican candidate was nominated.

Commemorations: the contested site of legitimacy

The area of commemorations was essential for Sinn Féin, as they represented a central party activity and a theme at the heart of many of its discourses. Yet how could some key dates be remembered when there was obvious competition from different quarters as to who those events 'belonged' to? Possibly the date that presented most difficulties was 1916. As in the case of Wolfe Tone, numerous groups claimed its legacy, but many of the participants in the Rising were still alive and active on the political scene. Having taken part in the Rising was essential when establishing the credentials of those who went forward for public office, as shown by the list of candidates published by the *Irish Times* before the 1933 general elections, which mentioned whether they had participated in the Rising (*IT*, 21/10/33). Fianna Fáil and Sinn Féin took quite differing views on how to go about commemorating these events. The former was prepared, for a duration at least, to share the legacy with its former ally, whereas Sinn Féin refused to have anything to do with any event that would involve its rival, on the grounds that they had betrayed the cause for which the men and women of 1916 had fought.

The 1932 celebration of 1916 was an interesting showcase of apparent unity. Republican groups, ranging from the smaller Cumann na mBan to the newly elected Fianna Fáil TDs, participated in a unified ceremony, and even more interestingly, most of the speakers were known IRA activists (Maurice Twomey in Dublin, Seán Russell in Tipperary, Peadar O'Donnell in Waterford). According to the *Irish Times* report, 'two thousand members of the IRA, with their supporters, paraded the principal streets of Dublin' (*IT*, 28/03/32), which indicated how blurred the boundaries still were between the different Republican factions. Moss Twomey, chief of staff of the IRA, declared on that occasion that 'the objects for which so many brave men and women have generously given their lives still remain to be achieved [...] until they are the 1916 proclamation of the Republic will remain for us the fundamental declaration of the right and authority of our nation to fight for its inalienable right to sovereign independence' (*IT*, 28/03/32). A few weeks later, at the funeral of Margaret Pearse, mother of Pádraig and William who had both been executed in the aftermath of the Rising, the oration was delivered by de Valera, in front of an impressive representation of all shades of political opinion ranging from Cumann na nGaedheal (Mulcahy, Duggan, Cosgrave) to the IRA. Sinn Féin was, possibly, the only party absent from the proceeding (*IT*, 27/04/32).

Yet from 1933, the division among Republican ranks was visible. Whereas the IRA, Cumann na mBan and Sinn Féin paraded jointly, Fianna Fáil organised its own celebration involving troops of the Free State Army and other organisations such as the Citizen Army and the Gaelic League (*IT*, 29/04/33), which in itself indicated the new dimension that those commemorations would take and heralded the competition that would characterise that event over the following years. Eoin O'Duffy's recently created ACA claimed in a meeting that the role of the organisation was to 'achieve in a less hazardous way the objects of the

Volunteers of 1916', supplying what O'Duffy termed a 'counter movement to that which put forward a perverted view of the national necessities of the country' (*IT*, 20/05/33), further indicating how the legacy of 1916 was open to interpretation.[16]

By 1934 the hostility between Fianna Fáil and the remaining Republican organisations was complete and overt. On Easter Sunday of that year, two competing parades were held, one at Arbour Hill cemetery where the executed leaders of the Rising were buried, with the old Dublin Brigade IRA, the other at Glasnevin cemetery Republican plot, where the orator, Seán Russell, strongly criticised the government for, in his words, 'asking the IRA to hand over its arms, and instituting an adjunct to the Free State Army. Both were national insults' (*IT*, 07/04/34).

The manner in which 1916 ought to be commemorated also created internal problems within Fianna Fáil.[17] In 1935, some discontent was voiced within the ranks of the party over the decision by its national executive that the Easter symbol worn by its members be the Easter torch.[18] A cumann in Carrick-on-Shannon stated that the change from the Easter lily was 'a weakening of the spirit of Republicanism'; it also criticised the government for the suppression of *An Phoblacht*, seen as the continuation of the tactics of the previous regime, and asked that the 'same freedom of circulation is accorded to it as is to the Blue Shirt organs, which have been even more extreme in their criticism of President de Valera and the Fianna Fáil party' (*IT*, 16/04/35). However, de Valera's unveiling of a memorial in the General Post Office, Sheppard's *Death of Cúchulainn*, seemed to restore some unity among the ranks of his organisation.[19]

Sinn Féin's position in that domain was in line with all other matters involving the recognition of the Free State. This became problematic with the celebration of the twentieth anniversary of the Rising, for which the government had decided upon a Roll of Honour to be signed by all who had taken part in the Rising. But loyalty to the Republic meant, according to Sinn Féin, that no Republican could have anything to do with the official commemoration because, as was explained in a letter to the *Irish Press* by members of the Second Dáil including former Sinn Féin President Brian O'Higgins,[20] '[the Roll] includes the names of traitors to the Republic'. The statement went further, indicating that 'most of its signatories are men and women who, after the 1916 Rising, fought against the Treaty and are today staunch supporters of the Proclamation of 1916 and are equally staunch supporters of the present effort to put an end to England's Treaty and England's interference in our National Affairs' (*IP*, 26/05/36). The interpretation of the authors of the letter gave an interesting insight into the manner in which 1916 would be viewed and remembered among future generations of Republicans, putting forward a narrative in which the majority of those who had taken part in 1916 had then followed the path taken by Sinn Féin and the IRA after 1926. This served to legitimise their struggle as it constructed a vision in which they were the true heirs of 1916. That this reading of history was blatantly inaccurate, given that a number of those signatories were members of other parties, was not taken into account. However, Sinn Féin were not the only ones to claim a bigger share of the 1916 legacy. It would indeed seem that the composition of the Roll which was officially presented to the government on 24 May 1936, amidst what the pro-Fianna Fáil press qualified as a 1,000-strong military parade with 'hundreds of spectators who swelled the already huge parade' (*IP*, 25/05/36), was problematic.[21] Indeed, there was a clear discrepancy between those who claimed a military service pension and the names that featured on the Roll, indicating that some had not signed the document, particularly within Cumann na nGaedheal, as names such as Richard Mulcahy's were conspicuously absent from the list of signatories. Although the editorial of the *Irish Press* chose to see it as 'the performance of a pious duty of patriotism' which would 'be treasured as one of our proudest heritages and heirlooms' (*IP*, 25/05/36), it was anything but a consensual event, as it showed the 'divisions that had dominated Irish politics until recently' (Joye and Malone, 2006, 11).

In view of the position that Sinn Féin had taken on this issue, it was unthinkable that anyone within their ranks should contemplate signing the Roll. This form of boycott evidently presented a dilemma for those who wished to see their role in the events officially recognised. Those whose participation in the Rising could not be registered other than within the confines of their party were at risk of being by-passed by history, that history which would be part of the national narrative. Several members of Sinn Féin thus decided to ignore the instruction and signed the Roll of Honour. To the Standing Committee, this represented no less than a 'national crisis', and it appealed to Dáil Éireann to 'rally all the forces of the Republic in support of Dáil Éireann, Government of the Republic' (SC, 20/06/36). Two of those members were Dr Kathleen Lynn, a medical doctor, and Madeleine ffrench-Mullen, both of whom had taken part in the 1916 Rising within the Irish Citizen Army and had subsequently founded the first infant hospital in Dublin. The Standing Committee, however, expected a public repudiation of their names being included on the list as they were both members of the Rathmines cumann at the time. However, they retorted that they did 'of course' sign the 1916 Roll of Honour as members of the Citizen Army and that they had 'neither traitors nor murderers among our members', but Sinn Féin replied that the Roll was put in the hands of a man who had betrayed the Republic (SC, 08/12/36). Both women resigned, and Kathleen Lynn subsequently testified at the court hearings in the Sinn Féin Funds Case.

In the context of this twentieth anniversary, O'Flanagan had been invited to take part in a radio broadcast on the inauguration of Dáil Éireann. He had already aroused a certain amount of controversy within the party the previous year, when he had been approached to work on the Placenames Commission; this involved taking part in a body financed by the Free State. To some, this was unacceptable. 'Sinn Féin tramples on its own constitution when it fails to expel O'Flanagan' (Garda Report, n.d.), wrote an irate American correspondent Sean C. Riada, who advocated the expulsion of all those who, in one way or another, benefited from Free State pensions or jobs. 'You may say "If we expel all those people we will have no members left", well it is better to have no members, and no Sinn Féin, rather than have members who will surely vote at some Sinn Féin Convention before long to accept the Free State' (Garda report, n.d.). Although O'Flanagan was no longer president of the party, his participation in a national radio programme was strongly disapproved of by the Standing Committee, which 'repudiates the proposed reconstitution of the inauguration of Dáil Éireann in 1919 with its declaration of independence, with those who have violated the national position of independence, so steadfastly maintained by the loyal citizens of the Republic since that date. The government of the living Republic, being the successors of the First Dáil Éireann, and to whom we give allegiance, have the sole right to authorise the reconstitution of such a ceremony'. As a consequence, 'any member taking part in the broadcast from the Free State radio on 21 January shall automatically cease to be a member' (SC, 13/01/36). O'Flanagan was excluded from the party which he had served for over twenty years.

Sinn Féin therefore kept its distance from the official commemorations, choosing instead to organise its own events. It published that year a small, sixteen-page pamphlet which was a collection of documents on the Rising: the proclamation itself, some small excerpts of famous speeches by Tone or Casement, and some calls for men and women to join the IRA or Cumann na mBan in order to finish the work started in 1916. Interestingly, it also contained a Roll of Honour which consisted of the names of those who were killed in action, representing an alternative to that of the government, which had the advantage of being uncontroversial. This pamphlet was published a number of times in subsequent years, until 1946, and certainly represented a source of revenue for the party, as it contained a high number of advertisements, some political (such as that for *An Phoblacht* or the *Irish Press*) but most of a commercial nature.[22]

Estrangement

The IRA's support for Fianna Fáil in 1932 and again in 1933 was seen as an act of disloyalty, if not betrayal, by Sinn Féin. The differences openly surfaced in May 1932 when, referring to the annual pilgrimage to Bodenstown, Sinn Féin set out its conditions for the holding of a joint parade: 'that organisations that have compromised on the Republican position will be excluded' (SC, 27/05/32). The wording of the statement offended those who, like Mary MacSwiney, saw Cumann na mBan as a staunch supporter of the Republican cause. In order to try and find a compromise, a conference of the Second Dáil, Óglaigh na hÉireann, Cumann na mBan, Fianna Éireann and Sinn Féin was organised and held its first sitting in November 1932. This initiative was short lived. According to Sinn Féin, not only had the main purpose of the conference, to discuss the draft constitution of Dáil Éireann and its possible amendments, not been considered, but the requirement by the IRA that Sinn Féin 'withdraw its allegiance from Dáil Éireann' and accept what it considered 'practically the main clause of Saor Éire' was unacceptable (SC, 02/12/32).

The tone went up a notch the following year, with the approaching commemoration of the Easter Rising. The attitude of the IRA was considered 'not as friendly' as in previous years, Sinn Féin resenting the fact that the 'Army HQ had departed from their usual practice to furnish Sinn Féin with copy of Army orders issued in connection with the Easter commemoration' (SC, 21/04/33). But the heart of the matter certainly was the IRA's support of Fianna Fáil in the elections. The Standing Committee therefore asked for clarification on 'the attitude of the Army of supporting political parties in future elections to the usurping legislatures in Dublin and Belfast' (SC, 21/04/33).

However, there were clear signs that the initial amiable relations between Fianna Fáil and the IRA were under strain. In April 1933, at a public meeting, de Valera warned young people not to join either the Blueshirts or, more importantly, the IRA. According to the *Irish Times* report, de Valera was quoted as saying that 'They should not be misled by 1921, as now they had the vote. In his view, they were most successful in 1919 and 1921 because they were an armed nation maintaining the policy that the elected government of that day was putting into operation. The only outcome of possession of firearms by unauthorised persons was civil war. The position and policies of the present government were those of Sinn Féin 1917–1922' (*IT*, 14/04/33). Interestingly, de Valera was already somehow repudiating the legacy of the party over which he had himself presided, the third Sinn Féin, as he clearly drew a line at 1922. This in itself might have been an indication of the approach that Fianna Fáil would take to Republicanism in years to come. Minister for Posts and Telegraphs Gerry Boland made it even more explicit that Fianna Fáil had every intention of severing the links that it had maintained with the IRA, disowned as not being the true heirs of the historical organisations. In May 1933, he warned: 'Another organisation which is causing us trouble is the IRA, a new organisation as far as I see. They have new objects; they have interfered in politics in the North of Ireland [...] they will realise anyway they cannot go around shooting people; that game has got to stop in this country. We tolerated it as long as we could, but they have gone too far' (*IP*, 02/05/33).

The obvious distance that Fianna Fáil was taking from the IRA did not prevent the drift between Sinn Féin and the IRA coming to a head in June 1933 for the Wolfe Tone commemoration. Three different processions were held, one by Sinn Féin, one by the IRA and one by Fianna Fáil. All had their reasons for holding a separate event. Sinn Féin explained that this decision was taken 'after correspondence with the promoters of the Bodenstown pilgrimage announced for June 18th, and failure to obtain assurances as to the exclusion of certain undesirable parties from that pilgrimage' (*IP*, 15/05/33). Fianna Fáil considered that

> it is the organisation to which the vast body of Irish Republicans look for leadership, and to permit any ambiguity to be created as to its name or status would do irreparable harm. Fianna Fáil has no hostility to any other demonstrations arranged for Bodenstown. On the contrary, it desires their unqualified success. But on Fianna Fáil, as the largest organised body of Republicans, rests the responsibility of arranging a demonstration of its members under its own leaders, so that no difficulty or difference will deter them from participating in the pilgrimage. (*IP*, 27/05/33)

The competition for the Republican constituency was taking on a new dimension, with Fianna Fáil determined to occupy the front stage and have its legitimacy as the Republican party recognised once and for all (*IT*, 06/06/33). However, Sinn Féin softened its stance, deciding to recommend that their members and supporters participate in a joint parade with Óglaigh na hÉireann, Cumann na mBan and Clan na Gael, therefore refraining from holding their own pilgrimage (*IT*, 08/06/33). The statement, signed 'by order of the Executive Council of Dáil Éireann', showed some signs of rapprochement between the different Republican factions:

> The present Free State Government claims to be Republican, but what hinders them from restoring the rule of the Republic? Until Ireland is free from English domination the IRA will remain. The Irish people when free will perfect their economic system on real Christian justice, and not on injustice, exploitation,

confiscation, corruption and hypocrisy, which bring discredit on nationals like English professions to be Christian. Until that the IRA will carefully train to fit themselves physically and otherwise for the task at hand. (SC, 30/06/33)

Republican unity was fragile. This was made clear with the decision by Cumann na mBan to break away from the Second Dáil. A message read by Mary MacSwiney at the Sinn Féin Ard Fheis showed how this was seen as one more betrayal: 'It is regrettable that among those hitherto loyal and uncompromising, disruptive influences have crept in. Cumann na mBan, until lately foremost in loyalty and unerring rectitude of judgment, has failed in that tradition of loyalty to the established Republic' (*IP*, 02/10/33).

The increasing bitterness between the different Republican organisations was creating internal problems for Sinn Féin. Some of its members were reluctant to accept this state of affairs, and two cumainn sent a letter to the Standing Committee asking for 'another effort to be made to bring Sinn Féin and the IRA together', to which Sinn Féin replied that 'no good thing could be achieved by doing so at present' (SC, 20/10/33). But the leadership of both organisations slowly relented, and the issue of the relationship between the IRA and Sinn Féin was again raised in April 1934, when the Standing Committee proposed that both organisations meet through three representatives each (SC, 20/04/34). Sceilg, as former president of Sinn Féin, held a preliminary meeting with the IRA Army Council, which expressed willingness to renew collaboration but refused that the army give allegiance to the Second Dáil. However, the negotiations between the representatives of the three Republican groups soon ended in an impasse. Fundamentally, it was considered that the IRA and Sinn Féin were too far apart on matters of principle such as the recognition of Dáil Éireann and voting at Free State elections to make an alliance possible. The working group recommended that their executives appoint representatives to work out a constitution (SC, 25/04/34).

Within the ranks of the IRA, some continued to battle for a political group that would unite all the left-wing forces. During the 1934 convention, this proposal was put to a vote, but the leadership refused to approve it and decided instead to put the matter on stand-by until the following convention. The supporters of the motion ignored this decision and left the IRA to form their own organisation, Republican Congress.[23] This new movement held its first convention on 8 April 1934, publishing a manifesto which accused the IRA, among other things, of being incapable of mobilising support on anti-capitalistic issues: 'Had the IRA leadership understood that the economic war was not being fought to free Ireland but to serve Irish capitalism they would have carried out this mobilisation first before giving any support to that war. On account of their failure the Republican issue had been pushed farther into the background' (*IP*, 10/04/34).[24] In the same statement it affirmed that 'The Republican movement, to be successful in smashing the British grip on Ireland, must attack those interests and destroy their power'. This ran contrary to the tenets of the 1929 Dáil Éireann Constitution which Sinn Féin had endorsed. MacSwiney had made this point clear when putting forward an amendment to the Constitution the previous year: 'The class in this country who demands social justice is the class for whom national independence is a primal necessity. That class is the Irish nation, still submerged but ever struggling' (SC, 05/01/34). The discourse held by Republican Congress was rejected by Sinn Féin which, when approached by a local cumann asking whether it was possible for a member of Sinn Féin to support the new organisation, sternly replied: 'a political organisation that accepts all fundamental principles of Sinn Féin has no reason for separate existence except as a disturbing faction, therefore no member of the organisation can give it support. It is also obvious that if it is not going to accept all the fundamental principles of Sinn Féin no member of the Sinn Féin organisation can give it support either' (SC, 11/05/34). Republican Congress did attempt to enlist Sinn Féin's support by inviting the Standing Committee to send representatives to their congress to be held at the end of September 1934. Predictably, the reply was negative, as Sinn Féin 'could not enter into political association with any party except on the basis of the acceptance of the existing Irish Republic for which Connolly and the other martyrs of 1916 gave their lives' (SC, 08/09/34).

Some party members were becoming restless with the extreme dogmatism of their leadership, to the extent that one of the resolutions put forward by a Belfast cumann for the 1935 Ard Fheis was that 'Sinn Féin declare the Second Dáil defunct' (SC, 22/11/35). Obviously rejected by the Standing Committee, this showed the internal frictions that such a rigid stance was generating. Moreover, Sinn Féin was to be dealt a further blow when the IRA, realising that it was necessary to launch a political initiative to counter Republican Congress, communicated to the papers in September 1935 that a new separatist organisation would be formed. Sinn Féin's response was immediate: 'Surely Mr. MacBride must know that such a separatist organisation is already in existence. Sinn Féin is just the organisation that Mr. MacBride so eloquently describes. It is no new organisation. It has been tried and proved. It has the additional advantage that no one can suspect it of being a mere shadow controlled from behind the scenes by another group' (SC, 27/09/35). Sinn Féin was suspicious of the motives of the IRA which, in their view, was seeking to gain control of the Republican political organisation. This, ironically, would be the exact scenario that would take place in 1948. But in the 1930s, it was clearly felt that the two organisations had different functions and one same objective, 'namely Óglaigh na hÉireann for the military work and Sinn Féin for the political work, to restore the Republican position of 1918–1921' (SC, 04/10/35). This, however, was the third time that an alternative Republican political formation was created since 1926, but party leaders did not seem to understand the reasons why the IRA refused to make Sinn Féin the political front of the Republican movement. They preferred to ascribe this to the IRA's desire to have full control over political matters, which conveniently negated the state of disrepair in which the party found itself. O'Flanagan did admit at a public meeting to the stagnation of the organisation, which he attributed to a 'shortage of young blood. The old members who had rendered long and faithful service to the movement were willing to make room' (Garda report, 17/03/36).

In February 1936, a meeting was held between Dáil Éireann, the Army Council and Sinn Féin, but participants failed to reach an agreement. As a result, the IRA announced that they would proceed with the setting up of a new organisation, in spite of Sinn Féin's repeated statements that 'the field of civil authority belongs to the Sinn Féin organisation, as completely as the field of military activity is claimed by Óglaigh na hÉireann' (SC, 31/02/36). In March 1936, the formation of Cumann Poblachta na hÉireann was announced to the press, with Patrick McLogan (abstentionist MP for South Armagh) as chairman and Seán MacBride as secretary. This was an all-Ireland, abstentionist party which aimed at establishing 'a reign of social justice based on Christian principles by a just distribution of the Nation's wealth and resources' and which was to resuscitate *An Phoblacht* as its press organ (*IP*, 07/03/36). The first convention of the party was attended by representatives of the IRA, Cumann na mBan and Clann na Gael, but not Sinn Féin, who retained a level of suspicion. As a representative of the party put it to an *Irish Press* reporter, there was a possibility that entry into Dáil Éireann would eventually be decided upon, which would in turn lead to an understanding with Fianna Fáil. But more fundamentally, the formation of Cumann Poblachta na hÉireann was seen as yet another disloyal attempt to bypass Sinn Féin. Councillor Raul explained at a meeting that the members 'were giving up the Republic and that they were hoping to displace the Fianna Fáil party, get into the Dáil, and obtain good jobs' (Garda report, 17/03/36) . In response to the IRA's initiative, Sinn Féin asked Dáil Éireann to 'immediately appoint the responsible ministers to the Dáil so as to afford the people directions as to the legal and moral authority in all public affairs, particularly the

affairs of the Defence forces of the country' (SC, 14/02/36). It seemed that
the estrangement between the two bodies was now complete, as Sinn Féin was
sending a very clear signal that it no longer considered the Army Council represented the armed body of the Republican movement.

The new organisation soon became a source of concern for the authorities,
and two months after its renewed publication, seized *An Phoblacht*. In the eyes
of the new party leaders, this was but a mere continuation of the 'intimidation'
and 'scare tactics' inherited from the Cumann na nGaedheal years, and was a
'direct interference with the right of [our] organisation to put its policy freely
before the electorate' (*II*, 01/05/36). The founders of the party nevertheless
canvassed the country and set up branches, particularly throughout the west,
with meetings gathering an average of fifty people, according to newspaper
reports, prompting Maud Gonne to state that 'If you return a majority [at the
next general election] the Republic will be declared the next day, and we have
an army to support the Republic' (*IP*, 04/05/36). The party also vehemently
protested against the arrest of some of its members and supporters, some of
whom, such as Seán MacSwiney (brother of dead hunger striker Terence and of
Mary), embarked on a hunger strike in Arbour Hill (*IP*, 18/05/36). However,
as Patrick Keena was soon to find out, the state took a strong view against those
who harboured views which both supported the IRA and dissented from the
institutions. This member of Cumann Poblachta na hÉireann was thus sentenced
to eighteen months' imprisonment for having incited young men to join the IRA
at a public meeting (*II*, 01/07/36).

Possibly feeling that it was becoming too entrenched in its principled stances,
the Sinn Féin Standing Committee made an unexpected move in July 1936, when
it decided that it would support 'an agreed candidate to contest the by-election
now pending in Galway of a person who accepts the established republic and
is prepared if opportunity offers to take his or her seat in Dáil Éireann only'
(SC, 29/07/36). More important, however, was the conclusion at that same
meeting that Sinn Féin was prepared to 'work for the election of such a candidate in cooperation with the other Republican organisations'. Two candidates
were nominated, Count Plunkett for Galway and Stephen Hayes, future IRA
chief of staff, for Wexford. The elections were scheduled for 13 and 17 August
respectively.

The presence of those two candidates seemed to irritate Fianna Fáil, which
insisted on its Republican credentials and legitimacy. In a speech uttered in
Wexford on 13 August 1936, de Valera stated that the election would be a vote of
confidence in the government, and insisted on making the Republican position

of his party clear: they derived their legitimacy not from Britain but from the Irish people who had voted them into power, their allegiance was to the Irish people, and the twenty-six counties had the right to choose their representatives in parliament (*IT*, 22/08/36).

At the other end of the Republican spectrum, Count Plunkett's manifesto was not only an appeal to Republican sentiment, it was also a clear denunciation of what the new party considered the Free State's coercion and repression against Republicans. It claimed that 150 men were jailed and the prison conditions were such that a Commission of Inquiry had been set up, under the chairmanship of William Norton, Labour TD, but banned by Fianna Fáil (Republican election manifesto).[25] This document also insisted on the fact that being a Republican under Fianna Fáil had become as difficult, if not more so, as under the previous government.

Sinn Féin collaborated with Cumann Poblachta na hÉireann, holding joint meetings and endorsing Count Plunkett's electoral address. But such unity did not suffice to attract public opinion, as shown by the dismally poor results obtained by the candidates: 1,301 and 2,696 votes, therefore demonstrating that abstentionism and the ideals of the IRA did not respond to the political concerns of the times.

Nevertheless, the rapprochement between Sinn Féin and the IRA was gathering momentum, with Sinn Féin agreeing to further cooperate with the new organisation. A coordinating committee was established after the election, with representatives from the three parties. MacSwiney was co-opted as the representative of Dáil Éireann, although she declined, deeming that 'as a TD, her presence on the committee would not be advisable' (SC, 08/12/36). Meetings of the coordinating committee were held throughout the winter. However, one of the key issues discussed was that of premises, the debate centring on the issue of whether the new party should share Sinn Féin's headquarters. Nevertheless, Cumann Poblachta na hÉireann would soon cease to operate, in light of its failed attempt to make an impression on the Irish public, and the party slowly dissolved.

Fighting the 'British Empire' constitution

In 1937, de Valera announced the repeal of the 1922 Constitution and its replacement by a new Constitution for Ireland. Prior to this, the External Relations Act had been rushed through the Oireachtas following the abdication of Edward VIII in December of 1936. The Act removed, in effect, the role of the British monarch in Irish Affairs.[26] Sinn Féin rejected this new development, putting forward, instead, its own Constitution as drafted in 1929, which stated that 'The national sovereignty of Ireland resides, under God, in the citizens of the entire nation' and that 'The Republic guarantees civil and religious liberty, but no organisation aiming at the subordination of the Republic shall be tolerated' (Sinn Féin Constitution, 1929, in Funds Case, 1948). This last clause left little doubt as to how a Sinn Féin-led Republic would have treated its enemies, and was quite ironic in light of the party's criticism of the Free State's repression towards those who were, so to speak, trying to undermine the legitimacy of the state.

The coronation of George VI on 2 May 1937 presented Sinn Féin with an opportunity to protest against the event. It 'called upon the Irish people everywhere to refuse to identify themselves in any way with a function that seeks to renew the old insults directed against the faith of the majority of our people and to perpetuate the partition and subjection of our country' (*IP*, 20/04/37). It tried, much as it had done in 1932 for the royal visit to Northern Ireland, to put forward a resolution in the Dublin City Corporation, but the latter ruled it out of order 'as a political matter'. Sinn Féin's efforts were, however, concentrated on denigrating the new Constitution as just another, 'latest alternative to the Republic of Ireland', which called on people to 'live in amity with the foreign power that holds Ireland's territory and her ports' (SC, 04/07/37). Sinn Féin called on its cumainn to submit a memo to what it called 'document no. 3', in a reference to document no. 2 drafted in 1922 by de Valera in which an external association between the two countries had been suggested and rejected by Sinn Féin.

The articles of the Constitution that Sinn Féin found most problematic were those that, in its view, either undermined the Republican aspiration or curtailed the right of the opposition to continue to fight for such an aspiration. Thus, Article 3, which stated that the 'laws enacted by that Parliament shall have the like area and extent of application as the laws of Saorstát Éireann and the like extra-territorial effect', fell short of the demand for the end of partition; it resented the fact that Article 12, which laid down the functions of the President, should use this term when the Republic was not the one proclaimed in 1916; it criticised Article 38 which provided for special courts and military tribunals where trials could be held without a jury. Article 40, Section 6.2, which regulated the right to assemble peacefully and without arms, was also seen as problematic as this right was curtailed, in its view, by the possibility to 'prevent or control meetings which are determined in accordance with law to be calculated to cause a breach of the peace or to be a danger or nuisance to the general public' (*Bunreacht na hÉireann*, 1937). Mary MacSwiney saw it as 'a further amendment to the already much amended 1922 Constitution', which aimed at the subversion of the Republic and which was based on British acts of parliament. But she did have another criticism to make, one which might not have been very frequently articulated at the time, as she insisted also on the fact that it was not democratic because it gave 'power to discriminate against women in their economic life. Equal pay for equal work is the only just solution' (UCD, MacSwiney, 1937). Most of Sinn Féin's arguments therefore centred on the perception that the constitution was not democratic, whereas it has been argued that in effect it 'protected the principle of democracy, committed the state to a peaceful resolution of international disputes, and prevented the state from ratifying international treaties without referenda' (Kissane, 2007, 223).

Sinn Féin, however, decided to take part in neither the 1937 general election nor the plebiscite on the draft constitution that took place on the same day. The reasons given were mainly financial, explaining that the £100 deposit[27] and the funds impounded in Chancery made it impossible for the party to enter any campaign. On 1 July, 685,105 voters approved of the new Constitution, while 526,945 rejected it. Sinn Féin continued to protest at what it saw as the undemocratic nature of the Constitution, and called a rally on 29 December 1937 to mark 'the resentment of the citizens at the enforcement of the British Empire constitution, which subverts the Republic and maintains England's occupation of Ireland's territory and her ports, and to show their disapproval for the campaign for the recruitment of Irishmen in any of the armed forces of the British Crown' (Garda report, 30/12/37). On 28 December 1937, a black flag was hoisted above the Sinn Féin headquarters in Parnell Square to signify, presumably, the death of the 1916 Republic. On that occasion, according to police reports, three resolutions were passed, one condemning the Constitution as being subversive to the Irish Republic, another pledging support to the campaign against the enlistment of Irishmen in British army forces, and a final one pledging allegiance to the established republic. The security forces minimised the relevance of the meeting in no uncertain terms: 'Although there was a fairly large crowd present, there was a complete absence of enthusiasm. The people present with the exception of a small section appeared to have no interest in the proceedings', adding that 'if intended to be a demonstration against the enactment of the Constitution, [it] must be regarded as a complete failure' (Garda report, 30/12/37).

The following day, 29 December 1937, the label 'Free State' disappeared, the south of Ireland becoming Ireland or Éire. On 25 April 1938, after negotiations between the Taoiseach and the British Prime Minister, the Anglo-Irish Agreement was signed, putting an end to the economic war that had been ongoing since 1932, and giving back to Ireland the control over the harbours that it had lost with the 1921 Treaty, an essential move if Ireland intended to adopt a neutral position in any future international conflict.

The S-Plan and the Second World War

The IRA, for its part, was now in an even more difficult position as it had become obvious, at the close of 1935, that its very existence was now intolerable for de Valera's government. This was partly due to the repeated interventions of the organisation in the trade union movement, having announced its 'willingness to assist the workers in their struggle' (*Irish Examiner*, 25/03/35). But more disturbing still was the fact that it was still active, even if its support was minimal, presenting an unacceptable challenge to the government. Tensions led to numerous arrests, and to the banning of *An Phoblacht* on several occasions. On 21 May 1936, chief of staff Maurice Twomey was arrested and sentenced to three years of hard labour. On 18 June 1936, the IRA was declared an unlawful organisation. This did not prevent it from defying the authorities. Indeed, at the June 1937 Bodenstown ceremony, its volunteers marched in military formation in front of approximately 1,500 Republicans, according to the report in the *Irish Times*, parading 'under military orders, the majority of which were issued, sergeant-major style, in Irish' and marching 'openly, under the banners of the proclaimed military organisation' (*IT*, 21/07/37).

The years that followed Twomey's arrest were characterised, on the one hand, by the power struggles inside the IRA's leadership and on the other hand, by an inactivity that the grassroots of the movement started to blame on the leadership. Some eighty volunteers decided to answer Frank Ryan's call to join the Connolly Column of the International Brigades to defend the Spanish Republic. However, perhaps as a result of the rising discontent within the ranks of the organisation, the April 1938 annual convention gave Seán Russell,[28] chief of staff, its support for the launch of a military campaign in Britain, albeit reluctantly. Some members, such as Tom Barry, thought that there were sufficient British in the six counties for the IRA to fight against. The disagreement that opposed both men extended to several members of the IRA who left the movement. In December, Russell went to the members of the Second Dáil to put his plans forward and secure their agreement. Russell's manoeuvre was unexpected, given that the IRA had removed its allegiance to the Second Dáil a decade earlier. However, strategically speaking, this initiative was not entirely contradictory. Faced with an organisation which was divided on the military tactic to adopt, and faced with a strong opposition to his military plans, Russell probably thought it best to obtain the approval of the living symbols of the legitimacy of the Republican cause. Therefore, in December 1938, the magazine *Wolfe Tone Weekly* gave the outcome of the agreement. The members of the Second Dáil accepted to transfer their authority to the Army Council as well as the power to enforce the 1916 Proclamation and the Declaration of Independence. 'Confident, in delegating this sacred trust to the Army of the Republic that, in their every action towards its consummation, they will be inspired by the high ideals and the chivalry of our martyred comrades, we, as Executive Council of Dáil Éireann, Government of the Republic, append our names', read the statement, signed by all seven members (*Wolfe Tone Weekly*, 17 December 1938). According to future Provisional Sinn Féin president Ruairí Ó Brádaigh, however, this was only a transfer of executive powers. Sinn Féin kept its legislative and judiciary prerogatives in order to avoid investing the IRA with too much power (Ó Brádaigh, interview, 1986).

The reason that led the Second Dáil to renounce part of its authority could have been its growing isolation. On a symbolic level at least, Russell was restoring its consultative role as well as its function as guardian of the principles of the Republic. 'The Dáil members felt that the IRA request gave them the moral recognition so long denied by all factions and that their conditional devolution of power would in turn give the IRA the moral basis for the impending campaign' (Bowyer Bell, 1983, 154). But obviously, Sinn Féin took serious offence at this, and decided in January 1939 that if the implications of this agreement did not extend to Sinn Féin (military affairs under IRA command, civil affairs under Sinn Féin control), the party would not pledge an oath to the new government of the Republic. Some years later, when giving her testimony to the court for the Funds Case hearings, Margaret Buckley gave her interpretation of this episode. The transfer of powers was owed, according to her, to the imminent war. After the war, she claimed that the members of the Second Dáil could take back those powers, although this was never done. The IRA would consider itself the embodiment of the Republic for decades to come.

This episode concerned the government enough to bring the matter to the Dáil and to reproduce the entire article of the *Wolfe Tone Weekly*. Particularly worrying was the IRA statement which read, indeed, like an ultimatum: 'The time has come to make that fight. There is no need to declare the Republic of Ireland, now or in the future. There is no need to reaffirm the declaration of Irish independence. But the hour has come for the supreme effort to make both effective. So in the name of the unconquered dead and the faithful living, we pledge

ourselves to that task' (*Dáil Debates*, 02/03/39). Minister for Justice Gerry
Boland concluded: 'Now we know that that armed body exists. It may not be a
large group, or a very large body, but there does exist in this country an organisation which has arms and war material at its disposal. It has been training and
organising, and it has been receiving funds from outside sources for the explicit
and sole purpose of using that position militarily' (*Dáil Debates*, 02/03/39).

Indeed, on 12 January 1939, the IRA had sent an ultimatum to the British
Secretary of Foreign Affairs calling on the British to withdraw from Ireland. It
launched its offensive, the S-Plan, or Sabotage plan, three days later, exploding
several bombs simultaneously in different locations in England. This initiative
generated some concern among Irish and British political circles. With the
intensification of the bombing campaign, emergency measures were introduced,
such as the Prevention of Violence Act, in June 1939.[29] The previous month, the
Treason Act had been introduced to complement Clause 39 of the Constitution
regarding Treason, which was now punishable by death and concerned those
who committed that offence within or outside the state (Treason Act, 1939).
The Offences Against the State Act of June 1939 reintroduced the military
courts, and gave an insightful definition of what an 'unlawful organisation'
consisted of: any group that encouraged treason, promoted the alteration of the
Constitution by the use of force or other unconstitutional means, maintained
an armed force, commissioned criminal offences or the obstruction of or interference with the administration of justice, and finally, promoted violence and
the non-payment of monies payable to the public funds. Anyone who was a
member of an unlawful organisation could be summarily convicted with a fine
not exceeding £50 and a sentence not exceeding three months (*Irish Statute
Book*, Offences Against the State Act, 1939).

Although the IRA never officially ended its campaign,[30] the bombings in
early 1940, which injured more than twenty people in London, were the last
operation of the S-Plan, which claimed seven lives and left 200 injured. The
campaign, which might not have received the academic and historical attention that it deserves (Craig, 2010, 310–11), was important if only because of the
level of security measures and emergency legislation it generated, both in Britain
and in Ireland, that almost succeeded in wiping out the Republican movement
altogether. Given the context of severe repression against Republicanism, Sinn
Féin's role, although minimal, did serve a purpose, as it became the only voice
that could still express opposition. It therefore stated the day following the introduction of the Offences Against the State Act that 'It is an amazing thing that
men who were once soldiers of the Republic and have lived most of their lives in

Ireland should show so little knowledge of the psychology of the Irish people as to imagine they can frighten the Irish people into submission by coercion Acts' (*IT*, 08/03/39). Calling it a 'panic legislation', Margaret Buckley, president of Sinn Féin since 1937, saw it as proof that Chamberlain and de Valera were in cahoots in trying to limit the IRA activities to Ireland. An attempt was made by IRA leader Stephen Hayes to reorganise Sinn Féin in Wexford, in order 'to ask for the support of the people of Wexford for the expeditionary force of the IRA who are at present engaged in the final struggle for the separation from the British empire' and voted a resolution that Sinn Féin clubs be established throughout Co. Wexford. The meeting, which was 'large' according to *The Echo* and small according to the Gardaí (forty-six people), did not generate a surge of sympathy or support for Sinn Féin, which stood on the margins of the system.

On 3 September 1939, Britain and France declared war on Germany. The previous day, de Valera had asked the Dáil to 'hereby resolv[e], pursuant to sub-section 3° of section 3 of Article 28 of the Constitution, that, arising out of the armed conflict now taking place in Europe, a national emergency exists affecting the vital interests of the State' (*Dáil Debates*, 02/09/39). The episodic relationships that Republicans had maintained with Berlin constituted a threat to the neutrality that Ireland wanted to keep. On 3 September 1939, the government moved to activate parts of the Offences Against the State Act, establishing the Special Criminal Court and introducing internment without trial.

Sinn Féin's position on the war was quite similar to that which it had held before and during the First World War, thereby displaying a visible lack of international awareness and political astuteness. Shortly before the outbreak of the war, a Sinn Féin statement read: 'If the war had come, he [de Valera] would have found himself in the position of John Redmond: ready to commit Irishmen to fight for England. But like Redmond, he would find that although he was willing to sell Ireland he would not deliver the goods and would get short shrift from even those who are now his supporters' (Garda report, 20/08/39). The parallel with the First World War had already been made on a number of occasions by some Sinn Féin speakers from 1935 onward, showing an ambivalent discourse towards the axis forces. What underlay this analysis was the preoccupation with the role of Britain in any future war, which obliterated all other political considerations. In 1935, O'Flanagan had stated that 'If England were involved in another war [...] the Irish Nation would not make the mistake she made in 1914, by waiting until the war was nearly over until she began her fight for independence'. Relying on the old adage that England's difficulty was Ireland's opportunity to secure her freedom, he formulated the hope that if Britain and Italy did go to war Ireland's old enemy would come out worst (Garda report, 02/10/35). In a meeting in March 1939, in the middle of the IRA campaign in England, Councillor Raul talked of the support given by the *Irish Independent* to General Franco and hoped they would now champion the cause of the IRA in the same manner, stating that the nations of Europe 'should combine and drive England from every country and put them back on their own island and keep them there as they were the only warmongers in the world' (Garda report, 08/03/39). Raul's inflammatory rhetoric also had rabid anti-Semitic connotations, as he qualified the First World War as having been fought between Freemasons and Catholics and hoped that in the next one 'the Catholics of the world would wipe out the agents of Satan' (Garda report, 07/08/35).

The period of the Second World War was characterised by an almost total absence of Republicans on the political front. *An Phoblacht* had ceased to appear in 1938, and apart from a short period when *Republican File* was published, the Republican movement no longer had a press organ. However, its reputation as a front for subversion justified the maintenance of a level of surveillance. Hence, British intelligence agent 'Captain Collinson sent agents to its public meetings and asked the Stubbs agency to provide the names and addresses of its executive committee so that they could be put under postal censorship' (McMahon, 2008, 360).[31] The Irish state also kept a close watch on Sinn Féin, even though there was not much activity to monitor, but the occasional meetings that were held were still attended by Gardaí. Given the level of censorship that existed throughout the period of the war, and the level of insecurity and anxiety that the government promoted,[32] Sinn Féin was one of the organisations that were closely monitored by the state. Whether there was much to spy on as far as Republican political activism was concerned is doubtful. Sinn Féin's situation was critical. Its 1939 Ard Fheis was held in November in the Parnell Square head office, an indication in itself of how modest in terms of membership the party had become. Its activity consisted for most of the period of defending prisoners' rights and condemning conditions within the prisons, which exceptionally translated into more than a statement. Thus, in one instance, the persistent efforts of a local cumann had led the Cork corporation to vote, by eight votes to six, for a resolution protesting against the detentions in Arbour Hill prison (*IP*, 15/11/39). The party also continued to organise public lectures and commemorations. The themes and speakers were varied, ranging from speeches on partition (SC, 22/01/40) to lectures celebrating patriot poets.

For much of the period, most news items concerning Sinn Féin were to be found in the obituary section. Some of the most loyal and dedicated members of the Sinn Féin Standing Committee died within months of each other: Liam Gilmore, who was honorary secretary of the organisation, Fr Michael O'Flanagan and Mary MacSwiney. The latter two were praised by the *Irish Press* for their commitment to the cause, MacSwiney's life being described as one of 'endeavour and self-sacrifice for Ireland [...] whose rigidity of principles even those who disagreed with her could only but admire' (*IP*, 03/03/42). Both had left the organisation, the former because of his participation in a radio broadcast, and the latter because of a disagreement over the acceptance of pensions by Sinn Féin members.[33] Mary MacSwiney's political trajectory could be seen as one of dedicated idealism characterised by a lack of political realism. She was adamant that her cause was just, and according to her biographer Charlotte Fallon, 'her Republicanism was religious in tone and in quality' (Fallon, 1986, 129). But her integrity and refusal to compromise also led her to make choices that would further isolate her. She fell out with most of her former colleagues, resigned from Cumann na mBan in 1933, when the latter organisation stated that 'To ask young girls and women to render allegiance to a government which does not and cannot function is simply taking their powers of credibility beyond reason' (Fallon, 1986, 129). She left Sinn Féin the following year, when the party authorised the membership of those who benefited from state pensions. Her funeral was a relatively low-key affair, in contrast to that of O'Flanagan, who was given the full honours owed to a national figure, his coffin draped in the tricolour and his requiem mass attended by a number of state representatives and politicians.[34] On this occasion, former Sinn Féin president O'Kelly delivered an impassioned speech, praising a man who 'adhered to his national ideals to the last and never dreamt of exploiting any of the great causes with which he identified' (O'Kelly, 1942).

With most IRA active members imprisoned and Sinn Féin absent from the political scene, Republicans no longer had a voice. Therefore, in February 1940, a number of former IRA volunteers decided to launch a new political formation, Córas na Poblachta, which aimed at establishing the Irish Republic.[35] At a meeting in the Mansion House on 11 February 1941, Seán Fitzpatrick reiterated the old Griffith adage that 'political freedom without economic independence was a mockery' (*IT*, 12/02/41). The message of this new organisation was, however, somewhat ambivalent and confusing. It stressed, on the one hand, that 'a political party had not, and could not have, a national outlook', and on the other, talked about Irish national interests, which should not be 'inevitably linked with sterling' (*IT*, 12/02/41). Its analysis was based on a simplistic anti-capitalistic rhetoric – Hugh O'Neill stated for instance that 'unemployment was part of the capitalist system, and no adjustment of that system could cure it' (*IT*, 12/02/41) – with anti-semitic overtones, as the organisation believed that those in power were controlled by 'key men' in other countries where the Freemasons, the 'Jewry' and the ascendancy gang controlled banks and big business (*IT*, 29/04/41). This type of rhetoric was reminiscent of other discourses where the enemy was an invisible and ill-defined mass of banker, Jews and Freemasons who controlled politics. In this sense, it could be said that Córas na Poblachta flirted with a type of nationalism that was not solely Irish in its sources but borrowed from other European discourses that flourished in the 1930s.

Córas na Poblachta put forward five candidates in the 1943 general election. Seán Dowling, the candidate for Dublin South, explained that his party would, through a five-year plan, establish an investment control policy which would liquidate foreign investments and use the capital to put Irish people to work (*II*, 19/06/43). He stated, however, that Ireland would get nothing from whichever country won the war and urged the Irish people to have their own plans and policy (*IP*, 08/03/43). Candidates had agreed, if elected, not to derive any personal gain from their salaries. However, a major departure from the traditional Republican dogma was that they did not seek to abstain from taking their seats.

The results of the elections showed that there was no place in the country at that time for a fringe Nationalist party. With a total of 2,600 votes, Córas na Poblachta's candidates lost their deposit.[36] Evidently, the ultra-Nationalist theories of the party had not appealed to the electorate, but the leaders attributed their electoral fiasco to the lack of unity within Republican ranks, explaining that the strength of Irish Nationalism was being dissipated because of so many small groups (*II*, 03/12/43). Indeed, for such a small number of people, the number of organisations was high: at the commemoration of the Easter Week, no less than six different groups were present.[37] By the following general election, called in 1944, Córas na Poblachta decided to bow out: 'the atmosphere in the country at present precludes the possibility of the electorate giving clear consideration to the national, financial, economic and social questions and to the great problems of reconstruction and development which are the main concern of Córas na Poblachta and which must sooner or later be faced if the Irish nation is to survive. For these reasons it was decided by the Central Committee not to put forward any candidates' (statement signed by honorary secretaries Roger MacCorley and Seán Mac Giobúin, *II*, 18/05/44).

Córas na Poblachta's 'raison d'être was wholly predicated upon an Axis victory in the war, and this, in conjunction with its corporatist economic doctrines, soon attracted to its ranks a substantial – and, ultimately, predominant – contingent of pro-German activists' (Douglas, 2006, 1173). It was yet another organisation that seemed tempted to drift towards more extreme versions of Nationalism which were expanding on the continent, being part of the nebula of extreme right-wing movements that were present in Ireland during the war. One such group was Ailtirí na hAiséirghe, which sought to merge fascism and Christianity and whose slogan was 'A New Order in a New Ireland'. Whereas some connections with Sinn Féin are mentioned in the only book that analyses this party (Douglas, 2009, 174), the group is not mentioned in any Sinn Féin document, no more than Córas na Poblachta, which was only referred to once by Buckley, on 17 March 1940, when she affirmed that there was no need for such an organisation, as Sinn Féin was open to all Republicans. She appealed to all those who had drifted away from their party to return to it.

The last battle?

As Córas na Poblachta's programme sank into oblivion,[38] the IRA was battling for its own survival. The Second World War was undoubtedly the darkest period ever experienced by the Republican movement. De Valera was keen to preserve neutrality during the conflict, a position that had been announced as early as April 1939, as he 'believed that small states only suffered in large states' wars. It was not for Ireland to take part in this great power struggle. Neutrality aimed to keep Ireland out of the conflict and find her destiny in a world at war [...] Though neutral, the State was still functioning within the world system' (Kennedy, 2011, 47). But there were other, more pragmatic reasons for Ireland's neutrality: its potential to give the country the possibility to act independently of Britain, and the fact that it was the least divisive policy in political terms. And last but not least, 'A genuine fear that if Ireland joined the war on the British side, it could provoke a German-backed IRA revolt and perhaps another civil war' (Ó Drisceoil, 2006, 246). Ireland would, nevertheless, implicitly side with the Allied Forces, as it let British planes fly over the territory and as Irish citizens were allowed to join the British armed forces. The government maintained good relations with the German representative in Dublin, but interned the agents who tried to make contact with the IRA. The Germans bombed Ireland several times, such as on 26 August 1940 in Wexford, killing three people, and on 30 and 31 May 1941 in Dublin, leaving twenty-eight dead and forty-five injured. The German government subsequently paid compensation for personal injuries (*IT*, 14/02/46). On the other hand, the north of the country was badly affected by the German raids, which killed hundreds of people in Belfast alone and led approximately 10,000 to cross the border (Barton, 1995, 49).

In this context, IRA activities, not only in England but also in Ireland, were seen as a danger that had to be prevented at all costs. Indeed, the IRA still showed signs of resilience in spite of the emergency legislation and was linked to a number of attacks in Éire, including ten murders. Moreover, according to MI5 files, it had made contact with the German authorities as early as 1937.[39] Therefore, in 1939, an agent of the German military services came to Ireland and made contact with the IRA. Early in 1940, Seán Russell went to Germany and was sent back to Ireland after having been trained in espionage in an operation codenamed 'Operation Dove'. However, he died at sea on the way back. His legacy is a contested one, as shown by the debate spurred by the vandalising of his statue in Fairview, Dublin, in 2005.[40]

The repression against the IRA was severe. Many arrests led Republicans to focus their attention on what was happening inside the prisons, where hunger strikes were embarked upon in order to protest against prison conditions.[41] Two prisoners died as a result of their protest: Tony D'Arcy, who was captured in February 1940, and Jack McNeela, chief of IRA publicity who published the magazine *War News* in Belfast, arrested on 29 December 1939 and later charged with 'conspiracy to usurp a function of government' by a special court and sentenced to two years' imprisonment. Both men, who had originally been detained in Mountjoy prison, were sent to Arbour Hill. They embarked on a hunger strike as a protest against the manner in which some of their fellow prisoners were treated, and not in order to obtain political status. Four other men had joined the hunger strike, including Tómas Óg Mac Curtain, son of the Cork Lord Mayor who had been killed in 1920, and Jack Plunkett, son of Count Plunkett and brother of Joseph Mary Plunkett, one of the signatories of the 1916 Proclamation. According to an article published in *An Phoblacht* for the sixty-fifth anniversary of his death, McNeela was visited by his uncle, a Fianna Fáil TD, who asked him to put an end to his action as he was 'embarrassing de Valera', the 'heaven-sent leader' (*AP*, 14/04/05). Whether the story is true or not, it nevertheless shows the deep resentment that existed between the two former allies turned enemies. McNeela died on 19 April 1943, just hours after the hunger strike had been called off (*IT*, 20/04/40).

The Fianna Fáil government did not hesitate to resort to capital punishment. In August 1940, three men were arrested and judged by a military court, which sentenced them to death. One sentence was commuted, the other two men becoming the first to be executed by the Fianna Fáil government in 1941. In total, six men were executed between 1940 and 1944, in Mountjoy and Portlaoise, the last one being Charlie Kerins, then chief of staff of the IRA, convicted of murdering a garda in Dublin. In spite of a campaign, in which Kerry county council took an active part, to have his sentence commuted, the prisoner, who refused to recognise the court, was denied leave to appeal his conviction by the Court of Appeal. His lawyer, Seán MacBride, as well as members of the public attempted to convince the Fianna Fáil government to commute his sentence, but Kerins was executed on 1 December 1944.

The IRA was, moreover, badly affected by the internal divisions that led to the so-called court-martialling and sentencing of the chief of staff, Stephen Hayes, who was accused of treason by some members. This was quite an extraordinary story, which started when Hayes was arrested by his own men in June 1941, and questioned repeatedly before being eventually 'court-martialled'.[42] After two months of imprisonment, Hayes managed to escape the vigilance of his warden and to get hold of his revolver, with which he escaped. Running with his feet chained, he approached a garda at the Rathmines garda station, explaining that he was 'the chief of staff of the IRA'. He was subsequently brought before the military tribunal, and the statement that he delivered retraced two long months of interrogation, harsh treatment and attempts on his part to gain time by making up 'imaginary incidents'. In these, a Free State agent, called De Lacy, turned out to be his brother-in-law, and Hayes provided information to him on the activities of his own organisation. His testimony contributed to the conviction of Seán McCaughey, a twenty-one-year-old man from Belfast who was adjutant-general of the IRA, who was sentenced to death. The statement of the landlady in whose house Hayes had been detained was equally as confusing and disconcerting, as she claimed not to have been aware of what was going on, explaining that she was under the impression that the man living in her house, Hayes, was an elderly man recovering from a drink problem (*IT*, 19/09/41). In June 1942, Hayes was, in turn, found guilty of having 'usurped a function of government by maintaining and being a member and officer of the IRA, an armed force not authorised by the Constitution' (*IT*, 20/06/42). He was sentenced to five years. The leadership of the movement was from then on in the hands of northern leaders.

The military campaign of the IRA in England led the Northern Ireland government to take strong repressive measures. On 28 December 1938, internment without trial was reintroduced, and was maintained until the end of the war. The Offences Against the State Act had become permanent in 1933. The IRA nevertheless kept a level of activity. Its leadership had decided to launch a campaign in Northern Ireland during its 1941 convention. A newspaper, *Republican News*, was irregularly published after the closure of *War News*, but the experience was short lived. In September 1941, the Royal Ulster Constabulary (RUC) raided the office of the paper and arrested its editor, John Graham. The activities of the IRA were almost as short lived. On 5 May 1942, a street battle opposed some IRA volunteers and members of the RUC. Six men were subsequently accused of the murder of an officer and were sentenced to death. Five of those sentences were commuted, but the sixth man was executed on 2 September 1942. The activities of the IRA seemed to get a new lease of life when four Republican prisoners, among whom Jimmy Steele and Hugh McAteer, managed to escape from Crumlin Road prison in January 1943. Two of them entered a Belfast cinema in April, interrupted the show, and read out the 1916 Proclamation, then managed to escape. They were both captured, one in October and the second in November.

The history of Sinn Féin during the Second World War was dominated by Margaret Buckley. According to Ruairí Ó Brádaigh, 'Mrs Buckley was Sinn Féin' (Ó Brádaigh, interview, 1986). Very few documents were published during this period, and therefore the history of the party is patchy. Before the beginning of the war, Sinn Féin organised meetings on a fortnightly basis, which would gather approximately ten people, testifying to the loss of influence the party was experiencing. In the years that followed, the numbers declined even further as the repression against the Republican movement intensified. Nevertheless, the party maintained a minimal level of activity. It held its Standing Committee meetings with regularity, and according to the minutes, those in attendance varied between five and seven. Not much business was carried out, and not much of a political agenda was discussed. Its executive was, by 1941, almost exclusively Dublin-based. At the instruction of the Minister for Justice, the Crime Branch of the Gardaí compiled the list of the Sinn Féin executive on 22 July 1942. While the report was deemed by its authors 'not very informative', it listed all members of Sinn Féin (which in itself was an indication of how small the party had become), nine in total, on which it had information. Most held ordinary jobs and there was little to report on their activities. So poor had attendance at its regular Standing Committee meetings become that the first to be held in 1943 had to be adjourned and 'Great dissatisfaction was expressed' by those present (SC, 04/01/43).

The Ard Fheiseanna were held every year, whatever the circumstances. In 1941 it was attended by eighty delegates (*IT*, 03/11/41). This slight increase in interest might have been due to the fact that on this occasion, the Sinn Féin funds issue was mentioned for the first time, Buckley indicating that the original amount of £8,610 had grown to £15,183 by 1937 through investment in national loans. In her view, the withholding of these monies explained 'the standstill in organisation'. The following year, 'the question of contesting the next general election received full attention' (*IP*, 09/11/42) but nothing was done about it. Relenting on its rule not to collaborate with any other organisation, Buckley attended a meeting some months later where it was proposed to hold a national convention to bring back the Irish Republic and to draft a new constitution. This was organised by the IRA Old Comrades, Labour and Old IRA elements and presided over by Seán MacBride. The objectives were, predictably, the restoration of a de facto Republic for the whole of Ireland, the end of partition, the restoration of the Irish language and the restoration and preservation of democratic institutions (*IT*, 19/03/43). This was wishful thinking, even to the most passionate advocates of the Republican cause. However, one of the Sinn Féin president's roles seemed to be to boost the morale of her few supporters. Thus she declared in 1944: 'We need never despair or be disheartened because we have reached a minority position. Minorities are nearly always right' (*IP*, 20/11/44).

The organisation of commemorations proved an arduous task. The Bodenstown annual event was limited in 1941 by an order issued by the 'body usurping the style and function of Dáil Éireann' forbidding the hiring of buses for private parties' (*SC*, 10/02/41). The following year, the numbers were so low that it was decided that, given the transport difficulties in the country, 'the [Sinn Féin] President and four others would travel by taxi' (*SC*, 08/06/43). Nevertheless, the tradition was never broken, and there was always a handful of committed members to lay a wreath to 'non-compromising Republicans' (*IT*, 19/06/43). Sinn Féin was on the verge of extinction, but it was still resilient. It therefore proceeded, in a David and Goliath-like combat, to sue the Irish state, through the Attorney General, for the monies that had been impounded in the courts since 1924. The story of the Funds Case was to provide, through the eyes of defendants and plaintiffs alike, a unique and insightful account of the country's recent past.

Notes

1 This Act enabled the unemployed, under specific circumstances, to apply for a 'qualification certificate', the rate of which was calculated according to a complex schedule. See www.irishstatutebook.ie/1933/en/act/pub/0046/print.html#sched1.
2 The 1933 Act transferred responsibility to the central government and harmonised means tests (Nolan, 1995, 27).

3 The *Irish Press* had been founded by de Valera a few months beforehand, in September, in order to counter what was seen as the hostile press coverage of both the Independent newsgroup and the *Irish Times*. Described by O'Brien as being dominated by de Valera rather than by Fianna Fáil, it ceased publishing in May 1995.

4 http://irishelectionliterature.wordpress.com/?s=Fianna+Fail+1932. This website (irishelectionliterature.wordpress.com) contains a large amount of electoral literature from the early twentieth century up to the present. Posters and pamphlets are classified by party and date and the website contains a useful index.

5 Jeffrey Prager observes that 'the election of 1932, which produced the first transfer of power between the parties in the Free State, has frequently been identified as the most important political demonstration of the success of Irish democracy' (Prager, 1986, 195).

6 This is an extract from a much-quoted statement made by Theobald Wolfe Tone in 1798 (in Lyons, 1983, 15).

7 'Will you vote for Fianna Fáil?' Election poster by Cumann na nGaedheal, 1932, irishe-lectionliterature.wordpress.com/category/cumann-na-gaerdhael/.

8 This was the amount that the British had lent to Irish farmers to give them the possibility of buying their lands. The 1921 Treaty had given the Free State the responsibility of collecting those annuities and then repaying them to the British Exchequer.

9 For an analysis of O'Donnell's contribution to the land annuities campaign and the decision by Fianna Fáil to put an end to their payments, see O'Neill, 2008, 19–40.

10 Giblin et al. conclude that the Fianna Fáil government 'made use of the Economic War once it had begun to hasten that government's policy [of self-sufficiency]. What is undeniable is that the severity of the British government reaction rallied Irish public opinion behind the actions of the Irish government to a degree that would otherwise have been difficult to achieve' (Giblin et al. 1988, 46).

11 The 1934 Act introduced a first critical date (11 July 1921) and a second critical date (2 July 1922 or any date between 2 July 1922 and 30 September 1923).

12 According to the figures compiled by Joye and Malone, 'There were 86,608 applications under the 1924, 1934 and 1949 Army Pensions Acts, of which 17,849 pensions were awarded to those who had proven service between 23 April 1916 and 30 September 1923' (Joye and Malone, 2006, 11).

13 It was also suggested, at the time and afterwards, that de Valera had been under severe pressure to dismiss O'Duffy, from within his own party and from the IRA. Maurice Manning, however, concluded that 'there is no evidence to show to what extent, if at all, de Valera was influenced in his decision by this sort of thing, and, on balance, it is very possible that the explanation given under pressure in the Dáil is the most accurate, that is, that he did not have full confidence in O'Duffy' (Manning, 1971, 67).

14 This position was termed by *An Phoblacht*, in a 2008 article paying tribute to O'Flanagan, as 'ultra-abstentionist' (AP, 07/08/08).

15 In Republican parlance, Dáil Éireann could only mean the Second Dáil and not any assembly elected subsequently.

16 O'Duffy subsequently tried to forge links with the IRA, by announcing in 1935 that he would establish a constitution based on 1916. His attempts proved, however, unsuccessful. See McGarry, 1999, 119–20.

17 This was not the only area in which the government's attitude towards Republicanism

was the source of discontent among some of its grassroots. In January 1935, for instance, a number of cumainn in Waterford, Donegal and Offaly called on the government to set up an investigation into the treatment of prisoners, the Offaly resolution going as far as demanding the release of all prisoners and protesting against 'the unfair and discriminating treatment meted out to them' (*IP*, 11/01/35).

18 The decision not to sell Easter lilies had been taken as a sign of repudiation of the IRA. See Fanning, 1983b, 165.

19 According to Turpin, 'Sheppard opposed using portrait figures as a vehicle for commemorating an idea. Instead, he favoured symbolic images. Death of Cúchulainn draws deeply on the romanticism of the Celtic Revival as articulated, for instance, in the early poetry of W. B. Yeats. Powerfully suggestive of the dead Christ of the Pietà, the statue's imagery appeals to those who saw the struggle for independence in sacred terms, and particularly in terms of Christian sacrifice. It also connects with the idealism of Patrick Pearse, poet and leader of the 1916 Rising, who linked the Celtic Revival to the political and military struggles for the new Ireland. Sheppard's sculpture performed the function normally attributed to a war memorial' (Turpin, 2007, 110–11).

20 The other signatories included members of Sinn Féin such as Count Plunkett and of the IRA such as Seán Russell.

21 It could be argued that the Roll of Honour was also an attempt by Fianna Fáil to give an official and somehow definitive interpretation to the legacy of 1916, which was an integral part of its history but which was also a 'problematic one for an organization increasingly committed to constitutional politics', as noted by Ó Beacháin, 2003, 116.

22 All these pamphlets are available on the National Library of Ireland website.

23 This split had a profound effect on the IRA, according to Dunphy, as not only did it weaken it from a numerical perspective, but it also led to a 'decline into sheer militarism', which would in turn hasten the movement's suppression (Dunphy, 1995, 189).

24 The Congress, which did not see itself as a party but as a national movement, was soon confronted with problems of internal cohesion, generating in turn conflicts between those who saw the establishment of a Workers' Republic as a fundamental priority, and those who sought first to fight imperialism and to gather support around this issue. The Congress slowly disintegrated and was disbanded in 1935.

25 http://catalogue.nli.ie/Record/vtls000510558.

26 De Valera's intention was 'to bring the law and the constitution of the Irish Free State into accord with existing political realities by removing the Crown from the Legislature, the Executive and generally from the constitution' (Mansergh, 1991, 294).

27 This was indeed a substantial sum, which moreover was non-refundable if the candidate did not obtain one third of the quota needed for election.

28 Seán Russell was a controversial figure within Irish Republicanism, both for his military convictions and for the connections he maintained with Germany during the Second World War.

29 Craig sees the Prevention of Violence Act as 'the direct ancestor of the 1973 Prevention of Terrorism Act and arguably all proceeding counter-terror legislation in the UK, thus it had a major impact on how Britain has dealt with terrorism right up to the present day. Certainly the British government did not, at the time, treat the 1939 campaign with the same lack of interest as historians now' (Craig, 2010, 315).

30 In 1945, it still described this campaign as ongoing. See Chapter 4.

31 Stubbs Ltd was a private commercial investigation firm based in Dublin, which Collinson used to carry out surveillance on specific individuals and groups.

32 Girvin's assessment is that 'this was a deliberate attempt to orchestrate support for the government and to undermine challenges from opposition parties' (Girvin, 2006, 221).

33 This had already caused a level of debate within the party when Mary MacSwiney's assertion that the Ard Fheis had condoned those payments was denied. Again, in 1942, the Standing Committee of Sinn Féin wrote a letter to the *Irish Press* maintaining that 'No Ard Fheis of Sinn Féin ever sanctioned that acceptance of pensions for its members' (*IP*, 03/03/42).

34 Captain T. Manning represented de Valera; former IRA leaders Peadar O'Donnell and Seán McBride were among those in attendance.

35 The organisers, although some had been clearly affiliated with the IRA before the war, denied any such connection: 'an attempt has been made to trap Córas na Poblachta into two alternative answers. We are to proclaim that we are the over-ground arm of the IRA, or we are to denounce and repudiate them', but have no affiliation, secret or otherwise, with any other organisation (*II*, 12/11/41).

36 Fianna Fáil got 557,574 votes, a sizeable drop of almost 150,000 from the previous elections in 1938, while Fine Gael also registered a decrease of almost 140,000 votes, with 307,631. Those who benefited were Labour (208,813, up from 128,945), the Farmers' Party (142,651) and 'Others' (115,652 from 60,693 in 1938) (*II*, 25/06/43).

37 These were Sinn Féin, Cumann na mBan, Córas na Poblachta, National Graves Committee, Clann na nGaedheal (Girl Scouts) and Fianna Éireann.

38 Interestingly, this party was mentioned only once in the *Dáil Debates*, in an exchange about petrol allowance for candidates at the 1943 general election, which is an indication of the level of interest that the political organisation actually aroused.

39 For more details on the links between the IRA and Nazi Germany, see O'Donoghue, 2011.

40 See Hanley, 2005, 31–5.

41 Girvin puts the number of internees at 1,130, of which 1,013 were brought before the Special Criminal Court and 914 were convicted (Girvin, 2006, 84).

42 Hayes signed a confession which was subsequently published by the IRA in a special communiqué in 1941. For a detailed account of the so-called Hayes court-martial episode, see Coogan, 1995, 150–8.

3

The Funds Case, 1941–48

Those who continued on in the organisation which we left can claim exactly the same continuity that we claimed up to 1925.
(Éamon de Valera, *Dáil Debates*, 14 March 1929)

Among the many battles that Sinn Féin had to face in order to ensure its own survival, possibly one of the toughest was fought on the financial front. As the years went by, the party's revenue shrank at an alarming rate, and the time and energy dedicated to the financial situation show a constant preoccupation with finding ways to avoid bankruptcy, to such an extent that this came to take precedence over political matters. Indeed, the minutes of Sinn Féin's Standing Committee meetings all tell a story of financial duress and list some of the desperate measures that had to be taken in order to tackle this issue. In January 1930, for instance, the party remarked that the lack of funds prevented HQ from sending speakers to the provinces (SC, 31/01/30), which was seen to considerably jeopardise the development of a party that was already heavily concentrated in the capital. It was thus suggested that the bicycle, property of the Standing Committee, that was used by the courier and which was 'in bad need of repair', be sold for a price of £3.10.0 (SC, 24/10/30). A decade later the outlook was equally bleak, and desperate situations called for desperate measures. In an effort to gather funds, the party agreed, in July 1941, to rent out the front room of its headquarters to Brian O'Higgins for theatrical rehearsals for one week, bringing a total of £3, to which were added £7 'for the sale of a typewriter no longer needed by headquarters' (SC, 28/07/41). But these ad hoc measures were far from sufficient to save the party from bankruptcy. Given the extent of the problem, a special meeting of the Standing Committee was called at the end of August 1941 to discuss manners in which the financial situation could be addressed (SC, 26/08/41).

The party's financial difficulties mirrored its gradual fall into oblivion. Its income came from different sources: the members' and cumainn's affiliation fees, the donations from friends and supporters, the fund-raising events and the selling of emblems, which took place at regular dates throughout the year (such as the flag collection during Wolfe Tone week or the selling of Easter lilies to which other organisations, such as Cumann na mBan, contributed). As the party further declined, so did the funds. However, there was a third potential income source that was available to the party and which hadn't yet been tapped into: the Sinn Féin funds, the monies that had been raised throughout the independence period and then deposited in the Free State Courts. There was no automatic entitlement to those funds, as the controversy that ensued would prove. Claiming the money involved not only lengthy and costly legal proceedings, but the opening of a Pandora's box in which Sinn Féin was not the only interested party. While the funds had been lying dormant for more than two decades, the issue gathered momentum in the early 1940s; indeed, as stated in the Standing Committee meeting minutes of August of 1941, 'it had come to the [Sinn Féin] President's knowledge that it was likely there would shortly be a move by the Prime Minister of the usurping Dáil Éireann to have these funds disbursed away from Sinn Féin' (SC, 26/08/41). Some speedy intervention was thus essential in order to prevent de Valera's government from getting hold of the money.

Therefore, Margaret Buckley, president of the quasi-extinct Sinn Féin, became the main plaintiff in a lawsuit that would oppose Sinn Féin to the state's Attorney General in the High Court. The funds that the party was claiming as belonging to the organisation corresponded to donations made by the general public throughout the independence period, from 1917, when the first subscription was opened, to the eve of the Civil War, when they were frozen until such time as the Irish population had made a decision on the Treaty and therefore, on the future of Sinn Féin; the two treasurers of the party, Jennie Wyse Power and Éamonn Duggan, lodged them in the Free State Courts after the Civil War. The amount was not in itself substantial at the time (£8,610), but with the interest that had been accrued throughout those two decades, it totalled more than £24,000 in 1941. Not an insignificant sum for a party on the verge of bankruptcy; indeed, its financial statement showed that for that same year, it disposed of a total of £86.

What became known as the Sinn Féin Funds Case thus started during the Second World War and spanned over several years, as the court hearings started in April 1948. The case attracted a level of journalistic attention which was quite disproportionate to the coverage that Sinn Féin actually got at the time. Indeed, the newspaper reports on the party were few and far between from the year

1926 onwards; the increase in the number of articles for the years 1947 to 1948 was in all probability not so much due to a renewed interest in Sinn Féin itself as due to what the case said about the interpretation of the country's history by its main protagonists. Indeed, it offered an insight into how the Irish state viewed its recent past. The statements of key witnesses such as former Sinn Féin presidents Éamon de Valera (1917–26) and John O'Kelly 'Sceilg' (1927–31) provided a unique appraisal, or reappraisal, of the role that Sinn Féin had played throughout the process of independence and thereafter.

The case represented an endeavour by a small, forgotten and to some extent despised party to reclaim its name, its reputation and its place in contemporary history. It was an attempt to be seen as the true successor of the party that had dominated the independence period, as the only party that had not fundamentally deviated from the original goal. On a more pragmatic level, obviously, Sinn Féin embarked on this lawsuit in light of its disastrous financial circumstances.

Unfinished business

The history of the Sinn Féin funds started three decades before the actual court case. In May 1917, as the second Sinn Féin was undergoing major changes, members of its leadership decided to set up a fund to secure financing for the upcoming Westminster general elections. Obviously, only candidates who were committed to uphold the abstentionist policy if elected were to be financed:

> It is essential that Sinn Féin should be organised to secure the return at the elections or at general election of candidates pledged to the principle of Irish independence and to the policy of abstentionism from the British parliament and the presentation of Sinn Féin's case to the forthcoming peace conference. (Extract from *Nationality*, 26/05/17, Funds Case, 1948, 87)

Therefore, a subscription was opened for those among the general public who were willing to support the Sinn Féin programme. It was originally started with the sum of two 100-shilling and one 20-shilling subscriptions. This became the 'shilling fund' and every Sinn Féin club was required to put its full weight behind the fund-raising operation: 'It is largely a question of money. We have now organised enthusiasm. We require to make it effective. Organisation costs money. Propaganda costs money. To achieve National Freedom costs money. But to fail to achieve it will be a much more costly business' (Extract from *Nationality*, 12/01/18, Funds Case, 1948, 88). More subscriptions were subsequently launched, such as the anti-conscription and the self-determination funds. These were complemented by the money paid by the local cumainn; as there were, in February 1922, 1,185 clubs or cumainn affiliated in Ireland, eight in England and sixty-five in Scotland, this represented a healthy revenue for the party.

By early 1922, the funds totalled £8,610, according to an audit commissioned by Sinn Féin. However, with the signing of the Treaty in December 1921, divisions were emerging within the party, and the question of the finances surfaced. On 9 December 1921, a resolution proposed by Michael Collins to the Standing Committee had been unanimously passed: 'That in view of the possible cleavage in the organisation, the funds and other property be vested in the President, Éamon de Valera, as sole trustee' (Letter from de Valera to Sinn Féin treasurers, 15/11/22, Funds Case, 1948, 47). When Jennie Wyse Power, one of the two treasurers of the organisation, asked whether she should hand over the funds to him, de Valera replied that 'there was "no hurry" or something like that but anyway I did not press for them or indicate that I was particularly anxious to get them. I did not want to give the impression that I was anxious to get hold of the funds' (de Valera, Witness Statement, 1948, B32). An agreement was then signed by de Valera, Austin Stack and Arthur Griffith and passed at the Ard Fheis, according to de Valera, which allowed for an officer board[1] to carry on the work of the organisation, although the implications of this were not clearly evident to those in charge at the time, as de Valera explained to the court twenty-six years later: 'I am worried about whether it was within our power to set aside the Standing Committee like that. This was a special Ard Fheis summoned for a special purpose. I am looking back on it now – it did not occur to me at the time'. In the words of the judge, however, 'certain things were done in a hurry and so forth' (de Valera, Witness Statement, 1948, B53).

The pact that was reached included an agreement on elections which would see the setting up of a national coalition panel for the election of a Third Dáil, after which an executive would be nominated, consisting of a president, a minister for defence and nine other ministers, five from the majority and four from the minority (Extract fom *The Freeman's Journal*, 16/06/22, Funds Case, 1948, 91). But in spite of this pact, the two factions that emerged, pro-Treaty (Cumann na nGaedheal) and anti-Treaty (Cumann na Poblachta), left the question of the Treaty and its effect on Sinn Féin undecided, and consequently, also, that of the funds. When asked by the judge in 1948 whether there was a 'clear-cut idea' as to what do with the funds, de Valera replied: 'The idea was to put them in the hands of a trustee and not in the hands of an organisation' (i.e. the treasurers) (de Valera, Witness Statement, 1948, B52). In the belief that the treasurers would be subject to the vote of the Standing Committee, the preferred option was, according to de Valera, to nominate him as trustee, although this particular choice was questioned by the judge, who pointed out that the 1917 Sinn Féin constitution provided for four trustees.[2] De Valera's response was somewhat unconvincing: 'I am surprised at that. It shows how fallible one's memory is [...] I do not remember. I may be wrong. The word "sole" would account for it. One trustee instead of four [...] I do not remember there were any at the time because I would have questioned my relationship to them' (de Valera, Witness Statement, 1948, B53).

As the country further sank into the Civil War, the future of Sinn Féin was increasingly unclear. De Valera, in a letter to Kathleen Lynn, vice-president of Sinn Féin, expressed his concern over 'the attempt that has been made to destroy the Sinn Féin organisation'[3] (Letter from de Valera to Kathleen Lynn, 02/10/22, Funds Case, 1948, 48). He was of the opinion that the funds should now be handed over to him as sole trustee. In a letter sent to the two treasurers, Éamonn Duggan and Jennie Wyse Power, he unambiguously stated: 'I was chosen trustee in the anticipation of a possible split, and it is on the same ground exactly that I demand now that the Treasurers fulfil their obligations', namely, that 'they send [me] a detailed list of all the assets of the Organisation, together with such deposit receipts and cheques, duly endorsed, as are held by you, as well as a cheque for the amount of the current account' (Letter from de Valera to treasurers of Sinn Féin, 10/10/22, Funds Case, 1948, 47). He then instructed Lynn to attend the next Standing Committee meeting in his place, as he could not be present, so as to avoid at all costs the rescinding of the January resolution making him sole trustee. Lynn replied: 'They are in the majority and they can do what they like on the Standing Committee. Our only logical position would be to make our protest and go. How can we stay and by our presence agree to the Standing Committee meeting instead of the officer board?' (Letter from Kathleen Lynn to de Valera, 30/10/22, Funds Case, 1948, 48).

The disagreement between the two factions centred around the issue of who held the supreme authority within the party. For the pro-Treatyists, it was the Ard Fheis; for de Valera, the Standing Committee, which was therefore entitled to control the funds. Treasurer Éamonn Duggan clearly disagreed with de Valera's interpretation, claiming that 'the resolution passed at the Ard Fheise-anna superseded the Standing Committee for a definite period which has long since expired, and [...] the Officer Board as then constituted no longer exists' (Letter from Éamonn Duggan to de Valera, 07/11/22, Funds Case, 1948, 43).

Interestingly, both sides had specific ideas as to what to do with the funds. The pro-Treaty faction had indicated that it favoured using them for charitable and broad national purposes, while the anti-Treaty faction wanted the funds, after payment of certain debts, to be allocated 'to the released prisoners and their dependents' (Brief for the Taoiseach for First Reading of Bill, 1947, Dept of Taoiseach, TSCH/3/S12110 /C). None of these paths was further explored. What complicated the debate on the future of these funds was that both Sinn Féin treasurers in 1922 had sided with the pro-Treaty forces. In a statement sworn in 1924 in front of their solicitors, Corrigan and Corrigan, they stated that, as they had been 'properly and constitutionally elected', they were 'now in possession of the funds belonging to the organisation. Both the Treaty and the Anti-treaty party are claiming this fund as theirs, the Treasurers are extremely anxious to get a legal and full discharge for the money and are anxious that same be lodged in Court and a decision be obtained with regard to same' (Affidavit signed by Wyse Power and Duggan, 15/01/24, Dept of Taoiseach, TSCH/3/S12110 /C). There-fore, they lodged the money in the Free State Courts in January 1924 (under the Trustee Act of 1893). It is possible that their main motivation for doing so was their lack of trust in de Valera who no longer agreed with their position. Jennie Wyse Power explained: 'I lodged the money in self-defence as the only way of terminating the campaign of threats, violence and petrol raids to which I was subjected when I refused to hand the funds over to the persons who had no title to them' (Letter to the *Sunday Independent*, 1925, Funds Case, 1948).[4]

From then on, the funds were held in the Free State Courts. Several plans were made as to their future use. In November 1925, Éamonn Duggan and Jennie Wyse Power jointly signed a document agreeing to hand them over to the Gaelic League to be invested in a trust for the promotion of the Irish language (Memo from Wyse Power and Duggan, 16/11/25, Dept of Taoiseach, 90/116/773). This did not go ahead. Just before the 1926 split, the Ard Fheis appointed a committee to look into the proposal, but nothing came of this. When in 1933, representatives from the Gaelic League attended a Standing Committee meeting in connection with this issue, being under the impression that they could apply for the £11,000 that the funds amounted to at that stage, they were told in no uncertain terms that those funds were 'the sole property' of Sinn Féin (SC, 08/01/33).

The question resurfaced on a regular basis. In July 1934, Seán Ó hUadhaigh, member of the Sinn Féin Standing Committee, had written to a counsel on behalf of his party regarding the matter, who had replied that he was willing to go deeper into the matter as long as he obtained assurance that the costs and fees of the procedure would be paid in full. More to the point, he wanted the Standing Committee to confirm, should the case be brought to court, that the party would not object on 'grounds of principles or otherwise to the matter being pursued to its logical conclusion' (SC, 10/08/34). Indeed, retrieving the funds raised a number of questions, not least that of the recognition, albeit implicit, of the courts. At a time when participating in a radio broadcast was sanctioned with expulsion from the party, this was undoubtedly a difficult line to cross. The matter therefore lay dormant for the next few years. It resurfaced in 1937 when an internal memo summarised the financial position of those funds. According to this document, the sum originally lodged was calculated at £15,183.[5] This was in sharp contrast to Sinn Féin's own financial situation, as shown by a letter from the National City Bank 'drawing attention to the overdraft and to the dormant state of the account' (SC, 20/5/37). Under such financial pressure, the temptation to recover those funds was indeed high.

The party's statement in June of that year concerning the general elections in which it did not participate contained what was probably the first public reference to the funds. Blaming the authorities, and more particularly Fianna Fáil, for its incapacity to run a proper electoral campaign, it explained the situation as follows:

> Yet the leader of the Merrion Street Assembly […] persists in repeating the false assertion that 'there are no groups or individuals now who are not free to submit themselves or their policies to the electorate'. He knows that the arbitrary £100 deposit imposed by England mainly for paralysing Sinn Féin must still accompany each nomination. He knows that funds (now amounting to £15,000) which he himself claimed as the property of Sinn Féin are withheld from the organisation. He knows that thousands of pounds of other Sinn Féin monies are utilised by the seceder of Sinn Féin to establish themselves and their parties in Leinster House, and that these monies have not been restored to the organisation. He knows, moreover, that Sinn Féin would contest the elections if it had even a fraction of those monies, despite his coercion acts, the banning of Republican organisations and Republican functions, the political censorship and suppression of Republican newspapers, the seizure of Republican funds, the man-hunting and jailing of Republicans, and all the other 'essentials' of a free election. (*IP*, 22/06/37)[6]

Who owns Sinn Féin?

Sinn Féin was not the only party interested in these funds. From 1938 onward, according to some reports, de Valera was in contact with Jennie Wyse Power as sole surviving treasurer, as Éamonn Duggan had died in 1936. He contacted two solicitors in 1940 to discuss the disposal of the funds, which in his view had to be used in a manner that was 'in harmony with the objects of the old

Sinn Féin organisation and with the views of the various groups into which the old organisation had been divided', such as for the Irish language. However, the Attorney General advised in 1941 that legislation would be required in order to dispose of the funds for a charitable organisation. Upon the death of Jennie Wyse Power in January 1941, the Taoiseach met her son, judge Charles Wyse Power, executor of his mother's will, and it was decided that he would summon and preside over a meeting of the surviving members (or their representatives) of the Standing Committee elected at the special Ard Fheis of 1922, with a view to nominating trustees who would compensate those who were entitled to claim part of the funds. These included Fr O'Flanagan, Dr K. Lynn, Mrs Ceannt, Mrs Stack and Mrs Sheehy Skeffington. Judge Wyse Power met with O'Flanagan in early September 1941 to expose the options that he was facing: abstaining from accepting the responsibility of the funds; asking the court to appoint trustees who would return the money to the original subscribers;[7] and seeking to have the matter dealt with by the legislature. As he was convinced that the right course of action was not to leave the funds dormant in the court but to use them for some 'useful purpose', he had chosen the third option, seeking the Taoiseach's support for the drafting of the necessary legislation. O'Flanagan then reported back to the Sinn Féin Standing Committee and the minutes of his meeting with Wyse Power were consigned in the appendix to the minutes of the meeting of 4 September (SC, 04/09/41).

According to the information provided to the Taoiseach in preparation for the legislation, all members, with the exception of O'Flanagan, approved of the disposal of the funds through legislation. Unsurprisingly, O'Flanagan would prove the most difficult member of this group to deal with, as shown by the memo written by Wyse Power. Indeed, even if he was no longer a member of Sinn Féin, he still held strong sympathies. Although not opposed in principle to the establishment of a trust to distribute the money to those who had fought in the revolutionary period, his personal resentment against de Valera remained intact and threatened to complicate the proceedings. He stressed that he would refuse to be summoned to a meeting by the head of government and that he therefore would not attend. Wyse Power nevertheless concluded his memo on an optimistic note: 'I have a feeling that if he is not got to by one of his friends we could have secured his adhesion' (Memo to de Valera, 05/09/41, Dept of Taoiseach, TSCH/3/S12110 A). Whether he was indeed 'got to' or whether he simply changed his mind, as shown by a memo written the following day, O'Flanagan described the taking of the monies by legislation a 'violent means' and stated that he would never find anyone who would agree to act as trustee

(Memo to de Valera, 06/09/41, Dept of Taoiseach, TSCH/3/S12110 A). Wyse Power interviewed the remaining members of the then advisory board, who seemed to be quite amenable to the proposal. Kathleen Lynn still wanted to ensure that this move was not a government move (Memo to de Valera, 02/09/41, Dept of Taoiseach, TSCH/3/S12110 A). Áine Ceannt was more pragmatic than her colleagues, when she suggested that a line be drawn at 1921, as subscribers 'could not have visualised Civil war and its consequences' (Dept of Taoiseach, TSCH/3/S12110 A). As to Hanna Sheehy Skeffington, according to a memo addressed to the Taoiseach, 'she started by stating that the funds should be released to the existing Sinn Féin organisation. I had the impression that she had put her proposition merely because she felt bound to do so, but realising that there was no hope of it being adopted either by the courts or the legislature' (Dept of Taoiseach, TSCH/3/S12110 A). It would seem that judge Wyse Power himself anticipated the outcome of a possible lawsuit, before it had even started.

As soon as de Valera made known his intention to legislate on the use of the funds, Sinn Féin realised that it was seriously at risk of losing the money altogether. It therefore agreed that a 'claim be made through a solicitor as soon as any public challenge to our right to our funds might appear' (SC, 19/08/41). This conclusion was reached in full knowledge of the fact that the case would have to be pursued 'even in the Free State Courts' and was backed by seven members and opposed by four (SC, 01/9/41). However, as the decision on the possible acceptance of the Free State Courts was deemed 'of vital importance to the organisation', it was deferred to the Ard Fheis (SC, 15/09/41). A message was subsequently sent to the five Dublin daily papers, stating that Sinn Féin had given authority to no one to make arrangements to claim the funds (SC, 29/09/41), but this was only published in the *Evening Mail*, showing the lack of interest which matters concerning Sinn Féin generated in the press. The Ard Fheis voted by twenty-two votes to nine in favour of the following resolution: 'That this Ard Fheis instructs the incoming Standing Committee to maintain the ownership of the Sinn Féin funds, even in the enemy's courts, if the right of the Sinn Féin organisation to the funds is challenged' (SC, 17/11/41). A sub-committee was nominated, including Margaret Buckley, Sceilg and the two secretaries, to 'obtain, examine and prepare all data necessary for the building up of the case' (SC, 17/11/41). Meanwhile, Sceilg opened a 'fighting fund', with £3 (himself, O'Flanagan and 'a friend') and wrote a letter to friends of Sinn Féin asking for the same amount. A solicitor's letter was then sent to judge Wyse Power informing him that the 'existing Sinn Féin organisation' intended to take legal action to obtain the payment of the funds. On 19 November 1941, therefore, Boyle Fawsitt, on behalf of the party, sent a letter to the Chief State Solicitor Corrigan, having been instructed by his client to 'take the necessary legal steps to have the said funds and money transferred and paid out to Mr Patrick Power and Miss C. McElroy, the Hon. Treasurers of the organisation' (Letter to Corrigan and Corrigan, 11/09/41, Dept of Taoiseach, TSCH/3/S12110 A). He also wanted to be informed as to whether the Attorney General would make any claim to the funds and if so, the nature of that claim. Corrigan replied that both the Attorney General and the government 'would have to reserve to themselves complete freedom to take any steps that the public interest might require in the event of proceedings being instituted in relations to these funds' (Letter from M. A. Corrigan to Boyle Fawsitt, 06/12/41, Dept of Taoiseach, TSCH/3/S12110 A).

The next Standing Committee meetings were dominated by this issue, and included reports of different communications with the solicitor. What transpires from the minutes is that the affidavit signed at the time of the lodgement in chancery was based on the denial of continuity of the organisation as there was an alleged breach between the pre- and post-Treaty Sinn Féin. The issue at the heart of the debate was whether post-1926 Sinn Féin was the heir of pre-1922 Sinn Féin and was consequently entitled to those funds. The party decided to draft a summary of the history of the organisation from 1905 to the present day in the hope of showing that there was indeed continuity and that the 1940s Sinn Féin was the legitimate owner of the funds in question.

In January 1942, the Standing Committee adopted a resolution which allowed its members to act as plaintiffs in the upcoming case: Margaret Buckley (president of the organisation), Seamus Mitchell and Seamus O'Neill (vice-presidents) as well as nine other party officials. On 19 January 1942, a summons was issued to the Attorney General, representing the people and government of Ireland, and circuit court judge Wyse Power, as personal representative of his mother, as defendants. The latter's main argument was that before the lodgement of the funds in court, the former Sinn Féin organisation had ceased to exist, and had not since existed; consequently, whatever organisation was in existence was not the same as the old organisation and was thus not entitled to the funds.

However, possibly due to the state of disarray, and even disintegration, of the party throughout the war period, nothing more was done for the following three years, which prompted the defendants to ask for the dismissal of the case for want of prosecution. Sinn Féin eventually served a notice of trial at the end of 1945, but having lost their original solicitor because the party had not been in a position to pay his fees, a new lawyer was contracted who asked for an adjournment in order to retrieve the documents. The government then decided to go ahead with the proposed legislation.

De Valera took a close, personal interest in the issue, as shown by several meetings he held, not only with the parties to the case (Jennie Wyse Power and the solicitors in 1938 and 1940 respectively), but also subsequently with judge Wyse Power: nine meetings between 1941 and 1945. Wyse Power's memos clearly show that the two men were in close contact over the issue, and that de Valera was, indirectly, acting as a behind-the-scenes adviser. After all, he knew well most of the people that the judge was about to contact and he was in a position to give some insight as to how they might react to some suggestions. For instance, when Wyse Power interviewed Kathleen Lynn, vice-president of Sinn Féin in 1922, he wrote: 'bearing in mind the hint that you dropped yesterday, I was at pains to explain to her that there was no hurry' (Memo to de Valera, 08/08/41, Dept of Taoiseach, TSCH/3/S12110 A).

De Valera's interest was hardly due to the amount involved as, while it was significant for Sinn Féin given the state of its finances, it was not a sum that warranted such a high-level implication by the state. What explains de Valera's determination and his haste in legislating on those funds was undoubtedly his repugnance at seeing the party that he had left and that he had come to disown claim the legacy of the 1916–22 Sinn Féin. This had therefore not so much to do with the redistribution of the funds to the victims of that period. Rather, it was a political manoeuvre to ensure that history would record the legitimacy of Fianna Fáil as the true heir of the 1922 period. Obviously, this had important implications and would influence the manner in which both parties were to deal with the case.

To ensure support for the upcoming legislation, the fact that Sinn Féin was not the heir of the pre-1922 party had to be established. Thus judge Wyse Power interviewed those who had been involved in the reorganisation of Sinn Féin. The interpretation that they gave in the 1940s of the reconstitution of Sinn Féin after the Civil War was undoubtedly tainted by the choice they made in 1926 to follow de Valera. Frank Aiken, who had taken over as chief of staff of the IRA in March 1923, recalled that although the old Sinn Féin was regarded as being dead, they thought that the name Sinn Féin was as good a name to call themselves as anything (Note of interview with Aiken, 01/10/42, Dept of Taoiseach, TSCH/3/S12110 /B). P. J. Little, Minister for Posts and Telegraphs in 1942, was of a similar opinion, estimating that the organisation reformed was using the name but that they intended to cut themselves from the old organisation, and that the old Sinn Féin was regarded as being dead. Therefore he did not feel it would be right to demand the transfer of the old funds (Memorandum of interview with P. J. Little, 24/09/42, Dept of Taoiseach, TSCH/3/S12110 /B). Some, such as S. T. O'Kelly (Tánaiste) differed in their recollection; although imprisoned during the process of reorganisation, he had assumed that it was a continuation of the old organisation (Note on interview with An Tánaiste, 23/09/42, Dept of Taoiseach, TSCH/3/S12110 /B). The fact that those very same people would have claimed, in 1923, to be the true heirs of the pre-Civil War Sinn Féin, as they considered those who had signed the Treaty as having departed from the true aims of the party, did not seem to enter into the equation. Interestingly, this take on what Sinn Féin actually meant for those men consti-tuted an interesting reappraisal of the years 1922–26, as if those years were a mistake in their political careers, a stain that needed to be erased. By doing so, they were concurring with the analysis that the pro-Treaty faction had put forward at the time, as stated by Éamonn Duggan. He had claimed that those who continued in Sinn Féin in 1923 were not the true representatives of the pre-Treaty party. In his words, 'In or about the month of August 1923, a group of people politically opposed to the Constitution and government established pursuant to the Treaty and to the views of the majority of the subscribers to the said monies, assembled in Dublin and purported to call themselves the Sinn Féin organisation and arrogated to themselves the right to represent themselves as being and constituting the Sinn Féin organisation referred to in paragraph three hereof' (Affidavit filed by Wyse Power and Duggan, 04/02/24, Dept of Taoiseach, TSCH/3/S12110 /B).

The Sinn Féin constitution, drafted in 1905 and amended both in 1917 when the party was reorganised and in 1919 when Dáil Éireann was established, was scrutinised. One of its fundamental clauses, as it constituted the core of the party's identity, stipulated Sinn Féin's 'undivided allegiance and entire support to Dáil Éireann, the duly elected parliament of Ireland' (Boyle Fawsitt, state-ment of claim, 17/06/42, Dept of Taoiseach, TSCH/3/S12110 /B). In this state-ment, the plaintiffs' solicitor also argued the difficulty to decide on the history of the party, particularly with the transition from the second to the third Sinn Féin.

A lot of preparatory work went into the drafting of legislation. All government departments were approached and asked for their advice on how the money should be spent. The Department of Defence estimated the sum involved too small in relation to the potential number of beneficiaries and suggested its use for objects of a more limited scope (Wyse Power, Summary of views of depart-ments, 18/10/41, Dept of the Taoiseach, TSCH/3/S12110 /A), such as the provision of a rest room for old IRA men or the endowment of beds in public hospitals. While most government departments approved of a scheme that would compensate 'those who had suffered in the national cause between 1916 and 1922', Fine Gael leaders were more sceptical. Richard Mulcahy disagreed with the contents of the proposed legislation, considering that the existing law already provided for such relief, and suggesting instead that the money be invested in a commemorative body such as the Wolfe Tone Memorial fund. Indeed, William Cosgrave, leader of Fine Gael, did not like the idea either.

'An insignificant little group': de Valera's controversial Bill

One of the reasons put forward by the government to proceed with the legislation was, in de Valera's words, to prevent the money from being 'frittered away in legal actions' so the aim was to secure the 'dismissal of the pending court action'. Indeed, the Bill provided that the costs both of judge Wyse Power and of the plaintiffs, which were evaluated at between £4,000 and £5,000, would be covered by the existing fund (Note on the Question of Costs, March 47, Dept of Taoiseach, TSCH/3/S12110 /B). However, the fact that the case was still pending, even if it was frozen for all intents or purposes at the end of the Second World War, adds an intriguing dimension to de Valera's haste with the legislation, a haste which would come back to haunt him in the months following the passing of the Bill in the Dáil. In essence, it proposed that the funds be made available to those 'in needy circumstances as a result of their activities during the national struggle'. However, de Valera stated that he was prepared to listen to any other suggestion, but he insisted on his personal conviction that the plaintiffs were not entitled to the money, 'either in equity or morally' (*Dáil Debates*, 11/03/47).

The text of the Sinn Féin Funds Bill was published on 12 March 1947.[8] It established a corporate body that would take charge of the funds, Bord Cistí Sinn Féin, under the chairmanship of the Chief Justice of the Supreme Court, and composed of six other members to be appointed by government. The money, £24,000 according to the Bill, was to be transferred to the board and a trust fund was to be established. Payments out of this fund would then be made to those 'qualified persons' who were either in needy circumstances as a result of service given during the 'critical period' from 1 April 1916 to 11 July 1921, or of having supported the activities of the forces, which comprised the IRA, the Irish Volunteers, the Irish Citizen Army, Fianna Éireann, the Hibernian Rifles and Cumann na mBan. Dependents, or those who would have been dependents of

members of the forces who had died as a result of their involvement, could also
be assisted. The board had power to accept donations, and would be dissolved
when the fund was exhausted. The Bill also contained a clause according to
which 'The High Court shall, if an application in that behalf is made *ex-parte*
by or on behalf of the Attorney General, make an order dismissing the pending
action without costs and pay all expenses incurred by both parties'.

The Sinn Féin Funds Bill provoked a heated debate within the Dáil, and the
arguments put forward by those who opposed it suggested just how sensitive that
chapter of Irish history continued to be. General Mulcahy (Fine Gael) protested
against the manner in which the Bill was introduced, without previous parliamentary consultation of any kind. In his opinion, 'other parties in the House
were as interested as the Government in this matter', a direct reference to the fact
that his party, now Fine Gael, was if anything equally entitled to the legacy of the
old Sinn Féin. As he claimed, 'he and anyone who had had any connection with
Sinn Féin or any knowledge of the law, would agree that the Courts could not
come to any settlement in such a case' (*IT*, 12/03/47). Sinn Féin also reacted
promptly, stating in a letter to the press:

> Our documents in this action number well over 5,000; very prominent persons
> will be called as witnesses in the Action, and the evidence of Mr de Valera will be
> very important. He must be aware that we propose to subpoena him as a witness in
> the action, as he was President of Sinn Féin from 1917 to 1926 when he resigned to
> found Fianna Fáil. In 1942, therefore, proceedings commenced in the High Court,
> and the Action now awaits fixing of a date for Trial. In such circumstances, to pass a
> Bill now, to deprive us of our rights to our funds, is nothing more or less than confis-
> cation of private property, and an infringement of the rights of private property
> and an interference with the Courts set up under Mr de Valera's much vaunted
> constitution. Trusting that public opinion will prevent this contemplated outrage.
> Dearmot O'Leary, James Russell, Hon Secs. (SC, 13/03/47)

On the second reading of the Bill, some disquiet was expressed by Patrick
McGilligan (Fine Gael) who scrutinised de Valera's stated reasons for introducing the Bill while a court action was pending. He expressed concern both
because the Taoiseach had not specified the amount involved in the costs
incurred until then, but more importantly, because no information had been
given on the actual case itself, other than that the plaintiff's assertion of being
the heir of the pre-1922 Sinn Féin was null and void. In his view,

> The information I have may not be accurate, but my information is that there
> are two pleas on which the defendants – that is, the State in this case – rely. The
> first is that the organisation was defunct prior to the date upon which the funds

were lodged in court, and that was early in 1924. That is the main plea, that the organisation was defunct, but it is well known, and nobody knows it better than the Taoiseach, that there were people parading themselves as heads of this organisation up to 1926 and the Taoiseach was one of them. How can he stand over a plea, in a defence to the action, that the organisation was defunct in 1924, when it is on record that he was associated with it later? (Dáil Debates, 19/03/47)

He further criticised the Taoiseach's contention that there were still people in 'needy circumstances': 'It is sad to think that there are. I thought we had made provision in various pieces of legislation for people affected in that way' (*Dáil Debates*, 19/03/47). Michael Donnellan (Clann na Talmhan, Farmers' Party) suggested that the Taoiseach had reasons for introducing the Bill other than those stated:

I am sure the Taoiseach is terribly worried when he realises that he himself will probably have to go before these courts. If he does, I hope that he will not state that the Sinn Féin organisation became defunct in 1924, because we find him taking a very important part in it in March, 1925. So far as we are concerned, we shall oppose this confiscation or attempted confiscation, because we believe it is nothing else. We believe that it is belittling the courts and that, in short, it is nothing but highway robbery. (Dáil Debates, 19/03/47)

The opposition also raised the issue of the balance of powers between the executive and the legislative. As William Norton (Labour Party) remarked, the courts had not yet decided that the Sinn Féin organisation was defunct and the case was still ongoing. Therefore, in his opinion, the Taoiseach and the cabinet had anticipated the decision of the court, somehow disregarding the independence of the legislature:

I am opposed to this Bill because it is nothing short of tyranny if a Cabinet or a Government, whatever its political complexion, being given the right to decide by a Parliamentary majority when a case is a good case and when a case is a bad case. That is not the function of a Government or a Cabinet. When a Government gets to the stage that it usurps the powers which properly belong to the courts, that Government is degenerating into a tyranny. (*Dáil Debates*, 19/03/47)

The case, in the view of the opposition, had been taken from the courts and brought to the Dáil, which prompted Patrick McGilligan (Fine Gael) to suggest that the reason for the Bill was that de Valera did not want to be called as a witness. 'His conscience will be in conflict with history' (*Dáil Debates*, 16/04/47). De Valera defended his position by reminding the deputies that the plaintiff had not done anything about the funds for over twenty years and had only reacted after the news that legislation would be introduced to dispose of them. He insisted

that the government had postponed the introduction of the Bill by five years
so as not to interfere with the law, but the plaintiff had been extremely slow.
Moreover, the body that spoke for the nation was the Oireachtas and it should
determine how the money should be spent. Finally, the court could end up
deciding to give back the money to the original subscribers, an option that had
been discarded from the outset as being too costly and complex. Very revealing,
however, was his opinion of the contemporary Sinn Féin:

> Sinn Féin was intended at the time to be a substitute for a national Parliament.
> When the national Parliament was set up, that national Parliament became the
> civil arm of the nation and these funds in my opinion were subscribed with the
> intention and for the purpose of establishing that national Parliament. To say
> that an insignificant little group, no matter what technical grounds they may put
> forward, could be regarded as entitled to the possession of these national funds is
> just absurd. (*Dáil Debates*, 20/03/47)

On that day, the Bill was carried, by forty-eight votes to twenty-nine. As a
result, on 10 June 1947, the Attorney General applied to the president of the
High Court to have the case dismissed. However, predictably perhaps, given the
arguments that had been developed in the Dáil, judge Gavan Duffy dismissed the
application, as in his view this raised 'a constitutional issue of an unprecedented
importance' (*IT*, 11/06/47), prompting the *Irish Times* editorial to state: 'The
few thousand pounds involved were surely not worth the risk of a battle between
legislative and judicial powers and privileges – a battle in which the Constitution of this country is bound to be cited, and more than likely to reveal hitherto
unsuspected shortcomings' (*IT*, 11/06/47). Richard McGonigal, senior counsel
for the Attorney General, then appealed the decision to the Supreme Court,
contending that the relevant passages in the Constitution were meant only to
prevent the total abolition of private property in the state, and that parliament
was quite competent to take away the property rights of any individual citizen or
citizens. Article 43, according to the counsel, was 'a declaration that the state will
never impose on this country a collectivist form of government; that the right of
mankind to private property will always be acknowledged, and that principles
of Communism or extreme socialism which would remove the general right
of the citizens to hold property of their own will never be put into force here'
(*IP*, 29/06/47). However, the Supreme Court was not of that opinion. What
became known as Buckley vs Attorney General (1947) was seen as 'a landmark in
Irish constitutional law' as 'the separation of powers doctrine had been robustly
upheld' (Keane, 2004, 8). In his judgement, judge O'Byrne deemed the Sinn
Féin Funds Act (1947) unconstitutional on two grounds, thereby confirming

High Court judge Gavan Duffy's decision. First, it infringed both on the rights of individuals and on the independence of the judiciary:

> In bringing these proceedings the plaintiffs were exercising their constitutional right and they were and are entitled to have the matter in dispute determined by the judicial organ of the state. The substantial effect of the Act is that the dispute is determined by the Oireachtas and the Court is required and directed by the Oireachtas to dismiss the plaintiffs' claim without any hearing and without forming any opinion as to the rights of the respective parties to the dispute. (Buckley vs Att. Gen., 1947, 12)

The first objectionable aspect of the legislation was thus that it was 'repugnant to the solemn declarations as to the rights to private property contained in Art. 43 of the Constitution and, accordingly, we are of opinion that it was not within the power of the Oireachtas to pass such an Act' (Buckley vs Att. Gen., 1947, 12). The second reason for rejecting the appeal by the Attorney General was that:

> the substantial effect of the Act is that the dispute is determined by the Oireachtas and the Court is required and directed by the Oireachtas to dismiss the plaintiffs' claim without any hearing and without forming any opinion as to the rights of the respective parties to the dispute. In our opinion this is clearly repugnant to the provisions of the Constitution, as being an unwarrantable interference by the Oireachtas with the operations of the Courts in a purely judicial domain. (Buckley vs Att. Gen., 1947, 11)

This episode was seen by the press as being a major blunder on the part of the Taoiseach who was personally identified with the case. In the *Sunday Independent*, P. S. O'Hegarty[9] clearly saw the incident as showing the undemocratic nature of the very foundations of Fianna Fáil: 'Let us remember that the whole anti-Treaty Fianna Fáil movement had its origin in a refusal to accept majority democratic decisions on a national issue and in a denial of popular liberties. It is hard to get away from one's origins' (*SI*, 11/08/47). The *Irish Times*, while being less severe, still argued that 'The truth is that the Government slipped up, and there is nothing more to be said or done. Even a general election would not change the situation, which must be accepted by the Taoiseach with the best possible grace' (*IT*, 01/08/47). The *Irish Independent* saw this move as a dangerous one for the country as a whole: 'The public must bear in mind that this arrogant claim to 'take any case from the courts' if once conceded to any government may be invoked tomorrow or the next day to prevent individual citizens or organisations of civil servants or teachers or trade unions asserting their rights against the executive. If this precedent were once established the Judiciary could no longer protect the rights of the citizen' (*II*, 01/08/47).

Defining continuity

This judgment paved the way for the case to be heard in the High Court. The counsels for the plaintiff had accumulated over 5,000 pages of documents to prove what was, in their view, at the heart of the matter: that there was continuity between the different Sinn Féin parties. The hearings started on 16 April 1948 and lasted for over two months, during which many former Sinn Féin officials were called upon to testify. The objective was to establish whether there was continuity between the two pre- and post-Civil War Sinn Féin parties and consequently, whether 1948 Sinn Féin was entitled to the funds. In total, nine lawyers examined and cross-examined the various witnesses, three for the plaintiffs, three for the Attorney General and three for judge Wyse Power.

An analysis of the transcripts of the case provides an enlightening perspective on how history was recorded, memorised and transmitted. Each one of the witnesses was asked to remember events that had taken place more than two decades earlier, as well as to authenticate the many documents that had been produced both by the plaintiffs and the defendants. These were scrutinised by the lawyers and the judge, and the narrative of the various actors of the period painted a unique and at times confusing picture of how the party had operated for the years that were under examination, mainly, 1917–22.

Those called to the witness stand ranged from high-ranking figures to individuals who had played, at one time or another and in very different capacities, a role in the fortunes of the party. Hence the contribution of the party's typist, Vera McDonnell, was to give details on the administrative work that was carried out in 1923 by the reorganising committee (*IP*, 23/04/48), while Michael Ó Foghlughdha who had supplied goods to the party up to 1936, considered 'it was the same Sinn Féin organisation he was dealing with all the time' (*IP*, 07/05/48). Others, such as Dr Kathleen Lynn, vice-president of Sinn Féin prior to the 1922 split, or Patrick J. Ruttlege, acting president of the third Sinn Féin while de Valera was in prison in 1923–24, had played a more substantial role, as had Owen O'Keeffe, secretary to the reorganising committee of the third Sinn Féin. However, the two testimonies that attracted most attention were those of two former Sinn Féin presidents, Éamon de Valera and John J. O'Kelly, 'Sceilg', who gave a first-hand account of the workings of a party under quite extreme, and exceptional, circumstances. Their statements to the court represented significantly different interpretations of the history of the independence years. As de Valera had been trying to ensure that the funds be allocated to a different purpose, it was in his interest to show that there was no continuity between the second and third Sinn Féin, which put him in a difficult position as he had presided over the third Sinn Féin. On the other hand, O'Kelly had taken over the leadership of the party that refused to follow those who formed Fianna Fáil and could thus be considered a champion of the view that the fourth Sinn Féin was indeed entitled to the funds. Both men's recollections revealed how subjective, and even unreliable, memory could be, and how one's vision of history could be blurred not only by ideology but by time. Both insisted on the difficulty of recalling with accuracy the events of the 'troubled times', as they called them, for obvious reasons: both were imprisoned on a number of occasions, both were absent for lengthy periods of time due to their travels to the US, Australia and Canada in order to collect funds, and the party was an illegal organisation, hence not always in a position to function in a very transparent or regular manner. As Sceilg put it, 'whether it was possible to have an Ard Fheis in 1920 I am not sure, because it was a very disturbed period' (Sceilg, Witness Statement, 1948, 44).

The inaccuracies that surround the history of the party were not only due to the state of upheaval that dominated the period. They were at the core of what Sinn Féin stood for from the outset. Even its origins were blurred in the witnesses' eyes. O'Kelly, when asked to recollect the early stages of the party, could not give a specific founding date. Obviously 1905 was seen as a starting point, but he traced the beginnings of the party to the Gaelic revival and the 1898 centenary of Wolfe Tone's death. His account of the party's history was factual and precise, and his testimony read like a chronological account of both his individual itinerary and that of his party. The reorganisation of Sinn Féin in 1917 was seen as the coming together of various groups, such as the Irish Nation League from Omagh and the Released Prisoners Committee of the IRA; that body drafted the 1917 constitution of the party. In Sceilg's view, 'Sinn Féin at that time did not politically stand for very much, not as much as it did at an earlier date. They called them the Sinn Féin people but what, to my mind, explains mainly the great change that came about at the General Election of 1918 was the attitude that what was called the Sinn Féin element took against conscription' (Sceilg, Witness Statement, 1948, 21).

The party developed rapidly, becoming a complex and bureaucratic organisation. 'Every club, and there were over 1,000 cumainn all over the place, they all thought they should have some rule. There was a call for the creation of one thing or another. Personal interests entered into it and the rules were multiplied until we got fairly tired of them' (Sceilg, Witness Statement, 1948, 29), which prompted the lawyer to comment: 'those rules do impress me as being one of the most un-modern set of regulations that I have ever come across, even very ungrammatical at times. They bear all the marks of having been caused by particular resolutions by particular clubs' (Sceilg, Witness Statement, 1948, 29). De Valera being ten years younger than Sceilg explained that 1905 was 'all only history to [him]' (de Valera, Witness Statement, 1948, B46), but concurred with his former colleague on the vagueness of Sinn Féin's policy and objectives in the early days. 'The national ideal put forward in 1905 was quite unsatisfactory in 1917 [...] We tried to make the old Sinn Féin members come along with us so we tried to put in everything that was, that seemed to be advisable at that period, to be practicable at that period' (de Valera, Witness Statement, 1948, B48). What contributed to cementing this group, in O'Kelly's account, was the ideal of the Republic. Even if the Sinn Féin constitution was, in his words, 'hammered out' by a composite committee, it was 'proposed and passed unanimously' and contained a strong Republican element. However, he highlighted the fact that divergences in the party were clearly visible from the outset. 'Arthur Griffith did not desire the Republic, but Cathal Brugha would have nothing but the Republic' (Sceilg, Witness Statement, 1948, 22). It was possibly the composite nature of the party that enabled two diametrically opposed interpretations of the Treaty and allowed both sides to believe they were loyal to their objective: in de Valera's view, those against the Treaty 'felt that they were acting strictly in accordance with the Sinn Féin constitution in accepting the Treaty. We felt that was an altogether forced and unnatural interpretation of the Sinn Féin constitution' (de Valera, Witness Statement, 1948, B24).

The choice of the Republic as the form that an independent Ireland should take was not, according to the counsel, a deliberate and specific objective; rather, 'the Republic as an ideal was taken over coincidentally, though people hardly realised that, it happened to be Wolfe Tone's method that was adopted without any particular consideration for the various and different forms of government which might prevail in the country' (Sceilg, Witness Statement, 1948, 22). Sceilg nevertheless refuted this interpretation and when asked whether the Republican element in the constitution of Sinn Féin was exceptional or essential to the spirit of the organisation, he replied: 'It was my duty to summon every individual member of that Assembly one after the other before me, to take the oath of allegiance calling on the Almighty God to witness that they were prepared to defend the Republic and the Parliament of the Republic' (Sceilg, Witness Statement, 1948, 51). In his view, Cathal Brugha was the main driver behind the Republican ideal. To the question: 'Cathal Brugha was then a more important and bigger figure than Michael Collins?', he replied: 'Oh Yes! Well to my mind of course, there are different estimates of people and things at the time, but to my mind, Cathal Brugha was the organiser from the military point of view, in the same sense that Fr O'Flanagan was up to the 1918 election and thereabout from the political point of view' (Sceilg, Witness Statement, 1948, 53–4).

What also transpired from both testimonies was the extent to which, for the period between 1919 and 1922, the party and the state were seen, almost, as one. This confusion was probably unavoidable. All seventy-three members of Dáil Éireann, without exception, were also members of Sinn Féin (the twenty-six Unionists of different shades and the six Irish parliamentary party members who had also been elected in the 1918 general election had refused to take part in the newly created institutions). The same scenario repeated itself with the 1921 elections, Dáil Éireann being exclusively composed of members of Sinn Féin. Therefore, both bodies were at times confused and interchangeable. The members of Dáil Éireann were as answerable to their party as they were to their assembly.

Both men's account of the pre-Civil War division and the electoral pact that was reached between the two factions of the party showed how much unity was still considered essential, and they hoped that it could somehow be restored. 'The Pact, for instance, was one step in the direction of reaching a wider settlement, a very big step, as far as I know, for the anti-treaty body to which I belonged [...] They hoped to improve the situation. They hoped to restore national harmony, national unity' (Sceilg, Witness Statement, 1948, 60). For de Valera, 'there were no divisions in Sinn Féin. There were two sides, Republicans and the others. Then the idea was that Republicans would continue their memberships. That we would even go and recruit and get as many members for Sinn Féin as possible and that they would still continue in the organisation' (de Valera, Witness Statement, 1948, B7). How that unity was going to be attained was not clearly spelt out. For de Valera, the creation of Cumann na Poblachta served that very purpose, as none of the competing factions would go forward in the election on a Sinn Féin ticket. It was thus formed in a 'contingency in which it might be necessary to contest an election and in that case, Sinn Féin had not expressed its opinion one way as an organisation or another' (de Valera, Witness Statement, 1948, B4).

De Valera's appearance in court was undoubtedly the highlight of the case, not only because of the stature he had acquired in his country, but also because of the crucial role he had played in the party upon which he was now asked to reminisce. He was subjected to detailed questioning and cross-examination, and his involvement in the organisation between 1921, when the controversy over the funds started, and 1926, when he left the party, was scrutinised. His testimony was that of a man who hesitated, whose memory was patchy. He did not come across as a very reliable witness. That he would on several occasions state, 'I don't recollect with exactitude', 'I would need to have my memory refreshed', could be attributed to the fact that he was questioned about events dating back more than two decades. However, this type of rhetoric could also have been a tactic destined to keep some distance both from the proceedings and from the events about which he was called upon to comment. Perhaps his vague and sometimes even inaccurate statements had more to do with a defence strategy, aimed at saying as little as possible and not committing himself to any definitive answer. Therefore, when asked to authenticate documents, he hesitated. To the question, 'Do you remember receiving that letter [from Kathleen Lynn]?', he replied: 'No, I do not remember it'. Asked whether he remembered writing a reply, he stated: 'I don't remember writing it but there is nothing in it that would suggest I did not write it' (de Valera, Witness Statement, 1948, B3). Even when it came to events that concerned him personally, he remained quite nebulous: 'I think I was released some time in June or July of the following year' (de Valera, Witness Statement, 1948, B15) was his answer when asked about his imprisonment. Perhaps he was determined not to be held accountable for any specific event. Thus the 1925 Ard Fheis was a turning point in the history of the organisation, as it paved the way for a debate on the possible entry of Sinn Féin to Dáil Éireann. But de Valera again remained quite vague: 'I am never sure whether I presided at an Ard Fheis or not though I was president of the organisation very frequently I did not take the chair'. 'You were at the Ard Fheis of 1925?', asked the counsel. 'I expect I was. I do not remember it as a fact but I see no reason why I would not be present in 1925' (de Valera, Witness Statement, 1948, B21). On the origins of the 1926 split, which led to the creation of Fianna Fáil, he remained noncommittal. Sceilg talked of the Cahirciveen motion that was put forward in 1925 in an attempt to prevent a debate on abstentionism from taking place as having 'overshadowed everything else because, as you see, it overshadowed a split in the organisation. There was a good deal of manipulation of things, moving the previous question, and methods of that nature, and eventually it was altered by agreement to another form'. De Valera, for his part, was much less certain: 'from recollection I could not say [whether it was dealt with in 1925], not from recollection. We are talking about things that happened nearly a quarter of a century ago. I could not recollect' (de Valera, Witness Statement, 1948, B24). As for the resolution he put forward in 1926, which stated that abstentionism should become a matter of policy not of principle and which led to the split in Sinn Féin, his reply was non-committal; although he did acknowledge that there was some motion put forward, he could not remember its content. Whether this was indeed the case or whether he preferred to have erased some facts from his memory is open to interpretation. Whatever the situation might be, he seemed to be quite badly prepared for the court hearing.

His memory losses were sometimes puzzling. When asked about the reason why he was appointed sole trustee of the organisation in 1921 while there were provisions in the Sinn Féin constitution for four trustees, who were named by the judge, his reply is intriguing. 'I'm surprised at that. It shows how fallible one's memory is' (de Valera, Witness Statement, 1948, B55). Even more problematic was his failure to remember the name of the organisation that was founded by those who supported the Treaty: 'There was another political organisation at the time, Fine Gael I think? I do not know what name, they probably had some sort of organisation. I do not know what it was' (de Valera, Witness Statement, 1948, B57–8). To which the counsel replied: 'It was Cumman na nGael [sic]'. The period itself was undoubtedly extremely confused, and the pact that followed the Treaty allowed for two separate organisations to fight for their sides, Cumann na nGaedheal and Cumann na Poblachta. While de Valera insisted on the importance of the latter, as its purpose was to ensure 'that the Republican cause would have an organisation which could represent its interests in an election', he seemed to conveniently forget the very name of his opponents, therefore perhaps minimising both their legitimacy and their relevance during the period in question. Interestingly, his memory became quite sharp when it came to the oath of allegiance, which he maintained neither he nor any other Fianna Fáil TD took in 1927. He was therefore capable of quoting the exact line that the clerk of the Dáil pronounced when he entered the building as well as what he replied (de Valera, Witness Statement, 1948, C3).

What both de Valera and Sceilg were there to establish was whether the Sinn Féin that was reorganised in 1923 was the true heir of the pre-Civil War party. De Valera's position was a delicate one, as he could not openly state that this was not the case, but to state the opposite would have validated Buckley's claim. Predictably, just as had happened while the Sinn Féin Bill was being prepared, those who had followed him in 1926 felt that the party that they left then was different from the 1922 Sinn Féin. P. S. Ruttlege, who was a founder member of Fianna Fáil, explained: 'I did not regard it as re-organisation. I regarded it as an organisation to help with the election' (*IP*, 07/04/48). Similarly, Joseph Connolly, chairman of the reorganising committee, explained that:

to me the organisation had disappeared with everything else of that nature in the Civil War. It was my belief and my understanding that de Valera had the same notion, that the movement was dead, and that we wanted to reorganise a thing, an organisation that stood for all that Sinn Féin had stood for in the past; but the idea of getting continuity or thinking of looking for the funds or trying to get the old Standing Committee never occurred and was never discussed. It did not seem practical politically. (*IP*, 03/06/48)

On the other hand, Owen O'Keeffe, secretary of the 1923 reorganising committee, stated that 'many of the people in the reorganising committee believed they were reviving the old Sinn Féin' (*II*, 01/05/48).

Judge Kingsmill Moore made his decision known on 26 October 1948.[10] This lengthy document, which took one hour and three quarters to read (*IT*, 29/10/48), constituted an impressive narrative of the history of the troubled years; as he stated, 'there is yet no history of this period which ranks as a classic'. His conclusions were based on the views that had been expressed throughout the hearings, a task that he acknowledged was a difficult one as the period in question was still fresh in the memories of his contemporaries: 'the times with which we are dealing are sufficiently recent for most of us to bear them in our own personal recollections, sufficiently distant to make those recollections partial and untrustworthy, and yet not so far removed as to permit reference to any single historical work which would be accepted by everyone alike as authoritative and impartial'. His analysis was comprehensive and detailed, but some general points emerged. First, with the setting up of Dáil Éireann, 'Sinn Féin had done its work [...] Logically it might then have gone out of existence, its mission accomplished.' Second, he insisted on the fact that 'independence and the Republic had for so long been considered as essentially the same thing that numbers now found it difficult to conceive of one without the other'. His most insightful comments concerned the ideal of the Republic, and what it came to signify: 'the Republic captured the imagination of the people. It affected them not as an intellectual conception but as an emotional stimulus'. Thus, for the ordinary supporter, it was 'a battle-cry, a symbol, an evocative word of immense power. It released a long suppressed desire for national realisation, national independence'. Finally, he also made clear that the ideal held very different meanings for the various groups that coexisted within Sinn Féin, and therefore it couldn't be seen as the element of continuity between the different parties of that name:

> To some who held what I may call the transcendental view, the Republic was an article of faith; others considered that at that juncture in world affairs there were sober and valid reasons for thinking that an independent republic could be

obtained; still others, and those perhaps a majority, regarded the republic only as the best and most dramatic symbol of independence, a few accepted it cynically as a convenient place of political clap trap. Into the ranks of the national Sinn Féin organisation were to be gathered men who would have been content to accept as a first step towards independence: Home Rule, Dominion Home Rule Federalism, Devolution or any other form of government which would have given Ireland control of her own affairs to a greater or lesser degree and which could be used as a legitimate stepping stone to that ultimate independence which the majority certainly desired.

However, those were subjective criteria which were open to interpretation. The fact that the same name was kept, that the same constitution was observed, that the ideal remained unchanged, was not in itself sufficient to prove continuity. What judge Kingsmill Moore was trying to establish was whether there was continuity from a legal point of view, based upon a set of objective criteria, such as: that an Ard Fheis had been properly summoned between the second and third Sinn Féin and that the rules of the organisation were abided by. It was on that basis that he decided against the plaintiffs' quest, as the 1923 Ard Fheis had not been organised according to the regulations set out in the constitution of the party: 'A mere fraction of the delegates who appeared and debated and voted on Oct 16 [1923] had any right to be present even if their affiliation fees had been received in the right quarters. The Ard Fheis was not properly consti- tuted according to the Rules and its actions and resolutions can have no validity in preserving the continuity of the organisation' (NAI D/T S12100D/1). However, this did not amount to a denial of Sinn Féin's genuine belief in the validity of the cause, as the judge estimated that 'the plaintiffs appeared to me to be perfectly sincere, believing not only in the righteousness but also in the rightness of their cause [...] It would appear that all the required steps were taken to preserve the continuity of the organisation and that present-day Sinn Féin is legally the same organisation as that which was born in 1923' (NAI D/T S12100D/1). Fundamentally, then, whereas Sinn Féin in 1948 could claim to be the rightful heir of the organisation founded in 1923, there had been a clear break between the second (1917–22) and the third (1923–26) parties.

This episode had important repercussions within the party. The case had given rise to internal tensions, with some estimating that Sinn Féin ought not to have used the state's institutions under any circumstances, considering that any justice that would come out of this system would be by definition arbitrary. Two local councillors wrote, in a letter to the Standing Committee, dated 31 August 1942: 'it is with regret that we have read in the press that the Sinn Féin organisation has voluntarily entered the Free State Courts after so many years of loyalty to the Republic of Ireland and consequent refusal to recognise the Free State government or its institutions. True, we have witnessed desertions from the Republicans from time to time, but the present one is the most tragic of all' (Funds Case, 1948, 114). Sinn Féin's response was as strident: 'The civil arm of the Republic could no more refuse this challenge (from the usurper) than the military arm could refuse a challenge in the field, even though neither arm can recognise the usurper to have any right' (Funds Case, 1948, 115). However, one of the major consequences of the Funds Case for Sinn Féin was the confirmation of the ban (which existed until then in theory) on the pleading of cases in the state's courts, and at the 1948 Ard Fheis, the following amendment was added to the Constitution: 'The Sinn Féin Organisation may not make use of the courts of either partition assembly for civil actions' (quoted in *Saoirse*, 06/10/98). This principle was inscribed in the party's constitution, and remained in place for almost four decades. But there is no doubt that this case inflicted a blow to the organisation. Margaret Buckley had stated, in her testimony to the High Court, 'that the money in this case is not of prime importance to us. Establishing the continuity of our organisation comes first with us, not the money. We do not care about it' (*II*, 13/05/48).[11] Whether that was an accurate assessment of the reasons for going to court or not, it certainly left no doubt as to the symbolic importance of the case. Losing it vindicated those who refused to engage with the state. But ultimately, it meant that Sinn Féin was no longer only isolated from the society in which it operated. It was also, in the national narrative, estranged from its own history. The outcome of the Funds Case was a psychological setback for Sinn Féin, a test of its faith in its own legitimacy and legacy.

Notes

1 The officer board was comprised of: Éamon de Valera, president; Arthur Griffith, Michael Collins, Michael O'Flanagan and Kathleen Lynn, vice-presidents; Austin Stack and Harry Boland, secretaries; and Jennie Wyse Power and Éamonn Duggan, treasurers.

2 The names of four trustees were read out by counsel Bell, from 20 May 1918: George Nesbitt, James O'Reilly, Fr Flanagan, T. Waldron.

3 In her reply, on 30 October 1922, Lynn said that she would gladly follow instructions but ended her letter on a hopeless note: 'Personally I have always thought Sinn Féin unlucky, it held us together only to let us down at the critical moment. Now I think, it will be difficult to resuscitate it, for any real good Republicans won't touch it and the Free Staters are determined to kill it' (FC, 1948, 48).

4 A number of letters were indeed addressed to Jennie Wyse Power in protest at the closing of the Harcourt Street head offices in July 1922: 'Although dictatorship is now the rule

I hope you will not attempt to imitate "Mick", "Dick" and "Oweny" by arrogating to yourself the functions of the Ard Fheis as they have attempted to usurp the functions of government' (Letter from Harry Boland to Jennie Wyse Power, 27/02/22, Funds Case, 1948, 47).

5 The £8,610 lodged on 4 February 1924 in the accountant's office, Four Courts and in cash, was subsequently invested in a 4 per cent conversion loan and the second national loan. The interests had enabled the funds to almost double in value over the years (SC, 10/05/37).

6 The Merrion Street Assembly is where the Houses of the Oireachtas are located.

7 That option was rapidly disregarded. Indeed, although it was seen as 'possible' by Cecil Lavery, advisor to the solicitors Corrigan and Corrigan, it was also viewed as a highly difficult and expensive task.

8 The full text of the act is available at: www.irishstatutebook.ie/1947/en/act/pub/0013/print.html.

9 Patrick Sarsfield O'Hegarty was a writer. His Nationalist sympathies led him to become a member of the Supreme Council of the IRB, and a close friend of Terence MacSwiney on whom he wrote *A Short Memoir* in 1922. He also authored a number of works on Sinn Féin, among which was *The Victory of Sinn Féin*, published in 1924.

10 'Judgement of the Honourable Mr Justice Kingsmill Moore delivered on the 26th day of October, 1948'. The full text of this judgement is contained in the National Archive file NAI D/T S12100D/1.

11 Kingsmill Moore allowed all three parties the legal costs, which amounted to over £12,000. However, the question of who the funds actually belonged to was not resolved.

4

Sinn Féin, 'political wing' of the IRA, 1948–70

Sinn Féin is not, and never was, a political party. Sinn Féin is a national movement.
(Patrick McLogan 1954)

While the Funds Case was still pending in the High Court, Republicans were trying to recover from the difficulties that they had experienced during the war. Some signs of revival were visible as early as April 1945. A memo from the Special Section of the Gardaí Detective Branch stated on 23 April that 'reliable information had been received that an attempt to re-organise the IRA under a Sinn Féin cumann is at present under way' (Garda report, 23/04/45). Indeed, a local branch, the Joseph Mary Plunkett cumann of Dublin, had issued a newsletter for the Easter commemoration, *The Spark*, which then became the *Sinn Féin Bulletin*. Although a modest and limited publication, it afforded the leaders of the organisation the opportunity to have their messages published. The authorities deemed this newsletter 'subversive' and the police were asked to produce a report on the individuals behind its publication. Particularly offensive was the reference to 'our soldiers who are prisoners of the enemy', to the 'soldiers of the Republic of Ireland [who] have made the supreme sacrifice in giving their lives for the Republic of Ireland declared war on England on January 10th 1939', a clear reference to the S-Plan operations, although the campaign had been effectively over since early 1940. A Sinn Féin reorganising committee was up and running from the early months of 1945, formed of a group of ex-internees and members of the Standing Committee (Garda report, 19/07/45). But initially, the revival of the party was not as successful as Republicans had hoped for or as the security forces had feared. In the second issue of *The Spark*, there was an appeal for 'financial support' to keep the paper afloat. 'The response was nothing like what we expected. We again renew our request, so that Irishmen may have at least the one Republican paper per month, however small', pleaded the editorial of the paper. Progress was slow. A new cumann was opened in Glasnevin on 10 May 1945, at a meeting attended by six people, then twelve the following month.

Overall, however, there was little innovation in the discourse of the party, as shown by the publication of the first manifesto since the 1936 Galway by-election. 'The case for the Republic', published some time in 1945 (it is not precisely dated), retraced the history of the Republic, with a view to reaffirming 'the continuity of the struggle'. The fact that this came at a time when the Funds Case was still pending and where the stakes were to decide whether Sinn Féin was the heir of the pre-Treaty Sinn Féin was perhaps a coincidence, as the case at that particular time was frozen, but it was revealing of the profound Republican belief in the legitimacy and continuity of their cause. The second aim of the document was to generate some badly needed optimism after such a difficult era. Therefore it stated that 'soon the Government of the Republic will be functioning fully and in place in a United Ireland, and our long night of sorrow will give place to the dawn of a Glorious Freedom'.

The following year, at the November 1946 Ard Fheis, resolutions were passed calling for the release of all Republican prisoners, for action to remedy the slow progress of the Irish language, condemning emigration, urging a plan for a boycott of 'British propaganda through films, literature and the radio' and protesting against 'the demolition of Irish colleges in the Gaeltacht to make room for luxury hotels which are only blockhouses on the road to imperialism' (*IT*, 18/11/46). But in line with its isolationist tradition, Sinn Féin president Margaret Buckley described Ireland's application to join the UN as 'Seeking admission to join a thieves' kitchen' (*IT*, 18/11/46).

Defending prisoners

1946 was a key year for Republicans. It saw the end of internment without trial, which had been in place throughout the war. In early 1946, the Republican Prisoners' Release Association (RPRA) was created which, although it claimed no political affiliation, was supported by Clann na Poblachta, and more specifically by its founder Seán MacBride (McDermott, 1998, 37). Republicans were mobilised that year around the death of hunger striker Seán McCaughey on 11 May 1946. A former adjutant-general of the IRA, he had been imprisoned in the aftermath of the Hayes affair for physical assault and illegal imprisonment,[1] and sentenced to death by a military tribunal on 18 September 1942, his sentence having been commuted to life imprisonment later that year. The RPRA published a document in May 1946 calling the population to support their campaign on McCaughey's conditions within the prison. The text underlined the importance of political prisoners by reminding the readers that 'the political offenders of today may well be the leaders of tomorrow' (RPRA, 1946). In some ways, McCaughey's story would find an echo in that of the H-Block prisoners some forty years later. According to the pamphlet, he, along with other Republican prisoners, were held in 'solitary confinement and without clothes because they would not wear the convict garb'. He was, still according to that document, held from September 1941 until the middle of September 1943 and was 'not even allowed out to the lavatory', which again could be seen as setting the scene for the 1970s no-wash protest. Those concerned with prison conditions were also to be found among Republican sympathisers. A resolution was passed, for instance, at the annual convention of the Gaelic League on prisoners in Portlaoise, on 20 October 1945 expressing concern about their conditions. A few days later, the government information bureau issued a counterstatement:

> As a result of the refusal to grant them these privileges [right to wear own clothes and non-association with other prisoners, extra letters and visits] they refuse to wear prison clothing or to comply with the prison rules and regulations. They are provided with blankets out of which they have improvised garments. As they refuse to wear proper clothing they are not permitted to leave the main prison block for exercise in the open-air. They do, however, associate daily for about three hours. They are also deprived of the privilege of visits, but are permitted to communicate with their relatives and friends. They received the usual prison diet and are not compelled to work. (*II*, 23/10/45)

McCaughey eventually went on hunger strike on 19 April 1946 which he doubled with a thirst strike five days later. In Belfast, twenty-seven-year-old David Fleming was also protesting against prison conditions. At a public meeting in Dublin, calls were made to release McCaughey. One of the speakers, Jim Larkin Jr, stated that such a course of action would have no political significance beyond, perhaps, saving Fleming's life. But the government adopted an inflexible line. During a debate in the Dáil on 8 May, de Valera clearly announced that:

> The issue in all these cases is whether we are to carry out our primary duty as a government, to protect the lives and property of the citizens, or permit citizens and servants of the state to be murdered with impunity; whether we are to endeavour intelligently to preserve the means of maintaining public order or to revert to primitive anarchy by foolishly permitting to be taken from our hands the only methods short of capital punishment known to civilised man for the restraint of the wrongdoer, that of imprisonment. (*Dáil Debates*, 08/05/46)

He quoted a 'definitive and final decision' made by the government in 1943 that no prisoner on hunger strike would be released. As to whether the government would put pressure on the Northern Ireland government in the case of Fleming, a citizen of the Free State, de Valera replied that 'our hands are tied'.

McCaughey died on 11 May 1946.[2] His death was followed by quite a robust public mobilisation, showing renewed public sympathy for the first time in two decades. According to the *Irish Times*, his funeral in Belfast was attended by some 1,000 young men. Thirteen men in the US were reported to have embarked on a hunger strike in protest at McCaughey's death; 300 turf workers marched in protest along the route taken by President O'Kelly on his way to the Easter 1916 ceremony at Arbour Hill, joined later by fifty more men (*II*, 10/05/46). Meetings were organised throughout the country, calling for a public inquiry into McCaughey's death (*IT*, 16/0546). Limerick county council adopted a resolution of sympathy with McCaughey's relatives (*II*, 27/05/46), as did Longford and Louth where a resolution calling for a public inquiry was debated (*II*, 20/05/46). The Westmeath agricultural committee debated a resolution calling on the government to free all political prisoners, which was eventually amended to include only those held without charges. But like others it demanded the setting up of an inquiry over prison conditions (*IT*, 21/05/46).

McCaughey's lawyer was Seán MacBride, former IRA chief of staff and leading Republican activist throughout the 1930s. He blamed prison conditions on the government and asked for a public inquiry. However, Minister for Justice Gerry Boland immediately retorted:

> There is no need for such an inquiry. The prison conditions here are well known to compare favourably with those in other countries. For a long time the government pursued a policy of deliberate lenience towards the group to which these men belong. We failed to get them to respect or recognise the right of the community but we have no intention of allowing them to enforce their will by organised crime. (*IT*, 22/05/46)

The government's reason for refusing a public inquiry on prisons was that, in its view, McCaughey had not been seeking better conditions; he simply wanted to be released. In the Seanad, a motion expressing concern at the length of time McCaughey had spent in solitary confinement was put to the vote. Donnellan (Farmers' Party) handed in a notice of a motion asking for the appointment of a select committee to investigate McCaughey's prison conditions (*Dáil Debates*, 23/05/46). His motion was defeated, a vote which was welcomed in an *Irish Times* editorial, although the paper acknowledged that prison reform was probably necessary.

Upon McCaughey's death, some County Tyrone Republicans founded a newspaper, *Resurgence*, which was published between June and November/

December 1946. It contained local articles and critiqued quite strongly any change in Republican principles (*Resurgence*, NLI, O'Mahony Papers, MS 44,084 /1). It was also the sign of increasing tensions among Republicans, as a debate was ongoing on the political future of the movement. Seán MacBride was of the opinion that a political formation should be created, but he argued against abstentionism, which in his eyes had become unnecessary since the introduction of the 1937 Constitution. However, he failed to get majority support for his plan and left the IRA. His followers were subsequently expelled from the movement. He decided to found his own organisation, Clann na Poblachta, in July 1946. The party quickly reassured potential voters that in spite of its inclination towards left-wing politics, it would not seek too radical a change. At its first annual county convention in 1948, a motion was passed asserting that 'the social policy [of Clann na Poblachta] is based on two Papal Encyclicals, Rerum Novarum and Quandragesuno anno' (*Anglo-Celt*, 10/04/48), in an effort to defuse the perception that the organisation was tainted with communism. However, it also clearly called for the release of Republican prisoners. The creation of a new party profoundly tore the IRA apart, according to a letter to the editor published in the *Irish Independent* on the second anniversary of McCaughey's death, which explained that 'its formation disgusted all Republicans' (*II*, 11/05/48).

Resurrecting Sinn Féin

The formation of Clann na Poblachta might have prompted the IRA into actively seeking to form a political movement. During its September 1948 convention, the first since the war, an executive committee was elected, comprising three long-standing Republicans: Tony Magan, a former Second World War internee, as chief of staff, Patrick McLogan, former abstentionist MP for South Armagh, and Tomás Óg Mac Curtain, son of former Sinn Féin Lord Mayor of Cork killed by RIC officers in 1920. All three men had impeccable Republican credentials, and they were to form the 'triumvirate which was to dominate the IRA for the next decade' (Bowyer Bell, 1983, 246). On this occasion, the S-Plan, or England campaign, of the previous decade, was formally called off, although the IRA had ceased all operations in 1940. The convention also decided that it was fundamental for the Republican movement to have a political wing and a resolution enabling the IRA to infiltrate Sinn Féin was put to a vote and passed.

It was not the first time that the IRA acknowledged the need to have a political wing, and many attempts had been made between the two wars. The decision to turn to Sinn Féin, which was, so to speak, non-existent, was probably better explained by all the other failed attempts to gather Republicans under the same political banner, reflecting the incapacity of the organisation to put together a policy that would be sufficiently coherent to unite its own ranks. Nevertheless, the IRA needed political legitimacy in order to operate and justify its very existence, and Sinn Féin presented a number of advantages. The two organisations shared the same ideology and the same objectives, and given the state of disrepair of the party, it would be possible to control it from the outset. Nevertheless, choosing the name Sinn Féin was a gamble: on the one hand, it was a household name for the majority of people, even though it had sunk into oblivion for the most part of two decades. Its name was regularly mentioned in daily and provincial newspapers, more often than not in relation to the pre-Civil War old Sinn Féin or to an obituary. The name also carried a number of negative connotations that it had acquired throughout the years, but in Sinn Féin's favour was the fact that it had always supported the principle of armed action, in spite of the difficult relationships it had experienced with the IRA throughout the late 1920s and early 1930s. Therefore Sinn Féin would probably be ready to invest the armed organisation with any decision-making power, as the IRA had been handed down by the Second Dáil the highly symbolic role of government of the Irish Republic in 1938.

Sinn Féin in 1946 was not much of a political party. One of its main activities was the organisation of free classes of Irish in its Dublin headquarters (SC, 21/11/46), which spoke volumes about its relevance as a political organisation. Party president Buckley also kept the Republican spirit alive by giving public lectures (SC, 28/01/46), which aimed to reaffirm values and principles and to justify the existence of Sinn Féin. Her attitude towards the Fianna Fáil government was as virulent as ever, referring to de Valera's 'announcement of a Republic from English dictionaries and encyclopaedias' and reminding her audience that 'had Mr de Valera professed a like good-will towards the Republic in 1926, instead of hankering after external association with England, there need not then have been a Republican split'. She added that there would not have been any executions which had left 'an indelible stain on the Government over which he now wielded dictatorial power' (*II*, 30/01/46).

Margaret Buckley remained the president of the recently reinvigorated Sinn Féin. The actual restructuring of the party would require a number of years given its state of neglect, and it was at first mostly involved in its traditional activities: commemorations, speeches and lectures, as well as its Ard Fheis. Undoubtedly, this was a party under the influence of the IRA, having been literally recreated by them. Its main *raison d'*être was limited: to ensure that the IRA could reorganise and function. The speech pronounced during the Wolfe Tone commemoration in 1949 left no doubt as to the role that the IRA intended to give to the party:

> Sinn Féin's job will be two-fold. In the first place it will be up to Sinn Féin to see that the men that will be doing the fighting will not be stabbed in the back as the men who were risking their lives and liberty in England were stabbed in the back by Fianna Fáil [...]. The second part of Sinn Féin's job will be just as important, if not more so. It will be its duty to see that the cultural, social and economic principles of the Irish Republican movement are not forgotten or watered down. (*United Irishman* (*UI*), July–August 1949)

Another important step was taken with the launch of a new publication, whose name, *United Irishman*, was anchored within the Republican tradition of Wolfe Tone. It was not the first time that this name was used by Republicans. It was the title of the paper founded by John Mitchell in 1848 after he broke away from *The Nation*. Arthur Griffith also published an eponymous paper between 1899 and 1906. But it was probably to the former that the new publication gave its historical allegiance, as its first issue came out on the centenary of the launch of Mitchell's own paper, in March 1948, one month after the release of the last prisoners from Portlaoise. Its essential role was to 'preach the Republican gospel', showing that the movement had not broken away from its traditional roots where political ideology and the Catholic faith were closely intertwined. It was conservative in its general outlook, as shown by one of its editorials: 'Ireland, for centuries acknowledged leader of culture, is now ravished and wrecked by an effete generation that would substitute the shadow of Hollywood for the substance of Kells and Clonmacnoise' (*UI*, July–August 1948). It viewed communism as 'a foreign ideology, just as unsuited to Irish character and temperament as British imperialism'. To further reinforce this point, a joint IRA–Sinn Féin statement explained the following year that there was 'no connection whatsoever between the Republican movement and organisations known to be under the control of the Communist Party or its agents' (*UI*, January–February 1951). The launch of the *United Irishman* was followed in 1949 by the creation of the Republican Bureau, whose role was to publish the statements of the leadership in order to 'make known to the world the fact that Ireland is still a dismembered nation' and to counter anti-Republican strategy.

It was only from July–August 1949 that the paper started to mention the name Sinn Féin on a regular basis. It reported on the Ard Fheis of that same year, during which it had been decided that the party 'today again comes to the forefront, a virile, active force' (*UI*, December 1949). In February 1950,

Sinn Féin nominated three candidates to the Westminster general elections in Northern Ireland, as unlike in the case of Stormont it was possible to put forwards abstentionist candidates. Therefore, it had been decided to 'avail ourselves of the opportunity now offered, as it will not arise again for another 5 years' (*UI*, February 1950). Even though the results were insignificant – it obtained 0.3 per cent of the vote – this was an indication that the party was willing to take on a more active role. The last time candidates had been put forward in the north was in 1933, when two abstentionist Republicans, but not directly connected with Sinn Féin, had been elected to Stormont. For the first time since then, Sinn Féin reappeared in the political life of Northern Ireland.

Championing anti-partitionism

The priority of the party was now altered. At the end of 1948, the Irish Dáil voted the Republic of Ireland Act, officially granting the twenty-six counties the status of Republic and abolishing the 1936 External Relations Act, which devolved foreign policy to the Irish cabinet, and ending its membership of the Commonwealth. According to the new legislation, the 'description of the State would be the Republic of Ireland', which was officially proclaimed on Easter Monday 1949. But for Republicans, this fell short of the original aspiration, as it did not include the north-eastern counties. However, the discourse on the Free State which had fed an essential part of Sinn Féin's rhetoric had now become somewhat redundant,[3] and the main focus shifted to become the fight against partition. At a meeting in September 1949, attended according to police reports by up to 1,000 people, one of the speakers, Gearóid Mac Broin, explained that 'talk was useless and that force would have to be employed'. He urged all to join Sinn Féin, 'either the militant groups, that is the IRA, or the non-military group, the Cumainn throughout the country' (Garda report, 26/09/49).

The annual congresses still only gathered a handful of delegates, a mere forty according to future Provisional IRA[4] leader Joe Cahill (interview, 1987), although the report established by the *United Irishman* stating it had been attended by sixty delegates was more optimistic. During the 1950 Ard Fheis, Margaret Buckley gave her last presidential address, as she had decided not to stand for election again. She underlined that Sinn Féin 'had always drawn our inspiration from past history and the day when Ireland forgets the past, she will have ceased to be a nation' (Buckley, *Presidential Address*, 1950). She also reminded her audience that 'the fundamental principles of Sinn Féin remain unaltered, for though historical circumstances may change, principles never

change'. Buckley's speech was a condensed history of Sinn Féin, and it contained
interesting insights into how Sinn Féin viewed its own past. Set in the context of
the loss of the lawsuit against the Irish state, it was a reaffirmation of de Valera's
responsibility for the continuation of partition. 'The year 1925 showed a rising
Republican spirit [...]. The implementing of the Partition Crime was having its
effect and, if the loyalty of the past year had been maintained for even another
year, we would not have British troops on our soil today'. From 1932 onwards,
'executions and deaths on hunger strike soon became part of the Fianna Fáil
routine' (Buckley, *Presidential Address*, 1950).

A substantial part of the speech was dedicated to the issue of emigration.
Indeed, this was a major problem within Irish society. Figures indicated that
'between 1951 and 1961 the estimated net emigration from Ireland was 409,000
persons – an amount equivalent to about one-seventh of the total population in
Ireland in 1961' (Kennedy, 1973, 95). There were several reasons for this increase
in emigration: better employment opportunities in Britain considering the
post-war labour shortages, making emigration less permanent than it had been
when it was directed towards the US, and more importantly, the widespread
adoption of labour-saving agricultural techniques which meant that the number
of those employed in the agricultural sector decreased by 17 per cent in the
1950s while the productivity per farm worker rose by 20 per cent (Kennedy,
1973, 95). This was problematic, according to Buckley, as not only did this mean
that the 'chief export is now young women and men, the very life and blood of
the land', but also, that this heralded the arrival of 'foreign accents', which meant
not enough children were reared 'as Irish children should be reared'. The race
was dying out, she concluded (Buckley, *Presidential Address*, 1950).

Patrick McLogan replaced Buckley at the head of Sinn Féin, making the link
between the party and the IRA all the more obvious, with the leaders of the army
also taking over the control of the party. According to Joe Cahill, in those days,
Sinn Féin was confined to a limited number of tasks: 'The main concentration
was on building what would be called today a "Brits Out" movement. The policy
was reunification, and support for the IRA in the North. It was more political
pressure' (Cahill, interview, 1987). Energies were almost entirely centred on
the issue of partition. The activities of the IRA were transferred, geographi-
cally, when its annual convention decided in 1949 to put an end to any armed
action in the Republic. The central aim was the reunification of Ireland and the
destruction of both states, north and south. This did not represent a marked
change in objectives, but implied strategic adjustments, as the party's activities
would no longer exclusively be located in the south of the island as had been the

case in the previous two decades. This was also taking place in a more general context where Nationalist aspirations were affirmed on both sides of the border, and within which the issue of partition was becoming a priority for a number of political parties. Therefore, in November 1945, two Stormont Nationalist MPs, Eddie McAteer and Malachy Conlon, organised a convention of Nationalist MPs, at the end of which the Anti-Partition League was founded 'with the object of uniting all those opposed to partition into a solid block' (Farrell, 1980, 179). In the south of the country, anti-partitionism was steadily gaining ground. Clann na Poblachta had entered the Dublin parliament after Seán MacBride and one of his colleagues had won two by-elections. The 1948 general election put an end to sixteen years of Fianna Fáil government, as the party only secured sixty-eight seats, which meant it could not form a government. Therefore, an inter-party government was formed, comprised of the Labour Party, Fine Gael, Clann na Poblachta, Clann na Talmhan and National Labour and presided over by John A. Costello.

On 29 January 1949, a conference organised by the government gathered the leaders of all political parties: Costello for Fine Gael, de Valera for Fianna Fáil, MacBride for Clann na Poblachta, William Norton for the Labour Party and, finally, Frank Aiken. As a result, an anti-partition fund was established to collect money for the campaign for the abolition of the border and to provide funding for the Anti-Partition League candidates in Northern Ireland, which was viewed by Britain with 'silence and detachment' (Sloan, 1997, 248). The Stormont general election of February 1949 showed the popularity of the anti-partition movement, which won 106,459 votes (nine seats). But it also confirmed that the Northern Ireland parliament constituted a Unionist monolith, as with the Unionist parties getting an absolute majority (234,202 votes), no other organisation or party was in a position to represent a serious challenge.

In the Republic, the coalition government's position soon became untenable. The controversy which developed around the project of Health Minister, Noel Browne (Clann na Poblachta), concerning the 'Mother and Child Scheme', put the government under strain. This proposed legislation provided free healthcare for women during maternity and for children under the age of sixteen, regardless of financial means. This caused great anger within the Catholic Church, for whom the field of health and family could not be administered by the state. It considered this very project a direct threat to its power and authority.[5] With the resignation of several members of Clann na Poblachta, including Noel Browne, the government lost its majority. The elections of 1951 enabled Fianna Fáil to form a new government, with the support of ten independent TDs. Clann na

Poblachta, on the other hand, lost most of its support, as it only managed to retain two of the ten seats that it had held previously. This party was fading away.

Sinn Féin did not take any stance on this controversy, but instead released a statement entitled *Ireland, Partition and the Atlantic Pact* in the early 1950s (not dated), where it described itself as 'not a political party with an axe to grind. It is a national organisation founded on truth and justice, [which] seeks only the implementation of those virtues in Irish life'. The purpose of the pamphlet was to warn the Irish people not to bargain on the issue of partition and not to be lured into any deal that would undermine Irish sovereignty. According to the document, 'negotiations are proceeding to end Partition by involving Ireland in the next Imperial war', which would 'provide the Anglo-American forces with Air, Naval and Military bases, all the resources or Irish man-power, under a unified command [...] All the advantages of such a bargain are obviously with the Anglo-Americans', stated the document. This was undoubtedly a reference to NATO, which Lemass, as early as 1949, had unambiguously stated Ireland would not join.[6]

Sinn Féin, at the time, 'was not involved in the socio-economic problems of the people; that came later', according to Joe Cahill (interview, 1987). It was only in February 1954 that the party published its first *National Unity and Independence Programme*. There was indeed little in terms of an economic analysis, in a document that was more concerned with outlining the strategy of the movement. It suggested an electoral policy that would be based on the principle of abstentionism (except in the twenty-six counties local elections) and insisted on the necessity of educating the Irish people by keeping them informed of the political decisions and the activities of the movement. The only concrete proposal that the document contained, that of forming a national assembly and proclaiming the Republic if the majority was secured in an election, seemed so unrealistic that it is doubtful whether it attracted potential voters outside of Republican circles. This was a three-pronged strategy, which involved contesting all twelve seats in Westminster elections, putting forward candidates in '26 County' elections, and ending 'the farce of men allegedly representing sections of the Irish people either at Stormont, in corporation county councils, etc., taking an oath of allegiance to a foreign monarch' (*UI*, October 1954).

Sinn Féin was indeed ambivalent about its role in political life, as shown by the statement of its president, who remarked that his organisation was 'not, and never was, a political party. Sinn Féin is a national movement' (*UI*, October 1954). It nevertheless attempted to put together some sort of economic programme, part of which was published in the *United Irishman* for a number of consecutive months. The party admitted that 'If we are not able to plan to meet the economic needs of our people, freeing the country politically is not going to get us very far. The system that now exists and the evils that flow from it will continue, and if it is to be changed, we must have a grasp of the main factors involved' (*UI*, September 1956).

Borrowing seats

The year 1955 gave Sinn Féin the opportunity to play an active political role. In June 1954, the IRA had organised a successful arms raid on an Armagh barracks and had obtained an important military load. A similar expedition had been organised in Omagh on 16 October 1954. This time, the operation was unsuccessful and eight men were arrested, among them Philip Clarke and Tom Mitchell, both sentenced to six years' imprisonment. They were nominated by the party as candidates in the 1955 British general election, along with ten other Republican candidates; Sinn Féin was therefore contesting all twelve seats. In its electoral address, however, an ambivalence towards the process was manifest: 'The winning of seats in this election will not be regarded by Sinn Féin as an end in itself, nor will the results, whatever they be, affect in any way the determination of Republicans to forge ahead toward their objectives' (*Election Manifesto*, Sinn Féin, 1955).[7] This rhetoric aimed undoubtedly at preparing the party and the general public for the possibility of an electoral failure. It also showed how little politics counted for Sinn Féin, and how dismissive Republicans were of any electoral manifestation. This was partly due to their inexperience in that field, not having fought an election for over three decades, but also to their mistrust of electoral processes, particularly in the context of a state that they deemed illegitimate.

The two imprisoned candidates were elected on 25 May 1955, and Sinn Féin won a total of 152,310 votes. Whether one could interpret this result as a manifestation of the party's progress, as Sinn Féin clearly did, noting that it heralded a 'new spirit of cooperation and voluntary service to Ireland that has spread throughout the country' (*UI*, June 1956), is open to question, as this election was fought in a particular context where the two elected candidates were in prison. Moreover, Sinn Féin was the only non-Unionist party in all but four constituencies.[8] However, the Unionist candidate for the Fermanagh-South Tyrone constituency lodged a complaint regarding the legitimacy of the candidacy of his rival, Philip Clarke; both his and Mitchell's elections were cancelled by a vote in Westminster, and by-elections were called. This gave rise to a new electoral contest, between Charles Beattie (Unionist) and Tom Mitchell, on 11 August 1955. Tom Mitchell was re-elected, increasing his share of the vote by 0.5 per cent. Beattie decided in turn to lodge a complaint, and the electoral tribunals concluded that neither Mitchell nor Clarke could be elected to Westminster. This episode then took on a new twist when it was uncovered that Beattie himself was ineligible as he was a judge in an appeals tribunal. A second by-election was therefore staged on 8 May 1956, and Mitchell was once again the Sinn Féin candidate. However, the presence of a third candidate had the effect of splitting the Nationalist vote and giving the majority to the Unionist candidate. The matter was therefore closed, but it had shown that support for Republicans did exist, at least as long as there was no organised Nationalist opposition.

12 December 1956 marked the start of a decisive period for the Republican movement, with both short- and long-term consequences. It was the start of the IRA's Border Campaign, although the very term, according to Daithí Ó Conaill,[9] was fabricated and controversial: 'It's an expression we reject because most of the operations took place far from the border. It was a propaganda cliché' (Ó Conaill, interview, 1987). This was the first campaign after almost twenty years of nearly complete inactivity, and was decided upon for a number of reasons. The organisation had probably regained confidence after the electoral results of 1955 in Northern Ireland and the attacks on arms and ammunitions depots which had increased its arsenal. It also acted under the pressure of events, both internal and external to the movement.

The first half of the decade was characterised, for the IRA, by internal rivalries and by the formation of dissident groups. The most important one, Fianna Uladh, was founded in 1953 in Pomeroy, County Tyrone, by Liam Kelly, a former member of the IRA expelled in 1951 for having planned an operation in Derry without prior authorisation. Fianna Uladh, 'The soldiers of Ulster', was a small political formation, as it was exclusively limited to County Tyrone. The IRA disapproved of this group, not only because it represented an open dissidence, but also because its policy went against one of the Republican principles, as it recognised the parliament of the Republic of Ireland. Fianna Uladh made a small, and brief, incursion in Irish political life, with the election of its leader to the Stormont parliament in 1953, as an abstentionist deputy. He was arrested almost immediately after his election and sentenced to one year of imprisonment for sedition. During his incarceration, he was nominated to the Irish Senate in June 1954 with the support of Seán MacBride. His maiden – and only – speech in the Seanad was in support of a motion put forward by Senators

McHugh and O'Donnell which read 'that all elected parliamentary representatives of the people of the six occupied counties of Ireland will be given a right
of audience in the Dáil or in the Seanad or alternatively requests the Government to submit this question for the decision of the Irish people by means of a
plebiscite' (*Seanad Debates*, 25/10/54). In August 1954, Kelly gave his political
group an armed wing, Saor Uladh, also a local organisation.

The idea of an armed campaign was making headway, even outside Republican circles. This phenomenon is best illustrated by the creation of the group
Laochra Uladh by Brendan O'Boyle.[10] A member of the IRA in the 1940s,
O'Boyle was arrested and imprisoned in the Crumlin Road prison, Belfast,
in September 1941, but managed to escape in 1943 and disappear for a while,
probably in the US. When he came back to Dublin, he opened a jewellery shop
and with the money that he had made abroad funded a 'one-man bombing
campaign' (Bowyer Bell, 1983, 256). O'Boyle was killed by his own bomb as he
tried to plant it in a phone booth near Stormont on 2 July 1956, marking the end
of his own organisation. This episode was a sign of things to come. Saor Uladh
had gone on the offensive on 25 November, attacking the Rosslea barracks in
County Fermanagh, which cost the life of Connie Green, Kelly's right-hand
man. As a consequence, the Northern Irish government banned Saor Uladh,
and a few months later, Fianna Uladh and Sinn Féin.

In Dublin, the IRA headquarters was confronted with a new problem of
internal discipline, in the person of Joe Christle, known for his enthusiastic
activism, and described in 1998 by the current Sinn Féin's weekly paper *An
Phoblacht* as 'a Republican Socialist of the highest calibre who clashed often with
the Movement's leadership over his open calls for the Movement to become
pro-active and his open espousal of radical policies, such as dropping abstentionism and greater political involvement' (*AP*, 20/08/98). Christle founded his
own organisation, the Republican Party, and stood for election for Dublin South
West (*Republican Party*, n.d., NLI, O'Mahony Papers, MS 44,084 /7). Expelled
from the IRA in June 1956, he joined Saor Uladh in September, followed by
members of the IRA Dublin unit. These events, according to Joe Cahill, had a
marked influence on the IRA command. The larger-scale campaign that the IRA
was to engage in 'was forced on the IRA by a group called Saor Uladh' (Cahill,
interview, 1987).

The IRA had been considering an armed campaign for some time. A document
published in 1954, *Irish Resistance to British Aggression*, outlined the rationale
behind any future armed campaign. But the arrival of Seán Cronin from the US
in the autumn of 1955 accelerated the military preparations as, 'despite being a

new recruit to Republicanism, [he] brought a dynamism to preparations, partly because, as Garland recalls, he seemed to know "a lot more than most of us about military matters"' (Hanley and Millar, 2009, 12). The final strategy was named 'Operation Harvest' and consisted in sending four columns of twenty-five men each positioned south of the border with the mission of making incursions into Northern Ireland and creating links with the units based in the north. The main targets were to be the Crown forces and the objective was to paralyse the civil administration. The strategy was ambitious but presented two major faults. On the one hand, it underestimated the hostility of the Unionist population on the ground, and on the other, it had not defined how to exploit, politically, any possible gain from the campaign. On 1 November 1956, the forces of Kelly and Christle attacked six customs offices. The following 12 December, the IRA launched its own campaign by attacking various posts along the border as well as in Northern Ireland, such as a BBC transmitter in Derry and an army building in Enniskillen. The IRA justified its action in the following manner:

> Spearheaded by Ireland's freedom fighters, our people in the Six Counties have carried the fight to the enemy. Out of this national liberation struggle a New Ireland will emerge, upright and free. On that New Ireland we shall build a country fit for all our people to live in. That then is our aim: an independent, united, democratic Irish Republic. (*UI*, January 1957)

The IRA's initiative was soon countered by the governments on both sides of the border as well as by Britain. On 21 December 1956, internment without trial was reintroduced in Northern Ireland. The IRA campaign seemed, at its early stages, to elicit a sympathetic response among some sections of the Irish population. Indeed, when two IRA members, Seán South and Fergal O'Hanlon, were killed during an attack in Brookeborough, several councils, such as Cork, Dublin and Waterford corporations, voted motions of sympathy with their relatives. South was buried in his native County Limerick, and his funeral procession was followed, according to the *Irish Press*, by 'thousands of people' (*IP*, 05/01/57). The Costello government reacted promptly, ordering the arrest on 6 January 1957 of most of the IRA leaders, among them Seán Cronin, followed by Mac Curtain, Magan and two others on 12 January. Their sentences ranged from three to six months' imprisonment. This was made possible by the Offences Against the State Act, introduced in 1939 by the Fianna Fáil government and reinstated in January 1957 to respond to the IRA campaign. As a result, MacBride introduced a vote of no confidence against the government on 28 January, and Costello called for new general elections.

Sinn Féin, which had succeeded in the space of a few years in gaining some political ground, grasped the opportunity of the elections of 5 March to seek the electorate's support. The stakes were clear. Given the context of the military campaign, the assimilation between the Sinn Féin vote and the support for the armed struggle was inevitable. Interestingly, although the consistent attempt to dissociate support for the IRA from a Sinn Féin vote would become a familiar discourse in the 1980s, this was a new experience at the time, as the last general elections in which the party had taken part had been held in 1927.[11] In order to justify its position, Sinn Féin used a rhetoric of ambiguity while cleverly managing its core contradictions: 'We were represented to the people by politicians, wrongly, as supporters of force. Sinn Féin does not advocate force. It believes that if England imposes itself in this country by force of arms, the Irish have the right, and the duty, to resist' (*UI*, February 1957). This came only a month after the IRA had issued a 'final warning' to the Inspector General of the RUC informing him that any civilian casualty within RUC barracks would be his responsibility (IRA General Headquarters, 1956). Sinn Féin was therefore already putting together a rhetorical strategy which aimed at reconciling an inherent contradiction, as future provisional director of publicity Danny Morrison would describe it.

Sinn Féin nominated nineteen candidates, and four were elected as abstentionist candidates to the Dáil: Ruairí Ó Brádaigh (Longford-Westmeath), Eighneachán Ó hAnnluain (Monaghan), John Joe McGirl (Sligo-Leitrim) and Joe Rice (Kerry South). It did remind voters that its policy 'is not to overthrow Leinster House but to replace it by an All-Ireland parliamentary legislation for a free and enlightened people',[12] and reiterated that Sinn Féin was a 'constitutional organisation which seeks to achieve its aims by constitutional means' (*UI*, March 1957).

Sinn Féin secured 5 per cent of the vote, 65,640 votes, which would have been a symbolically important result had it heralded that the party intended to return to full political life. However, this dimension was only second to that of military action, as had been clearly stated by Seán Cronin, who believed in the 'use of part-time guerrillas who would continue in civilian occupations yet be available for active service when called on' (IRA General Headquarters, 1956). Moreover, the abstentionist strategy of the party was once more to prove its strategic limitations. An article published in a local newspaper *The Kerryman* of 10 August 1957 insisted on the fact that the elected candidates should immediately take their seats in the Irish parliament. The leadership seized that opportunity to affirm its abstentionist position and to put an end to any suggestion that would go against that fundamental principle, stating that the elected candidates had to respect the wishes of the electorate and conform to the constitution of the party. The statement issued by the Ard Chomhairle added nothing new to the debate, limiting itself to reinforcing the abstentionist position in the name of history and particularly of 1918 (*UI*, September 1957). This precision enabled the party to bury the debate before it had even taken place, but only momentarily, as the events to come would show.

The election saw the return to power of Fianna Fáil which, with seventy-eight seats, had an absolute majority. Clann na Poblachta disappeared from the political horizon, having won no seats, and Fine Gael lost a considerable level of support, obtaining only thirty-nine seats. The new government led by de Valera was determined to put an end to Republican dissension. Sinn Féin's headquarters and those of the *United Irishman* were raided, resulting in the arrest of more than 100 people, including some party leaders. Some days later, on 7 July, internment without trial was reintroduced in the Republic, leading the *United Irishman* to condemn de Valera's 'totalitarian action' and the confinement of its members 'in the Curragh concentration camp' (*UI*, August 1957). The newspaper talked of a conspiracy by the government and the press to ensure that none of this was made known to the public: 'Sinn Féin statements are not being carried in the press, reports of Sinn Féin meetings are not being carried by newspapers. The authorities obviously hope to steamroller Sinn Féin completely out of their path without one word of protest being heard anywhere' (*UI*, August 1957). While the Fianna Fáil government created a commission to which the detained men could appeal in order to prove their innocence, Sinn Féin Ard Chomhairle retorted that they would not be 'party to this travesty of justice' (*UI*, August 1957).

In Northern Ireland, the legislation in place regarding elections excluded the possibility of an abstentionist strategy, as any candidate going forward to the Stormont elections had to swear his or her intention to take their seats if elected, which meant, according to the party, that 'Stormont elections are thus restricted to party and sectarian politicians who are thus prepared to recognise partitionist institutions' (Sinn Féin, 1956). Sinn Féin attempted to circumvent the obstacle by putting forward an alternative voting system, which was obviously more symbolic than practical, according to which all voters were to sign lists of non-official representatives and, as a consequence, abstain from going to the polling stations. This detailed plan for the boycott of Stormont elections aimed to provide an alternative for electors who were to sign an undertaking signed in turn by representatives nominated at constituency conventions.

These forms were to be distributed 'on the approaches to church gates', in private houses and through house-to-house canvassing. Voters were therefore asked to nominate alternative representatives for their constituencies and were pledging not to vote for candidates who would either take their seats or boycott Stormont once elected (Sinn Féin, 1956), voting instead for representatives to a virtual all-Ireland parliament who would seek to put an end to 'British occupation of Irish territory, British rule over any part of Ireland, and British interference in affairs that are the sole concern of the Irish people' (Sinn Féin, 1956).

One of the main weaknesses of the Republican movement remained the lack of new ideas and even content in its politics. The electoral successes of the party were limited, as they did not necessarily reflect the adhesion of a section of the electorate to specific ideals and objections. This was illustrated by the November 1957 Dublin North by-election. On that occasion, the *United Irishman* reiterated the political objectives of Sinn Féin, which could be summarised in a few lines: national unity and independence, economic and social freedom (breaking the economic link with Great Britain), the end of emigration and unemployment (with agricultural and industrial expansion based on the needs of the Irish people), cultural freedom, the end of spending and corruption and, finally, the building of the nation, stating that 'Sinn Féin alone has the necessary drive and enthusiasm to take up again the task of building the nation' (*UI*, November 1957). However, the candidate, Seán Garland, who had been imprisoned in the Curragh internment camp since the raid on Brookeborough barracks in January 1957 in which Seán South and Fergal O'Hanlon had lost their lives,[13] failed to be elected, although he succeeded in obtaining 13.4 per cent of the first preference vote.

The limitations of the military strategy

During the summer of 1957, the Republican movement still felt it benefited from some support, as shown by the number of copies the paper claimed it sold: 120,000. But there were signs showing that the Border Campaign was weakening the IRA and was therefore being counter-productive.

On the one hand, the IRA had been badly affected by the emergency measures that had been implemented on both sides of the border at the start of the year. On the other hand, its actions were often curtailed by the RUC, which seemed well informed about its activities and had been gathering detailed intelligence on the personnel engaged in the campaign. Therefore the IRA lost the offensive, which it might only have had during the first month of the campaign, when the element of surprise had played in its favour. The death, on 11 November 1957, of four men killed by the premature explosion of their own bomb, as well as that of the owner of the house in which they found themselves, inflicted a serious blow to the organisation's morale. Finally, the IRA was running short of arms and ammunitions.

In spite of this, it seemed determined to continue its campaign. The arrest in September 1958 of the main members of the IRA's executive, and especially that of its chief of staff Seán Cronin, did not appear to discourage the organisation. A provisional Army Council was put in place, including Ruairí Ó Brádaigh and Daithí Ó Conaill who had escaped from prison on 27 September 1958.[14] Ó Brádaigh took on the role of chief of staff in the absence of Cronin. However, whether this new leadership was approved of by the movement as a whole is open to question. An IRA internal memo dated January 1959 to all the prisoners in the 'Curragh concentration camp' clearly implied that this was not the case and that some discontent might have been voiced:

> to emerge successfully from this generation's fight, we must have unity as well as discipline. Nothing else than our united efforts will suffice to achieve our common goal. The enemy will try ceaselessly to penetrate our solidarity but we must defeat his every design and stand 'shoulder to shoulder' in splendid and unbreakable unity behind the duly-elected Army authorities and their representatives, the Units O/Cs. We must do so regardless of the personnel that occupy such positions for the time being. (IRA, January 1959, NLI, O'Mahony Papers, MS 44,084 /2)

Their rhetoric remained defiant and victorious, in spite of all objective indications, as shown by the 1959 statement for the 1916 anniversary: 'The Irish nation is on the right way to freedom'. Ó Brádaigh therefore stated at the Wolfe Tone commemoration in the summer of 1959: 'The Volunteers and our people in the occupied North are prepared to pay the price of freedom – however high it may be' (*UI*, July 1959).

The optimism shown by Republicans was soon to suffer a setback with the British general election of 1959. Sinn Féin nominated twelve candidates, calling on the electorate to vote for 'the movement which personifies the continuance of the national tradition of opposition to the usurped rule of the foreigner' (*UI*, September 1959). This time, the situation presented greater difficulties, as the results achieved four years previously would no doubt heighten hopes; any significant loss of support would inevitably be interpreted as a loss of support for the IRA's campaign. The tactic used was identical to that of the previous elections: the successful experience of the prisoner-candidate was repeated in the twelve constituencies. The results were, to say the least, disappointing, if not alarming. Sinn Féin secured 63,415 votes, a loss of almost half of the support it had obtained in the 1955 election.

Such a result did not seem to alter the trust of the leadership in their own strategy, at least publicly. The analysis remained the same, as was shown in an editorial of the *United Irishman* congratulating Republicans on the fact that a large number of voters had gone to the polling stations in spite of conditions deemed very adverse: 'A proscribed organisation, a banned newspaper, local leaders either in jail or exiled, these were among the conditions of elections in British occupied Ireland'. Sinn Féin had a similar interpretation of the results:

> The conquest and result of the elections is testimony that Ireland's demand and the desire of the people for freedom is not local, is not even provincial but national in its scope, and the demand for freedom, supported in the elections by almost 64,000 voters within the 6 counties and by many others of the Irish race at home and overseas who rallied to the support of the Republican cause remains a greater power in Ireland than the institutions of partitioned government imposed by English conquest. (*UI*, October 1959)

The discourse of the leadership had over-optimistic, almost victorious, overtones when the results did not, apparently, justify such an analysis. Its apparent aim was to reaffirm the faith of the movement, its loyalty to the 'standard bearers of Republican Ireland'. Little did the results matter, in fact, as Sinn Féin was convinced of holding the absolute truth. From this stemmed the lack of doubt in and questioning of the strategy, which was to precipitate the movement, from a military as well as a political point of view, towards failure. The presidential address of McLogan at the 1959 Ard Fheis, confirmed this. Having quoted Pearse, he then added: 'In any effort which we in Sinn Féin make to indicate the objective of our organisation there is no need to outline in terms others than those stated in the words of Padraig Pearse', the volunteers were part, as was confirmed at Easter, of 'the great brotherhood of martyrs and heroes that mark the 750 years of struggle to drive British armed forces out of Ireland' (*UI*, May 1960).

The signs of increasing strain on the organisation were visible from early 1960. Still convinced it could muster public support, it decided to engage politically at all possible levels, adopting different strategies according to the situation at hand. Therefore, in May 1960, it took up the electoral challenge in the Republic, presenting a number of candidates to the local elections who would 'take their places in any local government bodies to which they may be elected, they will cooperate with any such other elected representatives as are sincerely and genuinely endeavoured to serve the interests of the Nation and its people'

(*UI*, October 1959). This election was important on several levels. It was the first time that Sinn Féin was showing an interest in local issues such as housing or the environment, in a practical manner. For their immediate resolution, Sinn Féin was even prepared to engage with the local institutions. The party was quick to dispel any notion that this might have constituted a breach of the principle of abstentionism, as this principle only concerned the parliaments of the three jurisdictions and the local councils were not considered to be tied to the partitionist system. However, the results were disappointing (Hanley and Millar, 2009, 19). At the 1960 Ard Fheis, McLogan attempted to undermine the electoral setbacks that his party had suffered. After having called for national unity on all fronts, he concluded: 'Sinn Féin does not aim at uniting our country and its people under the banner of political leadership because such leadership is only concerned with serving the interests of the party to the exclusion of the nation' (*UI*, December 1960). Such an assessment highlighted once again the mistrust of the party in political engagement.

The armed campaign of the IRA was no longer a priority in the politics of the Republic, and the end of internment on 15 March 1959 showed that the IRA was no longer considered a threat.[15] The Irish political scene had undergone important political changes. The three main parties had new leaderships, which heralded a renewal of the party personnel. On 17 June 1959, de Valera was elected President of the Republic, leaving his leadership of Fianna Fáil and of the government to Seán Lemass. This was the end of the political domination of de Valera over Irish political life. In October of that same year, Richard Mulcahy, veteran of the independence period, resigned from the leadership of Fine Gael and was replaced by James Dillon. Finally, in 1960, the Labour Party elected a new leader, Brendan Corish, who replaced William Norton.

The Lemass government gave priority to economic development. As early as 1958, the programme for economic expansion had been approved, planning a massive injection of state capital into productive companies over a five-year period, as well as the stimulation of the private sector. On an international level, Lemass sought to give the country a more significant place. Ireland joined the United Nations in December 1955, and the country's first main commitment on the international stage took place in 1960 when Irish troops joined the UNUC[16] forces in Congo. Lemass applied in July 1961 for EEC membership, following the lead of the UK.

In September 1961, Lemass called for a general election for 15 October 1961, in the wake of the country's application to join the EEC. It was characterised by the elimination of smaller parties, such as Clann na Talmhan, created in

1939 to fight for the small farmers from the west of the country, which had won fourteen seats in 1943 and seven in 1948. One of its representatives had been Minister for Lands and Fisheries for the coalition government. However, it only succeeded in maintaining two seats, while Clann na Poblachta only secured one and disappeared officially in 1965. For Sinn Féin, these elections were a disaster. Its twenty-one candidates only totalled 36,396 votes, a mere 3 per cent of the vote, halving its 1957 performance. None of the four abstentionist TDs was re-elected. Although Fianna Fáil no longer had an absolute majority, Seán Lemass formed a government with the support of two independent TDs.

The Border Campaign, although still ongoing in theory, was moribund. The IRA seemed to find it increasingly difficult to justify its action to its own supporters. Therefore, when its units blew up two bridges in April 1961, the explanation put forward by the headquarters sounded lame: 'It has been said that the IRA inconvenienced the 30 families [...]. In fact thirty families have been reunited with their fellow countrymen. They have been reunited with their natural hinterland and trading areas. They are no longer inconvenienced by the presence of British Crown forces travelling their roads, searching their farms, raiding their homes' ('Why the bridges were blown', IRA statement, August 1961, NLI, O'Mahony Papers, MS 44,084 /2). One last operation was carried out in November, during which an RUC officer lost his life. As a consequence, the Irish government reintroduced the military courts on 23 November. At the end of December 1961, the situation of the IRA was grim. Twenty-two men had been sentenced by these courts and funds had dried up. The leadership of the movement was forced to admit that the Border Campaign had failed. On 26 February 1962, a public statement put an end to an episode that had lasted more than five years, and during which eight members of the IRA, two civilian Republicans, two Saor Uladh men and six RUC officers had lost their lives. The lengthy statement addressed 'to the people or Ireland' was a covert admission of defeat: 'The resistance movement remains intact and in a position to continue its campaign in the occupied area indefinitely. It realises, however, that the situation obtained in the earlier stages of the campaign has altered radically and is convinced that the time has come to conserve its resources, to augment them, and to prepare a more favourable situation' (IRA statement, 26/02/62, NLI, O'Mahony Papers, MS 44,084 /2).

Indeed, from a strategic and political point of view, the campaign had back-fired on the movement. The implications for Sinn Féin were momentous, as its destiny was closely linked to that of the IRA; the failure of the IRA was to directly affect the political party, just as the party had benefited, in the earlier years, from the initial successes of the Border Campaign. Therefore, as enthusiasm for military action and the hopes that it might have given rise to were waning, support for the party dropped. The electoral results were a good indication not so much of the state of the party as of the decline of popularity of the IRA's activities.

The role of Sinn Féin during that campaign had been fundamental for the movement as a whole. It had promoted Republican ideals, kept enthusiasm alive and praised military action. But this was a limited role for a political party. Sinn Féin, during these years, was a machine that produced speeches, a structure useful for public relations and publicity. Never had it played so diligently its role as the political wing of the IRA. Very few efforts had been made in terms of policy, as all energies were being concentrated on the armed campaign as the affirmation of the inalienable right of the Irish people to resort to arms. The IRA was in no position to renew the political discourse, and therein probably resided the main weakness of the Republican strategy: the incapacity to give, on the one hand, a dimension to the armed struggle other than that of its very existence, and on the other hand, a political dynamic to its struggle.

The questioning that was emerging within the ranks of the armed organisation concerned not only the armed strategy, but also the role of a political party. Indeed, it became obvious that limiting Sinn Féin's role to that of supporting the IRA was not in itself enough. Since 1948, the party had only succeeded partially in creating an identity for itself, and the military campaign proved that too strong an identification of both components of the movement could be counterproductive. Following the end of the campaign, the IRA, much like Sinn Féin, was without any real direction, its personnel having lost credibility among its own ranks and with the public. A renewal of the composition of the movement, both from a political and personal perspective, was essential for its own survival.

Renewal was made possible by the departure of party president Patrick McLogan in the spring, having voiced concern as to the uneven relationship that existed between the party and the IRA. Ironically, the reason for leaving the party was precisely that it had become too subservient to the Army Council. He explained in a detailed memo dated 24 May 1962 that the party had been 'used' by the IRA for 'any purpose and in any way that suits the ideas of the Army Control'. Moreover, in his opinion, Sinn Féin was unjustly blamed for the ending of the Border Campaign and he refuted the 'false accusations' levied against the party and some of its leaders (Memo from McLogan to the Sinn Féin Ard Chomhairle, 24/05/62, NLI, O'Mahony Papers, MS 44,112 /2). McLogan followed up this memo by a number of other letters to headquarters where he further attempted to clarify his position, reiterating that Sinn Féin was not a subordinate organisation and should have equal control over the policies and decision-making process of the movement as a whole. This culminated in a statement dated 18 July 1962 signed by eight members of the Ard Chomhairle and circulated to all local Sinn Féin clubs. The reaction from the party headquarters was prompt and severe: Tom Mitchell, general secretary, informed them on 24 September that a court of inquiry would be held to determine whether their action constituted a 'breach of discipline', showing the extent to which the party was prepared to go to deal with internal dissidence. McLogan interpreted this decision as an attempt to 'side-track the issues at stake', and informed headquarters that he had no intention of attending what he saw as a 'farcical' court as no rule contained within the party's constitution had been breached (27/09/62, NLI, O'Mahony Papers, MS 44,112 /2). However, all eight men were expelled from the party and found guilty of showing 'disrespect and contempt' for the court. The party's headquarters informed McLogan that no further correspondence would be addressed and that the expulsion was final and in accordance with party rules.

Patrick McLogan was assassinated in June 1964 by what Republicans referred to as 'unknown forces'. Eleven years later, a tribute was organised in his memory. The press release, signed by Sinn Féin member Liam Cotter, talked of McLogan as 'a traditional IRA man in every sense of the term', but added, quite insightfully, that 'His departure from the movement in 1962 removed an obstacle to a new departure in policy that followed' (Copy of press release on memorial service to be held in New York for Paddy McLogan, 10/06/75, NLI, O'Mahony Papers, MS 44,112 /4). The McLogan episode sheds light on the internal operation of a party that could be ruthless with its most loyal and ardent supporters when it came to the perceived interests of the movement as a whole.

The Border Campaign had sowed the seeds of doubt among a number of Republicans. The armed strategy was questioned in certain quarters, some going as far as to consider that it could stand in the way of the movement's overall objectives if the strategy was not coupled with proper political thought. The first task at hand was that of analysing the reasons that had led to this situation. Both observers and actors seemed to agree that the campaign had been a failure, but their interpretations on the reasons for this differed. Seán Cronin, who had organised operations since the very start, observed later that 'Sinn Féin had put down few roots in the Nationalist areas' (Cronin, 1980, 171). Joe Cahill ascribed its failure mainly to the fact that the operations had been undertaken prematurely, the IRA not being ready at the time to engage in such a military campaign: 'In the fifties, the strategy of the IRA was to carry out spectacular operations, to obtain arms and to build up resistance. It was successful. It built faith in the IRA and showed it was capable. If that strategy had been continued for two more years, it would have been a successful military campaign' (Cahill, interview, 1987). Armed struggle, in its most traditional form, was not unanimously questioned.

In-depth restructuring

The story of the Republican movement in the aftermath of the Border Campaign has been told many times. The direction that was taken at both political and military levels led to the 1970 split between Officials and Provisionals, precipitated by the events unfolding in Northern Ireland in the second half of the 1960s. Many divergent and even at times contradictory interpretations have been put forward regarding the paths taken by the two factions of the movement and their reasons for doing so. For some, including the Provisionals, the movement in the 1960s fell under the influence of other political forces, particularly the Communist Party. For others, the leadership chose the only possible revolutionary route that could lead to the end of partition, even if this meant that some long-held objectives would need to be postponed. Others still saw the division that these developments generated as one between right and left, between socialism and modernism versus traditionalism and conservatism. Although none of these theses is sufficient per se to explain the split between Provisionals and Officials, all have some merit; but arguably, the primary reason for the split of the fourth Sinn Féin was contained in the very foundation of the party itself and its relationship to the IRA. Therefore, instead of exploring the events that led to the implosion of the movement in 1969–70, this section aims at analysing the transformations that took place and the manner in which they were assessed by those who either advocated or opposed them. The two narratives that emerge from such an analysis demonstrate the fault line that was inherent in the party from the outset and which explains both its lack of ideological consistency and why it was so prone to devastating splits.

At the 1962 Sinn Féin Ard Fheis, Tomás Mac Giolla was elected president of the party, a position which had remained vacant since McLogan's resignation. 'With Mac Giolla, it was the end of a period. A whole new situation arose', said Ó Brádaigh some years later (Ó Brádaigh, interview, 1986). Indeed, this change in leadership heralded an in-depth restructuring, both on a strategic and a political level, although it would only become visible some two years later; for the time being, traditionalism prevailed. Mac Giolla's speech at Bodenstown in June 1962 was rooted in continuity, as two of the issues that were to become most contentious within the movement, that of armed struggle and abstentionsim, remained seeped in a rhetoric which was habitual to Republicans: that of triumphalism ('this [the end of the Border Campaign] was not a step backwards but a step forward. It is an opportunity to observe our resources and consolidate our position and gird ourselves to move forward with enthusiasm and optimism to the next phase in the struggle for freedom') and outward rejection of the state ('No man can claim to be a Republican and a separatist while he accepts and works with the very institutions of government which were designed by Britain to keep Ireland divided and sundered and surrendered and under her dominion') (*UI*, July 1962). But Sinn Féin's attacks against what was still termed the 'Free State' took on a new dimension, as it was criticised for its anti-democratic ethos. This was visible, according to the party, in the very existence of the Offences Against the State Act (1939), which, according to a pamphlet published in April 1964, raised a fundamental question: 'Do we really have a democracy: "We are satisfied that any state that has a piece of legislation such as this cannot be classed as a democracy"' (May 1964, NLI, O'Mahony Papers, MS 44,084 /7).

One of the first initiatives taken by new IRA chief of staff Cathal Goulding was to nominate an internal commission to examine the attitudes of the past two generations regarding Republicanism, as he felt that it 'had drifted away from the original Republicanism' (Goulding, interview, 1987). The criticism which would later profoundly divide the movement already loomed: armed strategy had taken the lead over politics, which had contributed to destabilising the balance of the historical Republican foundations consisting precisely in harmonising, as much as possible, guerrilla tactics and political strategy. This commission was to reach its conclusions in 1967.

The new leadership of the movement, both within Sinn Féin and the IRA, was convinced of the pressing need to readjust political objectives. The shape that these would take was still, however, quite uncertain in 1962, as the discourse essentially consisted in reaffirming basic principles and in reassuring those for whom fundamental change might prove too difficult to accept. Moreover, the leaders themselves were not yet certain of the political route that they would travel. Therefore, according to one of main proponents of socialism, 'Mac Giolla started from a Catholic right-wing anti-communist and came to a moderate left-wing approach' (Johnston, interview, 1988). Mac Giolla's first speech, at the 1962 Ard Fheis, echoed a familiar rhetoric. The themes developed were the criticism of the Treaty, the aspiration to reunification, the demand to 'reassert our nationality and that pride in our race we have almost lost' (*UI*, December 1962). He was therefore reaffirming the primordial reading of the nation which still characterised his party, showing that in 1962, it was not ready to embark on a more novel and radical path. In spite of the split that was caused by the departure of men such as McLogan, some of the older generation remained within Sinn Féin, whose vision, according to Bowyer Bell:

> focused only on the single issue of national unity. Their limitations were often magnified within Sinn Féin, the depository of retired revolutionaries, clinging to the idols of their youth. The new ideas oozing out of the Dublin centre were rarely of interest unless there was a prospect of physical force. The dead weight of tradition, unimportant during a military campaign, made it difficult for the young men to chart an alternative course once the military option had aborted. (Bowyer Bell, 1983, 339–40)

Indeed, the first pamphlet published in 1963, entitled *Ireland: Nation or Province? Ireland and the Common Market* (Sinn Féin, 1963), illustrated the cautious approach of the leadership, which showed how far Republicans still were from embracing socialism. At the outset, it stated that 'the vast majority of Irish people reject communist imperialism and the sources from which it stems. By none among us is it more emphatically rejected than by members of the Republican movement' (Sinn Féin, 1963). The document then launched into a vigorous anti-communist diatribe, warning the country against joining the EEC, as 'no restriction can be placed on the entry to Ireland of communists from Italy, France or any other Common Market country'. There was an attempt to put forward the guiding principles of an economic programme. The proposals were contained in three points: a break of the link with sterling, the adoption of a monetary system which would balance the capital and economic needs of the country, and the repatriation of capital. The party was still, however, impregnated with a traditional outlook, as this pamphlet concluded that 'the administration of a sovereign independent 32-county Republic on Christian social principles will bring happiness and prosperity to all the people of Ireland'. Interestingly, Sinn Féin saw its role as stretching beyond that of a political party, as its mission also encompassed the moral well-being of its electorate.

Socialism and Republicanism

The more radical elements within the movement adopted a guarded attitude towards the introduction of new ideas, as the aim was, according to Goulding, to 'win the minds, not the votes' (Goulding, interview, 1987). When Mac Giolla addressed the Ard Fheis in 1963, a new trend could be seen, even if it was timid. The objectives were no longer simply stated as being the achievement of a Republic, but that of 'full political and economic freedom; [but] it also means control of the resources of the nation and of all factors of production that must be restored to Irish hands' (*UI*, December 1963). This formula was reminiscent of that contained in the 1916 Proclamation, making it possible for Sinn Féin to root its discourse within a historical line, while borrowing some basic Marxist rhetoric, therefore signalling a renewal of the political thinking.

The progress of the movement went hand in hand with the creation of the Wolfe Tone clubs in 1963 at the instigation of the IRA, and more particularly of its chief of staff, commemorating the birth of Theobald Wolfe Tone. They were 'an attempt to supply an intellectual think-tank and ideas to politicise the movement' (Johnston, interview, 1988), with a view to generating a reflection on the profound meaning of Republicanism as an ideology and its significance in society. According to Ó Conaill, these clubs 'did have an influence on the movement', as they offered a Republican and Marxist analysis, concluding with the necessity to break the sectarian barriers in order to proceed to unification (Ó Conaill, interview, 1987). The issue of partition was no longer simply put in territorial terms, but also in social and political terms. The main source of divisions was now identified as being the divergent interests of the social classes. The constitution of the Wolfe Tone Society insisted on the convergence of inter-ests of all the people of Ireland: 'No real conflict of interest exists between any section of the common people, either between different sections of the people of the north, or between north and south. Ultimately, the issue of partition would only be resolved once the proletariat had been reunited, but that process needed, as a prerequisite, the achievement of equality for Nationalists'. Among the objectives of the society was the establishment of a 'United Irish democratic Republic', and it sought to 'unite the scattered forces of discontent, be they farmers, trade Unionists or Catholics in the North' (Wolfe Tone Society, *Draft Constitution*, 1964, NLI, O'Mahony Papers, MS 44,090 /1).

Out of these clubs emerged several figures, among whom that of Roy Johnston, a young physicist from Trinity College, who was a fervent advocate of Marxist theories. His influence on the ideology of the movement was important, as he was able to develop an all-encompassing analysis. He became secretary of the Wolfe Tone Society in 1964, as well as a member of Sinn Féin. The arrival of such figures was to considerably alter the course of the movement which, according to some contemporary observers, 'fell under the influence of certain left-wing intellectuals and adopted the language of social revolution' (O'Brien, 1972, 209).

Johnston brought to the movement an innovative analysis of its role within society. According to him, it was Sinn Féin, more than the IRA, that held the key to political progress. However, he felt that this analysis was incompatible with the very nature of the movement: 'if anything was to be implemented, the IRA had to want it. A new Sinn Féin meant the transformation of the IRA to politics, and Sinn Féin had to be the activist' (Johnston, interview, 1988). Johnston sought to devolve an active political role to Sinn Féin, which in his view meant the modification of the very structures of the movement. Priority could no longer be given to armed struggle; the IRA had to revert to a more limited role, that of an army defending the political objectives designed by Sinn Féin. Since 1926, political thought had arisen from within the IRA, and not so much from the leadership as from individual leaders. Johnston considered that as long as the IRA remained in control of strategies and of the political decision-making process, the options of the movement as a whole were limited. Outside the movement, others recognised the potential fundamental change in thinking that the Wolfe Tone Society represented. 'It is known that Sinn Féin have been drawing up a social policy and if any of their ideas are like those of Roy Johnston and Uinseann Mac Eoin of the Wolfe Tone Committee then it marks a revolution in thinking', wrote an enthusiastic Michael McInerney, political correspondent of the *Irish Times* (*IT*, 15/08/64).

Sinn Féin's strategies were therefore reviewed, as it could no longer content itself with supporting long-term claims, but had to devote time and energy to more concrete and short-term issues. The party critically lacked any solid popular rank and file, on both sides of the border, as had been shown by the 1959 and 1961 electoral results. It had to prove its commitment to issues that had been until then neglected, thereby contributing to giving the movement an elitist profile. Mac Giolla explained this process in an interview that he gave to the *United Irishman* a few years later:

> I felt that in the previous years Sinn Féin had become somehow divorced from the ordinary everyday problems of the people. Sinn Féin has a tradition of single-minded purpose to end British rule in Ireland and they have maintained that tradition [...]. We had to become more active among the people and until such time as Sinn Féin did that we would not be in a position to solve the fundamental problem of freedom and sovereignty. (*UI*, January 1966)

As early as 1963, the movement approached Irish trade unions and other political formations with socialist tendencies, notably the Communist Party. It broadened its agenda, tackling issues such as unemployment, land exploitation, housing and social injustices. According to Goulding:

it was responsible for bringing in an awareness of social inequalities, among the first to pinpoint the reasons for unemployment, who owned the land and wealth. Previously, the Communist party had been the only one to do so, but because of the conservative nature of Ireland, it wasn't acceptable. (Goulding, interview, 1987)

Agitation campaigns were organised, taking the form of land occupations and demonstrations. Sinn Féin showed a particular interest in the fate of the farmers. A pamphlet published in 1964, *Who Owns the Land* (Sinn Féin, 1964), outlined the party's policy on land distribution, the final objective being its division and the formation of cooperatives, aiming to limit the size of farms and therefore help smaller farmers. These proposals were further developed at the Ard Fheis, when it was suggested that 'the land acquired by the State shouldn't be broken but leased to a number of families who would work as one cooperative unit' (*UI*, January 1965). It was also suggested that an organisation of farm workers be set up in order to group their lands in production units. The importance that Sinn Féin gave to this issue was reminiscent of the theories developed by Fintan Lalor in the nineteenth century, who had insisted on the fundamental role of the farm workers in the independence process: 'A secure and independent peasantry is the only base on which a people ever rises or ever can be raised, or on which a nation can safely rest' (in Lyons, 1983, 108). It was also one of the fundamental fights undertaken by Peadar O'Donnell in the late 1920s and early 1930s, the focus then being to put an end to the payment of land annuities to Britain. Parallel to this, Sinn Féin tackled the issues of housing, creating structures such as the Dublin Housing Committee, which included members of the Communist Party, and even members of the Labour Party, to put pressure on the government around these issues; according to a representative of the Communist Party, 'they were very successful in mobilising people' (Communist Party of Ireland, interview, 1987).

In its ideological transformation, Sinn Féin embraced, albeit slowly, socialist theories. These corresponded to the rising awareness of the need for the party to have its own identity in order to play an active role in Irish politics. The very choice of socialism could be seen as a bold one, as this ideology did not benefit from a positive image within the ranks of the movement, no more than it seemed in tune with the mood of a country which was, at that time, overwhelmingly conservative, as Goulding himself remarked (Goulding, interview, 1987). However, there was an attempt on the part of the leaders to root socialism within a traditional ideological trend going back to Tone and Connolly. The fact that socialism had never been consensual within the movement, but rather had frequently been a source of division, did not seem to deter those who sought to embrace its main theories. Nevertheless, this ideological transformation was slow and cautious. The leaders refrained in the first years from using too radical a terminology, 'nationalisation' and 'cooperative' being the most extreme terms of their repertoire. Mac Giolla therefore reminded his supporters in his 1965 presidential address to the party that communism, 'as it has manifested itself in many countries, is not an ideology which would commend itself to the Irish people' (*UI*, November 1965). The political references of the movement remained mainly Irish, at least as far as the official discourse was concerned; therefore, in that same address, Mac Giolla explained that the alternative to communism and capitalism was 'cooperativism as preached by James Connolly, that is, cooperative control of the means of production, distribution and exchange' (*UI*, November 1965).

The devolution of the wealth to the people of Ireland was not a new theme, as it was contained in the 1916 Proclamation. But the role of the state became more and more central in the analysis. As early as 1964, a manifesto stated that 'control over issues of money and credit should be taken over by the State' (*UI*, October 1964). Similarly, one of the objectives was the nationalisation of the key industries, which would lead to a system of cooperative property, financed by the nationalisation of banks and insurance companies. Sinn Féin also sought the creation of a free social security system, as well as a national fund for housing, both under state control. Undoubtedly, this presented the movement with a fundamental dilemma, as it brought to the fore one of the contradictions that would surface at the end of the decade: indeed, advocating the reinforcement of the role of the state meant an acceptance, however timid, of the legitimacy of the very state Republicans sought to destroy.

This newly found interest in socialism enabled Sinn Féin to engage with its environment in a manner that went beyond its traditional activities. The notion of economic resistance resurfaced. It had indeed been developed at the start of the century by Arthur Griffith and had constituted one of the founding stones of the Sinn Féin programme. This time, however, the objective was to organise a wide-scale mobilisation in order to oppose resistance to the existing economic system that Sinn Féin deemed rooted in British imperialism. Republicans were therefore encouraged to join trade unions and farming organisations, as well as to foster the development of cooperatives and of the Irish language.[17]

These new political and tactical objectives incited the party to seek a broader support basis beyond Republican circles, in order to put an end to the ostracism which had characterised its operation for numerous years. This approach constituted an important innovation for the movement which until then had expressed a great level of mistrust towards anything that was external to it. In July 1967, at the annual Wolfe Tone commemoration, Republicans were warned that:

> We can no longer look only within ourselves for our strength. We can no longer afford to depend on ourselves alone. We need all the commitment we can get from all the people of no matter what political persuasion in the pursuit of our national aims. Let us not exclude in a narrow and introverted fashion those whose goodwill is available if we seek it. (*UI*, July 1965)

This represented a radical change in Sinn Féin thinking. For the first time, the party acknowledged the limitations of its appeal and sought to reach out to other groups. This was not a totally new approach for the IRA, as Saor Éire, for instance, had represented an attempt to enlarge its political outlook, but this had been shunned by Sinn Féin. In 1965, however, the point was to collaborate with other political forces which were not necessarily Republican in outlook or ideology. Republicans were therefore reminded by Mac Giolla, on the occasion of the 1965 Ard Fheis, that 'we are a national organisation whose function is to strengthen the forces of resistance to British imperialism and weld them together into a powerful force dedicated to win the freedom of the Irish nation' (*UI*, January 1965).

Civil rights

The revision of theories and strategies within the Republican movement led its leaders to modify their positions and to adopt a new approach to the issue of Northern Ireland, and more specifically, to partition. Until 1962–63, the Republican response had been limited not only theoretically but strategically, as it had mainly involved demanding, by force of arms, the withdrawal of the British and the reunification of the country. Moreover, the party's situation in Northern Ireland was one of relative weakness. For some, this was due to the sectarian nature of society, which explained why social agitation was possible in the Republic but not in Northern Ireland: 'Suppression of Republicans and bigotry were complete drawbacks' (Goulding, interview, 1987) was how Cathal Goulding explained the lack of influence of his movement. Moreover, Sinn Féin had been officially banned since 1956. To counter this, it had put in place the Republican clubs, which would in turn be banned in 1967. However, what the party most lacked was a base and support.

According to Tony Heffernan, who joined Sinn Féin in 1969 and stayed with the Official leadership after the 1970 split, 'In the North, Sinn Féin and the IRA were not deliberately sectarian, but got their support from the Catholics.

If a united Ireland was to come about, the first need was for a united people'
(Heffernan, interview, 1986). Thus, if agitation campaigns were to be conducted
in the north on the model of those in the south, the first priority was to overcome
the sectarian divide of the Northern Irish proletariat. As Daithí Ó Conaill put
it, 'one thing was developed in the Six Counties between 1963 and 1969, and
that was a consciousness about how do you approach the problem, and it was
then that the thinking began to move into the area of civil rights' (Ó Conaill,
interview, 1987).

On 13 August 1966, at the end of a Wolfe Tone Society meeting, a text was
drafted and signed by Anthony Coughlan and Roy Johnston among others. 'It
advocated, among other tactics, the infiltration of Northern Ireland trade unions
as a precondition for creating a revolutionary class that would bind together the
Catholic and Protestant working class of Ulster' (Bishop and Mallie, 1987, 56).
This led to the creation of a Civil Rights movement, in February 1967, in Belfast.
Johnston insists on the fundamental role played by the Wolfe Tone Society,
which gave the initial impetus for such an organisation. 'Meetings were organ-
ized as early as 1966 through the activities of the Republican Clubs. Sinn Féin,
had, at this stage, no connection with the Civil Rights Movement' (Johnston,
interview, 1988).

NICRA (Northern Ireland Civil Rights Association) had five main objectives: 'To defend the basic freedoms of all citizens; to protect the rights of the
individual; to highlight all possible abuses of power; to demand guarantees
for freedom of speech, assembly and association; and to inform the public of
their lawful rights' (NICRA, 1978, 8). Whether the IRA was instrumental in
the creation of this body or whether it infiltrated it to its own ends is open to
question. Brian Faulkner, Prime Minister of Northern Ireland from March 1971
to March 1972, saw NICRA as a legal front for the IRA:

> The Civil Rights Association began as an ostensibly non-sectarian body seeking
> to have rectified certain alleged grievances, but with no overall political view on
> the situation [...]. It is a job for historians to decide at what stage the IRA took
> over the Civil Rights Movement, but it is quite clear, and it seemed quite clear to
> me at the time, that irrespective of the ideals of those who started it off, subversive
> elements were quick to realise the opportunity for exploitation, and to jump on
> the band wagon. (Faulkner, 1978, 47)

However, according to Republicans, the IRA was present within NICRA from
the outset, in collaboration with other groups. According to former chief of
staff Seán Cronin, 'the IRA did not just infiltrate and take over the Civil Rights
movement. It began it' (Cronin, 1980, 185). The conclusion of the Cameron

report, the aim of which was to 'Report on events leading to and since the 5 October 1968', was not as straightforward: 'While there is evidence that members of the IRA are active in the organization, there is no sign that they are in any sense dominant or in a position to control or direct policy of the Civil Rights Association' (Government of Northern Ireland, 1969, 86). Heffernan contended that 'Sinn Féin provided the organizational apparatus, the political platform. It was never the intention that it should be a Sinn Féin front. The success depended on the fact that it wouldn't be a traditional Republican organisation. There was a need to involve other people' (Heffernan, interview, 1986).

The Civil Rights movement was in line with the new thinking elaborated by the leadership, but represented a departure from traditional Republican thinking, which had reserved action to a small number of people and confined most supporters to a passive position. The most obvious schism at a theoretical level took place in the articulation of the demands, essentially founded on short-term reforms, which had never been a priority. The Civil Rights movement sought to obtain concessions and changes which were, at the start at least, reformist, and did not place at the top of its demands either the withdrawal of the British state or the reunification of the island, 'sticking rigidly to a policy of political reform and ignoring completely the issue of the State's existence' (NICRA, 1978, 13). In this manner, the IRA had, in theory, no active role to play, at least in a military capacity. A *Sunday Times* investigation concluded that 'if the IRA, instead of refusing as in the past to recognise the existence of Ulster, was now encouraging people to claim their full rights as citizens of it, only one conclusion – a correct one – could be drawn: the new-look IRA was prepared de facto to recognise partition and the separate existence of Northern Ireland' (*Sunday Times*, 1972, 49).

This was precisely what the future Provisionals were most concerned about. For them, the value of civil rights was undeniable, but only in the short term. Mac Stiofáin explained: 'We thought that if the Civil Rights Movement achieved their demands, good. We didn't think that they would but nevertheless they had a useful role, and perhaps they would awaken people on what was really going on in the North of Ireland, and also it shocked the political consciousness of people' (Mac Stiofáin, interview, 1988). His own view was mitigated by the fact that he was convinced that 'of course it was only a minor step on the road. If it helped to create a situation that we could exploit, well, then good, but from the beginning some and myself realised that there was great potential danger involved in that there could be a violent reaction from the Unionists' (Mac Stiofáin, interview, 1988).

Rising discontent

The changes in political thought in the Republican movement led to a revision of a number of strategies. The commission appointed by Goulding in 1962 to review the internal operation of the movement, which consisted, according to the IRA's Easter statement of 1965, of an 'internal examination of our movement in all its branches, a re-education of our people in the necessities of today and on an open-minded scrutiny of our present situation' (*UI*, May 1965), could only lead to the questioning of deeply rooted strategies until then taken for granted. Indeed, when the commission revealed the outcome of its investigations in 1967, some of its recommendations were bound to stir up a level of debate. The most important points of this report advocated, according to Seán Mac Stiofáin: 'the end of abstentionism; involvement in agitation, social, economic and cultural; Republicans should recognise the courts; they should apply for permits from the police, north and south, to hold parades and to distribute and sell Republican emblems; and the creation of a National Liberation Front with the Communist Party and other organisations' (Mac Stiofáin, interview, 1988).

The electoral policy of the party, which continued to be rooted in absten-tionism, started to be re-examined. The issue came to the fore during the Westminster general elections of 1964. While in 1956, the party had stressed that the electoral results, in themselves, did not count, this time 'there [could] be no doubt in the minds of Republicans everywhere that this is an important election for us' (*UI*, March 1964). Candidates were appointed in all twelve constituencies. None was elected, and Sinn Féin only secured 83,000 votes, which compared poorly with the 1956 results. However, in 1963, the Ard Fheis had introduced a clause into the party's constitution according to which, as Ó Brádaigh remembered, 'any member advocating the end of abstentionism should be expelled. There was already a clause that any anti-abstentionist shouldn't be admitted' (Ó Brádaigh, interview, 1986). This clause, representing a safeguard against reopening a Pandora's box, did not prevent the leadership from calling an extraordinary Ard Fheis in 1965 on this very issue. The anti-abstentionist position was not successful, as according to Ó Brádaigh its advocates only obtained thirteen votes, against a hundred for the defenders of abstentionism. Moreover, an article published in the Republican weekly affirmed: 'We will not enter Leinster House as a minority group, but given a majority we are prepared to take over the assembly, invite in all the elected representatives of the Irish people and proceed to legislate for all Ireland' (*UI*, March 1965). Abstentionism seemed confirmed and solidly anchored in the tactics of the party. However, the very fact that an extraordinary Ard Fheis had been held on this issue constituted a precedent and re-ignited a debate that had remained buried since 1926.

Sinn Féin was increasingly convinced that it had to fight electoral battles in order to achieve its aims. This amounted to a radical change of position, a recognition, albeit limited, of the importance of the electoral process to the very people whose support the party sought. A fundamental element of the party's reorganisation was to prepare it to 'contest 26-county elections within five years with the view to secure a majority of seats, and fill the political vacuum' (*UI*, February 1966). While the aim, to be in a position to form an alternative assembly once the majority of votes had been secured, was not in itself new, the fact that this was inscribed within the medium-term strategy of the movement was a radical innovation, as it pre-empted a redirection of energy and funds and showed a commitment to the electoral process. This was a double-edged strategy, as was shown with the general election in Northern Ireland in 1966, when Republican candidates obtained a total of 62,782 votes, down from 83,534 in 1964. However, in some instances, candidates increased their share of the vote, such as Tom Mitchell in Mid-Ulster whose score rose from 39.6 per cent in 1964 to 47.8 per cent in 1966, largely because of the absence of the NILP candidate who had secured 8.8 per cent of the vote in 1964. On the other hand, the Fermanagh-South Tyrone candidate's performance showed a sharp decline: with 19 per cent of the vote, he lost 10 per cent compared with the 1964 election, as there was a Unity candidate who obtained 29 per cent of the vote.

During the 1966 Ard Fheis, the leadership reaffirmed its loyalty towards abstentionism, stating that sitting in Leinster House was out of the question. But for those who read between the lines, Mac Giolla's speech was driven not so much by a belief in a principle as by a willingness to respect the wishes of the majority and not to rock the boat. He acknowledged the limitations of the strategy, as he believed that sitting in parliament 'might bring some temporary benefits to the organisation and even to some sections of the community'. But the leadership was not yet ready to give up the traditional policy, as this 'would gravely jeopardise the ultimate objective of establishing a sovereign independent Irish Republic' (*UI*, January 1967). For the first time since 1926, two analyses were confronted: that of pragmatism and its potential advantages, on the one hand, and that of the safeguard of principles, on the other. Even if abstentionism had prevailed that year, the days of the old electoral policy were numbered. A few months later, an editorial of the *United Irishman* warned Republicans against the fact that:

Power does not come to him who waits in the wings, no matter how strongly he feels that his general political attitude is correct or just. It is simply not enough to organise a body of workers at election times, to give one's time to the Republican Movement only. We must, if we are serious in our intent, involve ourselves with the people in every way open to us. (*UI*, July 1967)

The issue of the recognition of the state, at the heart of the abstentionist debate, underpinned the internal discussions within the party. The leadership was somehow caught between two antagonistic positions. Some, such as Tom Mitchell or Seamus Costello, according to Ó Brádaigh, called for a radical change in policy, whereas others reaffirmed their faith in traditional strategies. The internal commotion that this provoked was felt long before the issue openly became a bone of contention between the different factions within the movement. Seán Caughey, vice-president of Sinn Féin, resigned in 1965 'because the movement refused to give de facto recognition to both governments of Ireland' (Bowyer Bell, 1983, 346). The debate remained open, and the risks of a split were looming large.

In 1967, the Ard Fheis affirmed once more its adhesion to principles. But there was little doubt that the electoral strategy of the movement was bound to undergo substantial changes. In October 1968, a *United Irishman* editorial, 'Sinn Féin's dilemma', raised serious questions regarding the future of the movement. The problem, as the author saw it, was the following: in spite of the radical and successful campaigns undertaken by the party, such as that on housing,[18] its impact remained limited, insofar as the political gains benefited parties that were more solidly implanted in the political life of the country such as the Labour Party. Sinn Féin had not, it contended, succeeded in building a firm and stable basis of support: 'it is the lack of a corresponding base that is Sinn Féin's major problem'. The conclusion of the article was unequivocal: 'it remains to be seen who can ride the changes and who will be swept away by them. It will be no time for the uncertain, the disorganised or the politically half-committed' (*UI*, October 1968).

The events took an interesting turn with the by-election in Mid-Ulster in 1969. The party was divided on the approach to take. Some, such as Tom Mitchell, clearly voiced their preference for a non-abstentionist candidate. The debate, according to Bernadette Devlin, lasted for several hours at the end of which, 'when the stalemate between the abstentionist and the attendance factions was reached, one of the big guns of the party got up and said the policy was still abstentionism and anyone who worked against it should get out. Rather than risk a split, everyone fell into line' (Devlin, 1969, 160). An abstentionist candidate, Kevin Agnew, was nominated, but he subsequently withdrew his name in favour of Bernadette Devlin. On this occasion, six members of the Tyrone cumann resigned, justifying their decision in the following manner: 'We believe that the abstentionist policy bears no relevance to conditions in 1969 ... An abstentionist candidate ensures the return of the Unionist nominee. This would be a disaster for the Civil Rights Movement' (Bowyer Bell, 1983, 359).

The political process and its new orientations touched on a point that was perhaps even more sensitive than abstentionism within the movement: the role of armed struggle. Indeed, as the transformations in progress followed the upheaval generated by the Border Campaign, a questioning of the military strategy seemed inevitable. Once the failure of 1962 had been more or less accepted and digested by the movement, the question of the future of the IRA was bound to be raised. The divergences that had surfaced related, partly at least, to the potential of the IRA and its capacity. Joe Cahill was convinced that 'the IRA was fairly strong after the campaign' (Cahill, interview, 1987). But this did not square with the assessment of the leadership, which questioned armed struggle as it had been thought of until then. For Tony Heffernan, 'the traditional model of the Republican Movement was sporadic military campaigns, Sinn Féin being the propagandist and political wing. This was an inadequate response' (Heffernan, interview, 1986).

The leadership of the IRA, and more particularly Goulding, were still guarded in their discourse about the approach that would be taken regarding armed action. In August 1965, in a speech delivered in Drogheda, he stated that 'there will be a fight, there must be a fight. It will have to be a fight on many fronts. The battle on the economic front is second only in importance to the battle on the military front' (*UI*, September 1965). This rhetoric was undoubtedly intended to reassure the most disgruntled body of Republicans, and to show that there was no intention of sidelining armed struggle.

It would seem that the theoretical debates eclipsed part of its rank and file. Goulding believed that launching a military campaign was out of the question as long as the political ground had not been prepared. During his 1967 Bodenstown speech, he stated: 'In recognising that we have to fight for what we want, it is essential that the physical force phase be demanded and supported by the people' (*UI*, July 1967). The days when the IRA embarked on a military campaign with, as sole support, Sinn Féin, and as sole rhetoric, the legitimacy of the cause, were over.

The leadership of the Republican movement had not entirely abandoned the armed struggle, contrary to the accusation the Provisionals levied against them. Nevertheless, the strategy put forward certainly represented a departure from what the IRA had been accustomed to. For the leadership, the traditional manner in which the IRA operated was elitist and went against what they considered was the role of an army of liberation. 'To be victorious a struggle for freedom must be a struggle of the people. The role of the IRA is to assist the people in what is THEIR liberation struggle' stated a pamphlet published by the Officials in the aftermath of the split. This was no longer the case, as 'the IRA had become remote from the people. The people respected the stance which they were taking and indeed cheered them on from the sidelines. But they were spectators and not participants in the Republican struggle against British imperialism' (Official IRA, n.d., 1).

For the Irish Communist Party, the Republican leadership had not sidelined the army, but 'saw its role as defending the gains achieved in the political struggle and in an extreme situation as a role of defence' (ICP, interview, 1987). Priority was given to the political struggle, and military action was to be considered with caution, so as not to thwart the progress of the party. Moreover, whatever influence Johnston's theories actually had on the leadership, probably exaggerated by the dissident members of the movement, the very fact that they were voiced and listened to sufficed to alarm the most militarist. Johnston believed that 'there was no point in the armed struggle, which was an anachronism and counter-productive'. He went even further: 'as long as the IRA was there, no left-wing movement was possible' (Johnston, interview, 1988).

To break away from its isolation, the commission set up in 1962 by the leadership of the IRA considered the creation of a National Liberation Front, which according to Johnston consisted in forming a 'front similar to that in Vietnam, to include communists, Republicans, separatists, etc.' or in Johnston's analysis, 'an alliance between urban Socialists and rural radicals' (Johnston, interview, 1988). Several meetings were reported to have taken place, including with the Communist Party, as part of 'a particular strategy for a particular time' (Heffernan, interview, 1986). This alliance, however, never materialised, mainly according to the Communist Party because of the efforts of the Republican leadership to preserve unity within its own ranks: 'There was a strong anti-communist stand. They were afraid to lose support among the Catholic population of the North' (Communist Party of Ireland, interview, 1987). It is certain that such a project was far from generating unanimity in Republican ranks. 'We knew that the leadership would do everything possible to secure a majority for their proposals to reduce the IRA to a cog in a Marxist political machine', recalled Seán Mac Stiofáin (Mac Stiofáin, interview, 1988). Heffernan's explanation is more directly related to the events in Northern Ireland: 'It could have been possible in the South; it was out

of the question in the North. But the political situation in the South was inhib-
ited by that of the North' (Heffernan, interview, 1986). However, the opponents
to such a strategy held a different view. Joe Cahill pointed out that while the
struggle for civil rights was taking place in the north, the strategy was being
conceived in the south. The main modus operandi of the Civil Rights movement
had initially been constructed around peaceful demonstrations, but the situation threatened to escalate into an open conflict. For him, the political analysis
failed to take into account the priorities of the circumstances on the ground.
This pointed to an interesting dichotomy; that of a party organised throughout
two different jurisdictions with divergent needs and political cultures.

Moreover, the new political priorities needed energy and financial means,
and their implementations were carried out, according to some, at the expense
of the IRA. Joe Cahill spoke of a 'run-down of military strategy' (Cahill, interview, 1987). Ó Conaill was convinced that, because of the leadership's prior-
itising of political action, the IRA in 1969 'just didn't exist as such. The structure
was there, but the training had been eased off, there was no acquisition of equip-
ment' (Ó Conaill, interview, 1987). For some, the party had gone too far. Seán
Ó Brádaigh, brother of Ruairí and future Provisional Sinn Féin director of
publicity, estimated that:

> it was a healthy development, but it went off to one extreme, of getting involved in
> all kinds of agitation. Every strike that happened you had to support it, and we got
> involved in every kind of dog fight in the country and gradually we were moved
> away from any thought of using any kind of military force. That was the direction
> in which we went, and that came to a head then when the Civil Rights movement
> in the north came under attack from the B Specials, the RUC and so on, and the
> Nationalist people were left undefended in August 1969. That was the result of too
> much emphasis on the political side. (Ó Brádaigh, interview, 1988)

Thus some within the movement were convinced that the IRA should have
been on the alert, given that events could take a violent turn. The IRA, particularly in Belfast where there were Catholic enclaves in the middle of Protestant
areas, had taken on a defence role throughout the years, although, for those
who sought to transform the Republican movement, this was precisely part of
the problem. They saw the IRA as a force that played into the sectarian divide of
the region. 'The people of West Belfast saw the IRA as a Catholic defence force,
not a revolutionary force' (ICP, interview, 1987). The situation in which the
IRA found itself in 1969 was critical: lack of weapons, lack of trained personnel
and lack of structures. 'The IRA was non-existent except for a few groups here
and there', concluded Mac Stiofáin (Mac Stiofáin, interview, 1988), blaming the

leadership for its lack of foresight and considering its analysis of the Northern Irish situation totally inadequate. Joe Cahill agreed with this view: 'Us who lived in the North realised that in the political field you can only go so far and force should be used'. The priority of the movement should have been, in his view, the creation of a strong, well-equipped IRA: 'in the South they thought they had more time, and they wouldn't take the advice of the people on the ground. Sinn Féin had no great role to play in the North; the people were looking for means of survival' (Cahill, interview, 1987).

The issue of armed struggle crystallised many discontents. This found expression in a speech delivered by Belfast IRA activist Jimmy Drumm, in Belfast in 1969, in which he criticised what he considered a betrayal of Republican strategies, with the dangers that this presented for the future of the movement. In doing this, he was probably voicing the concern of many disillusioned Republicans. The reaction of the leadership was swift and severe: Jimmy Drumm was expelled from the movement. This was an unacceptable precedent for its adversaries, one on which they would subsequently capitalise. The anecdote marked the end of a fragile consensus and showed that, from both perspectives, cohabitation between the leadership and its opponents was no longer an option. The example of Joe Cahill who had left the party as early as 1967 in disagreement with the leadership, was to be followed by many more in the last months of 1969. The division that would oppose Officials – those loyal to the leadership – and Provisionals was imminent.

Notes

1 Stephen Hayes was then chief of staff of the IRA and McCaughey was accused of having unlawfully detained him between 30 June and 2 September 1941.

2 A website is dedicated to Seán McCaughey: www.seanmccaugheyhistoricalsociety.moonfruit.com.

3 Sinn Féin still used the term 'Free State' throughout most of the twentieth century, until it was decided in the mid-1980s to drop it from its vocabulary as the party acknowledged that the majority of the people recognised the legitimacy of the Republic.

4 When Sinn Féin and the IRA split in 1969–70 the two sides became known as Officials (those who accepted the reforms proposed by the leadership) and Provisionals (those who dissented and therefore left the party and the armed organisation to create new ones).

5 One of the arguments put forward in 1951 by Edward J. Coyne, professor of moral theology, against the scheme was precisely that the 'distinction between Church and State (though not their separation) is the best guarantee that there will be no clash between the two "true and perfect societies"' (Coyne [1951] 1998, 402).

6 The debate on NATO was triggered later, with the prospect of Ireland's membership of the

EEC, which was discussed in the early 1960s. This was an occasion for the leaders to assert their position on the North Atlantic Pact. Indeed, Lemass stated in the Dáil, in 1962, that 'The view of the Government in that regard has been made clear. We think the existence of NATO is necessary for the preservation of peace and for the defence of the countries of Western Europe, including this country. Although we are not members of NATO, we are in full agreement with its aims' (*Dáil Debates*, 14 February 1962, quoted in Keogh, 1997).

7 This manifesto, together with an important volume of literature concerning the 1955–62 period, is available on the Border Campaign website, laochrauladh.blogspot.fr, which contains reproductions of articles, manifestos and newspaper clippings, as well as the *Handbook for Volunteers of the Irish Republican Army: Notes on Guerrilla Warfare*, issued by General Headquarters but written by Seán Cronin in 1956. The blog also contains a number of links to archival video material on the Border Campaign and the main events throughout the 1950s and early 1960s.

8 The Northern Ireland Labour Party fought the election in the four Belfast constituencies.

9 Ó Conaill was IRA director of operations in 1958 after his escape from the Curragh internment camp with Ó Brádaigh that same year, before being captured by the RUC in 1959. He later became director of publicity for the Provisional IRA and was a prominent leader of Provisional Sinn Féin.

10 For more information on this group, see laochrauladh.blogspot.fr.

11 With the exception of the 1936 Wexford and Galway by-election in which Sinn Féin took part alongside Cumann Poblachta na hÉireann.

12 Leinster House is the seat of the national parliament (Houses of the Oireachtas).

13 For a detailed account of the operation and a portrait of Seán South, see Flynn, 2007, 36–41.

14 Escapes from prison were a problem for the IRA's Army Council. If successful, they could provide a valuable propaganda tool, but could be equally counter-productive in case of failure. Therefore they were carefully prepared and could only take place with prior authorisation from the headquarters. On 2 December 1958, twenty-seven men escaped from the Curragh internment camp, of whom thirteen were successful. This was a clear breach of discipline and was sanctionable by immediate suspension. However, all men involved subsequently applied for readmission, which was granted in all cases as this was deemed 'in the best interests of the Republican Movement' (IRA internal memo, 04/04/59, O'Mahony Papers, MS 44,084 /2).

15 According to Hanley and Millar, the number of IRA operations had declined dramatically, from 341 in 1957 to 27 in 1959 (Hanley and Millar, 2009, 17).

16 Opération des Nations Unies au Congo.

17 The Wolfe Tone Society was actively promoting a 'juncture of the forces of the labour and Republican movements' as 'such an alliance holds the seeds of the future' (*Tuarisc* (newsletter of the Wolfe Tone Society), January–February 1966, O'Mahony Papers, MS 44,090/2).

18 The Wolfe Tone Society had prioritised housing in the proposals put forward for the 1966 local election. Among its demands were cheaper housing loans, security of tenure for rented accommodation, end to eviction on arrival of first child, housing and building cooperatives, compulsory acquisition of central city land (*Tuarisc*, June 1966, O'Mahony Papers, MS 44,090 /2).

Conclusion

Official Sinn Féin was right too early. Provisional Sinn Féin is right too late. Ruairí
Ó Brádaigh will never be right. (Cathal Goulding, interview, 1988)

When Seán Mac Stiofáin and his supporters walked out of the IRA convention in 1969 and formed the Provisional Army Council, the path that Sinn Féin
would follow seemed already mapped out: the divisions that were tearing the
army apart were inevitably reflected within the party. At the Ard Fheis, on 11
January 1970, the delegates who opposed the end of abstentionism left the hall
and created the Caretaker Executive in the Intercontinental Hotel in Dublin,
thereby putting an end to the fourth Sinn Féin, which had beaten all records
of longevity as it had not experienced any major split since 1926. However,
contrary to what had happened in 1922 and 1926, both factions laid claim to
the same legacy and the same identity. What this actually meant to the two
parties differed considerably, although both claimed to represent the continuity
of the movement. Therefore, two rival parties faced each other: Official Sinn
Féin, which advocated class struggle and mass mobilisation, and Provisional
Sinn Féin, which justified its existence and legitimacy arguing that it was the
true heir of the previous two Sinn Féin parties.

The fourth Sinn Féin had existed for more than forty years, even if a substantial period had been spent out of the limelight. However, whether it remained
the same party throughout those years is open to question. While the criteria
for defining continuity that were used in the Funds Case – the holding of Ard
Fheiseanna, the observance of rules and regulations, and the regular meetings
of the Standing Committee – were clearly present, the shape and outlook of the
party had considerably evolved during those years. This enabled both Officials
and Provisionals to claim some form of legacy. The Officials had abided by the
rules of the party, had put the changes of policy to the vote of the Ard Fheis and
had every reason to believe they represented the 'official' face of Republicanism.
The Provisionals took a stance which blurred principle and tactic, one that had

been so characteristic of the inter-war years. What made them the true heirs, in their own eyes, was their strict observance of principles, particularly that of abstentionism, seen as one of the major causes of the split. The manner in which the issue was raised was similar to that of the previous split. Just like in 1926, the leadership advocated that the party embrace constitutional politics, an option which was rejected in identical terms to those developed in 1926, as shown by Mac Stiofáin's assessment: 'It was the parliamentary proposal that presented the clear-cut issue for all Republicans, who had now to choose between accepting the institutions of partition or upholding the basic principle of Ireland's right to national unity' (Mac Stiofáin, interview, 1988). Abstentionism was thus deemed inherent by some to the identity of Sinn Féin, as it constituted the main link to its historical continuity. Obviously, the nature of the debate had evolved. It was the founding stone of Griffith's strategy, as part of his non-violent approach, but it was then predicated on the fact that the boycott of Westminster would be far more efficient than armed action. It was, therefore, a tactic, seen as the best means to achieve self-determination. In the Free State that emerged as a result of the Treaty, abstentionism came to embody the rejection of the new institutions and the commitment to the Second Dáil as the only legitimate parliament, contributing to further amalgamating the tactic itself and the ideal of the Republic.

Abstentionism was the means of identification of Republicans to their ideology. It became the depository of a number of aspirations, the catalyst of discontent for those who decided to remain faithful to principles and refused any attempted change. In the statement following the 1969 split, the Provisional IRA listed the reasons why they had left the movement, among which was the 'Recognition of Westminster, Stormont and Leinster House' (An Phoblacht, February 1970). The symbolic weight of this issue was underestimated by the Official leadership of both Sinn Féin and the IRA, who saw it as a pretext used by the dissidents for refusing the new approach that they advocated. On a more pragmatic level, they deemed it obsolete, and even counter-productive, as it brought no immediate result in the context of the struggle that Republicans had embraced as part of the Civil Rights movement. But Provisional Sinn Féin in 1970, just like Sinn Féin in 1926, was not particularly interested in such political gains. What it wanted was a complete overhaul of the state. Electing individuals to parliaments that it deemed illegitimate was certainly not part of its strategy.

The debate that opposed both factions of the movement also had to do with how the final objective was to be achieved, through reform or through revolution. For the then leadership, the reformist aspect of the Civil Rights movement was not seen as a problem per se.

Certainly the Civil Rights programme is a reformist one. All the more reason, therefore, for the revolutionaries to be in the lead for reforms. For it is only if the revolutionaries lead a reformist movement that there can be a guarantee that reforms will not be betrayed and that when they are gained the mass of the movement will still go forward for further progressive change. (*UI*, June 1969)

Two theories faced each other: one which sought to fight the state from within, and one which did not contemplate any transitional phase. The main departure, however, was not so much the leadership's implicit acceptance of the medium-term objective to reform the state and the consequent admission that the state was reformable; it was that the situation was analysed in terms of class struggle, not Nationalism. 'If there was a situation where the rights were the same for all, then it would be possible to unite the working class' (Johnston, interview, 1988). The revolutionary work that they contemplated consisted of creating the conditions for a social revolution, and meant the organisation of the proletariat itself. Following this logic, the introduction of reforms would pave the way for the formation of a united working class capable of carrying forward the revolution.

Consequently, the strategies of the two main factions in the movement were antagonistic. On the one hand, the leadership stated in 1969 that 'there is no salvation for the Six counties in direct rule by Westminster. Strengthening Britain's hold on the North is not the way to a free, united Ireland' (*UI*, September 1969). If the objective was to obtain reforms, and to strike a blow at the Unionist administration, direct intervention by the British government was to be avoided at all costs, as it would be far more difficult to obtain its withdrawal if it became directly involved. The Provisionals came to the opposite conclusion: 'We find absolutely incomprehensible from any Republican standpoint the campaign in favour of retaining the Stormont parliament in August, September and October last when it was in danger of being abolished altogether by the British government' (*AP*, February 1970). This view was based on two arguments: it was preferable to provoke a direct confrontation with the British government than with Stormont; and the abolition of the Northern Irish parliament would be seen as a symbolic advance, as it would embody the fall of the Unionist political monolith.

The issue of abstentionism revealed a flaw in the party's ideological and strategic make-up: that of its composite nature. The fact that the 1970 split was seen as a division between the right- and left-wing tendencies within the movement shows the extent to which ideology was vague and at times inconsistent. What is interesting, however, is that the Republican movement in general, and the IRA in particular throughout the 1930s, were viewed in the early 1960s as potential vehicles for socialism, while there was little in their political outlook that would vindicate this analysis. Indeed, Sinn Féin had been, throughout the decades that preceded the introduction of socialism in the 1960s, rather conservative in nature. The issue of socialism had never been a consensual one within the IRA either, and its attempts at setting up radical organisations in the late 1920s and early 1930s were more divisive than unifying. The question that arises therefore is why socialists such as Johnston invested Sinn Féin with the potential to carry forward a socialist revolution? Perhaps the reason was Sinn Féin's subversive nature, seen through its refusal to recognise the state and its institutions, and its support for armed struggle. But this did not make them socially progressive and inclined to adhere to more radical views. The conclusion that Ó Brádaigh came to showed just how much what defined subversion was divisive. 'If people are totally socialist you can integrate them within the present set-up. If they are nationalists and especially if they are associated with a military organisation, they could become very upsetting for the status quo' (Ó Brádaigh, 1986, interview). Therefore, to be subversive meant two different things. For the Officials, it was about socialist engagement, while the Provisionals put the focus on the revolutionary nature of armed struggle per se, which was seen as an illustration of the lack of political sophistication of the Provisionals, and their 'a-political' stance. But Mac Stiofáin strongly objected to this: 'By that stage I had spent twenty years of my life working in a political movement. How could anyone say that we were a-political? We had one political objective, an Irish Socialist Republic, and we had our own social and economic programmes. It was a propaganda lie' (Mac Stiofáin, interview, 1988).

The Officials progressively put the emphasis on socialism, adopting the sub-title 'The Workers' Party' in 1977 and dropping the name Sinn Féin altogether in 1982. From then on, although the nickname 'Provos' or 'Provisionals' stuck for some time, they were established as the only Sinn Féin party in Ireland. Its current website no longer carries a historical dimension and therefore no longer claims to be 'the oldest party in Ireland', as it did some ten years ago,[1] even if the history of the Republican movement remains a contentious issue that resurfaces regularly within Irish political life. The only Sinn Féin party which currently claims a historical legacy is Sinn Féin Poblachtach (Republican Sinn Féin), who define themselves as

> the last remaining true Republican political organisation founded in 1905. Reformed in 1986 out of the walkout of the 86 Ard-Fheis by the true Republican leadership, who saw the failure of the new Provisional leadership's decision to enter into a partitionist assembly of the 26 County Southern Free State. This one

day would lead to a larger erosion of Republican principles, to the acceptance of entering a new Stormont and an acceptance of British Partition. Republican Sinn Féin uphold the right of the Irish people to oppose continued British occupation in Ireland.[2]

Republican Sinn Féin is possibly a more likely successor to the fourth Sinn Féin, and it exhibits the same weakness as its predecessor: its incapacity to adapt to changing circumstances. The current Sinn Féin party, on the other hand, has taken on board some of the lessons from the past to ensure that its existence is not merely a question of survival but one of expansion and progress. It shares with its ancestors a certain amount of resilience, but it has managed to shed the principles which constituted the core identity of the party without disintegrating. It has successfully adjusted to very different contexts, which allows it to be at the same time in government in the north of Ireland and in the opposition in the Republic, while still claiming some unity in programme, objectives and tone. This could be attributed to its ideological flexibility.

If there is one legacy that Sinn Féin still holds from its predecessors, it is the ideal of a united Ireland, which still features strongly in its strategies and discourses and which constitutes, perhaps, the principle that has been held onto over the years, one that has survived many splits, while other cornerstones of Republicanism have shifted. It has succeeded in becoming what its predecessors never quite achieved, an all-Ireland party, the only Irish political formation working on both sides of the border. Its relentless campaigning for reunification both links it to its past and differentiates it from its colleagues in the Republic who, although they still hold reunification as an aspiration, do not make it their priority. Against all odds, whether favourable or unfavourable, Sinn Féin continues to demand the end of partition, disregarding the circumstances and the desirability of such a demand. This might be not only because it is a genuinely held conviction, but also because it is the only remaining issue that links the party to its subversive past.

Notes

1 There are two websites for Sinn Féin. One is www.sinnfein.ie and the other www.sinnfein.org. The former is mainly focused on the contemporary party, with a focus on the current policies of the party. The latter explains that 'the movement founded almost 100 years ago by Arthur Griffith ... evolved into a number of organisations which carried the name'.
2 http://rsfnational.wordpress.com.

Bibliography

Primary sources

Archival material

National Archives of Ireland (NAI)
Department of the Taoiseach
Sinn Féin Funds: control and disposal of (1941) 90/116/773
Sinn Féin Funds; disposal of (1937–42), TSCH/3/S12110 A
Sinn Féin Funds; disposal of (1942–47) TSCH/3/S12110 /B
Sinn Féin Funds; disposal of (1947) TSCH/3/S12110 /C
Sinn Féin Funds; disposal of (1948–51) TSCH/3/S12110 //D1
Sinn Féin Funds; disposal (December 1951–April 1956), TSCH/3/S12110 E
'Judgment of the Honourable Mr Justice Kingsmill Moore delivered on the 26th day of October, 1948' (NAI D/T S12100D/1)

Four Courts, Sinn Féin Funds Case

Sinn Féin Standing Committee Meetings (SC), 1921–47
Funds Case: correspondence, documents and newspaper articles, gathered in one volume, 1917–48
De Valera's and Sceilg's Witness Statements, 1948 (transcripts)

Department of Justice

Evolution of Fianna Fáil and new Sinn Féin party (1926–1933) TSCH/3/S5880
Sinn Féin: Garda reports (1934–50) JUS/8/1053

National Library of Ireland (NLI)
Sean O'Mahony Papers (1880–2005) MS Collection, MSS 44,025–MS 44,310

UCD Archives
Papers of Mary MacSwiney (1872–1942) IE UCDA P48a

Newspapers

Anglo-Celt
An Phoblacht (1925–36), Dublin
An Phoblacht (1970–), Dublin
Connacht Tribune
Dundalk Examiner
Irish Independent
Irish Press
Irish Times
Meath Chronicle
Saoirse Freedom (1927–28), Dublin
Saoirse (Irish Freedom) (1987–)
Sinn Féin (1923–25)
Sunday Independent
United Irishman (1948–70), Dublin
Wolfe Tone Weekly (1937–39)

Political pamphlets (in chronological order)

Griffith, Arthur (1904), *The Resurrection of Hungary* (Dublin: James Duffy and Co.)
Sinn Féin (1905), *Constitution* (Dublin: Sinn Féin)
—— (1918), *Look at the Map – God Has Made Ireland One* (Dublin)
—— (1918), *The Policy of Abstentionism* (Dublin: Sinn Féin)
Ginnell, Laurence (1919?), *The Irish Republic, Why? Official Statement Prepared for Submission to the Peace Conference* (New York: Friends of Irish Freedom)
Sinn Féin (1921), *What the Treaty Means* (Dublin: SF Series)
Griffith, Arthur (1922), *Arguments for the Treaty* (Dublin: Martin Lester Ltd)
Collins, Michael (1922), *Free Treaty of Chaos?* (Dublin)
Sinn Féin Reorganising Committee (1923) (Dublin: Sinn Féin)
O'Kelly, John J. (1928), *Presidential Address* (Dublin)
—— (1930), *The Sinn Féin Outlook* (Dublin: Sinn Féin Standing Committee)
—— (1931), *The Republic of Ireland Vindicated* (Dublin: Fodhla Pr. Co.)
MacSwiney, Mary (1932), *The Republic of Ireland* (Cork: Leeless Printing Works)
Óglaigh na hÉireann (1933a), *Governmental Policy and Constitution of Óglaigh na h-Éireann* (Dublin: Republican Press Ltd)
—— (1933b), *Manifesto to the Irish People* (issued by the General Convention of Óglaigh na hÉireann)
O'Flanagan, Michael (1934), *The Strength of Sinn Féin* (Dublin: Standing Committee)
O'Kelly, John J. (1936), *The Republican Outlook* (Dublin: Sinn Féin Standing Committee)
Plunkett, Count Noble George (1936), *Electoral Manifesto* (Dublin: published by the candidate)Córas na Poblachta (1940), *The Republican Plan* (Dublin: Central Committee)

Óglaigh na hÉireann (1941), Special communiqué issued by the Army Council, http://catalogue.nli.ie/Record/vtls000123206 (accessed 25 November 2014)

O'Kelly, John J. (1942), *Graveside Oration*, 10 August, http://catalogue.nli.ie/Record/vtls000255031 (accessed 25 November 2014)

RPRA (Republican Prisoners' Release Association) (1946), *Seán McCaughey – The Truth* (Dublin)

Buckley, Margaret (1950), *Presidential Address at Annual Ard Fheis* (Dublin: Sinn Féin)

Sinn Féin (195?), *Ireland, Partition and the Atlantic Pact* (Dublin: Sinn Féin)

IRA Army Council (1954), *Irish Resistance to British Aggression* (Dublin: Marian Printing Ltd)

Sinn Féin (1954), *National Unity and Independence Programme* (Dublin: Sinn Féin)

—— (195?), *Social and Economic Programme* (Dublin: Sinn Féin)

—— (1955), *Election Manifesto*, laochrauladh.blogspot.fr/2013/10/sinn-fein-election-manifesto-1955.html (accessed 25 November 2014)

Buckley, Margaret (1956), *Sinn Féin 1905–1956: A Proud History* (Dublin: Sinn Féin Publications)

Sinn Féin (1956), *Alternative to Stormont Elections* (Dublin)

IRA General Headquarters (1956), *Handbook for Volunteers of the Irish Republican Army: Notes on Guerrilla Warfare*, www.scribd.com/doc/239074319/IRA-Volunteers-Handbook-Notes-on-Guerrilla-Warfare#download (accessed 25 November 2014)

Sinn Féin (1957), *Republican Policy* (Dublin: Publicity Committee)

—— (1958), *British Troops Must Go!* (Dublin)

—— (1961), *Instructions to Canvassers, Speakers and Organisers* (Dublin)

—— (1961), *What It Is All About* (Dublin)

—— (1963), *Ireland: Nation or Province? Ireland and the Common Market* (Dublin)

—— (1964), *Who Owns the Land?* (Dublin: Sinn Féin)

—— (1965), *Are You Satisfied?* (Dublin)

—— (1968), *Ireland Today: Some Questions on the Way Forward* (Dublin: Education Department)

NICRA (1978), *We Shall Oversome* (Belfast: Northern Ireland Civil Rights Association)

Official IRA (n.d.), *In the 70s: The IRA Speaks* (Dublin: Repsol Pamphlet)

Interviews

Cahill, Joe (Dublin, April 1987)

Communist Party of Ireland (spokesperson) (Dublin, April 1987)

Goulding, Cathal (Dublin, April 1987)

Heffernan, Tony (Dublin, January 1986)

Johnston, Roy (Dublin, July 1988)

Mac Stiofáin, Seán (Dublin, July 1988)
Ó Brádaigh, Ruairí (Roscommon, January 1986)
Ó Brádaigh, Seán (Dublin, July 1988)
Ó Conaill, Daithí (Dublin, April 1987)

Websites (all accessed 25 November 2014)

Border Campaign: laochrauladh.blogspot.fr
Bunreacht na hÉireann (1937): www.constitution.ie/Documents/Bhunreacht_na_ hEireann_web.pdf
Dáil Debates: http://debates.oireachtas.ie/dail
Election literature: http://irishelectionliterature.wordpress.com
Election results: ElectionsIreland.org
Irish Statute Book: www.irishstatutebook.ie
Irish Times digital archives (limited access): search.proquest.com
Irish newspapers archive (limited access): archive.irishnewsarchive.com
National Archives, Anglo-Irish Treaty: http://treaty.nationalarchives.ie/document-gallery/anglo-irish-treaty-6-december-1921/
National Graves Association: www.nga.ie/history.php
Republican Sinn Féin: http://rsfnational.wordpress.com
Seanad Debates: http://debates.oireachtas.ie/seanad
Seán McCaughey website: www.seanmccaugheyhistoricalsociety.moonfruit.com
Sinn Féin: www.sinnfein.ie www.sinnfein.org
Supreme Court Judgement Buckley vs Att. Gen., 1947: www.supremecourt.ie/ supremecourt/sclibrary3.nsf/pagecurrent/9FA0AA8E8D261FC48025765C00 42F6B3?opendocument&l=en

Secondary sources

Barton, Brian (1995), *Northern Ireland in the Second World War* (Belfast: Ulster Historical Foundation)
Bishop, Patrick and Mallie, Eamonn (1987), *The Provisional IRA* (London: Heine-mann)
Bowman, John (1982), *De Valera and the Ulster Question* (Oxford: Oxford University Press)
Bowyer Bell, John (1983), *The Secret Army: The IRA, 1916–1979* (Dublin: Academy Press)
Boyce, D. George (1995, 3rd edn), *Nationalism in Ireland* (London: Routledge)
Brown, Terence (2004), *Ireland: A Social and Cultural History, 1922–2002* (London: Harper Perennial)
Chubb, Basil (1992, 3rd edn), *The Government and Politics of Ireland* (London: Longman)

Coleman, Marie (2013), 'Military service pensions for veterans of the Irish Revolution, 1916–1923', *War in History*, 20 (2), pp. 201–21.

Colum, Padraig (1959), *Arthur Griffith* (Dublin: Browne and Nolan)

Coogan, T. P. (1966), *Ireland since the Rising* (London: Pall Mall Press)

—— (1995), *The IRA* (London: Harper Collins)

Coquelin, Olivier (2005), 'Politics in the Irish Free State: the legacy of a conservative revolution', *European Legacy*, 10 (1), pp. 29–39.

Corcoran, Donal P. (2013), *Freedom to Achieve Freedom: The Irish Free State 1922–1932* (Dublin: Gill and Macmillan)

Coughlan, Anthony J. (1977), *Austin Stack: Portrait of a Separatist* (Dublin: Kingdom Books)

Coyne, Edward J. ([1951] 1998), 'The Mother and Child Scheme', *Studies, An Irish Quarterly Review*, 87 (348), Winter, pp. 402–5.

Craig, Tony (2010), 'Sabotage! The origins, development and impact of the IRA's infrastructural bombing campaigns 1939–1997', *Intelligence and National Security*, 25 (3), pp. 309–26

Cronin, Mike (1995), 'The Blueshirt movement, 1932–5: Ireland's fascists', *Journal of Contemporary History*, 30 (2), pp. 311–32.

—— (1997), *The Blueshirts and Irish Politics* (Dublin and Portland, OR: Four Courts Press)

Cronin, Seán (1972), *The McGarrity Papers* (Tralee, Anvil Books Ltd)

—— (1980), *Irish Nationalism* (Dublin: Academy Press)

Davis, Richard P. (1974), *Arthur Griffith and Non-violent Sinn Féin* (Dublin: Anvil Books)

Devlin, Bernadette (1969), *The Price of My Soul* (London: Pan Books)

Dolan, Anne (2006), *Commemorating the Irish Civil War: History and Memory, 1923–2000* (New York: Cambridge)

Douglas, R. M. (2006), 'The Pro-Axis Underground in Ireland, 1939–1942', *The Historical Journal*, 49 (4), pp. 1155–83.

—— (2009), *Architects of the Resurrection: Ailtirí na hAisérghe and the Fascist 'New Order' in Ireland* (Manchester: Manchester University Press)

Dunphy, Richard (1995), *The Making of Fianna Fáil Power in Ireland, 1923–1948* (Dublin, Clarendon Press)

English, Richard (1994), *Radicals and the Republic: Socialist Republicanism in the Irish Free State, 1925–1937* (Oxford: Clarendon Press)

—— (2004), *Armed Struggle: The History of the IRA* (London: Pan Books)

—— (2007), *Irish Freedom: The History of Nationalism in Ireland* (London: Pan Books)

Fallon, C. (1986), *Soul of Fire: A Biography of Mary MacSwiney* (Cork: Mercier Press)

Fanning, Bryan (2012), *An Irish Century: Studies, 1912–2012* (Dublin: University College Press)

Fanning, Ronan (1983a), *Independent Ireland* (Dublin: Helicon)

—— (1983b), '"The Rule of Order": Éamon de Valera and the IRA, 1923–40', in Murphy, John A. and O'Carroll, John P. (eds), *De Valera and His Times* (Cork: Cork University Press)

Farrell, Brian (1971), *The Founding of Dáil Éireann: Parliament and Nation-Building* (Dublin, Gill and Macmillan)

Faulkner, Brian (1978), *Memoirs of a Statesman* (London: Weidenfeld and Nicolson)

Feeney, Brian (2002), *Sinn Féin: A Hundred Turbulent Years* (Dublin: O'Brien Press)

Feldman, Matthew, Turda, Marius and Georgescu, Tudor (eds) (2008), *Clerical Fascism in Interwar Europe (Totalitarianism Movements and Political Religions)* (London, Routledge)

Ferriter, Diarmaid (2005), *The Transformation of Ireland, 1900–2000* (London: Profile Books)

Fitzpatrick, David (2001), 'Commemoration in the Irish Free State: a chronicle of embarrassment', in McBride, Ian (ed.), *History and Memory in Modern Ireland* (Cambridge: Cambridge University Press), pp. 184–203

Flynn, Barry (2009), *Soldiers of Folly: The IRA Border Campaign 1956–1962* (Cork: The Collins Press)

Flynn, Kevin Haddick (2007), 'Seán South of Garryowen', *History Ireland*, 15 (1), pp. 36–41.

Foxton, David (2008), *Revolutionary Lawyers: Sinn Féin and Crown Courts in Ireland and Britain, 1916–1923* (Dublin: Four Courts Press)

French, Brigittine (2013), 'Ethnography and postconflict violence in the Irish Free State', *American Anthropologist*, 115 (2), pp. 160–73.

Garvin, Tom (1981), *The Evolution of Irish Nationalist Politics* (Dublin: Gill and Macmillan)

—— (1996), *1922: The Birth of Irish Democracy* (Dublin: Gill and Macmillan)

—— (2005), *Nationalist Revolutionaries in Ireland, 1858–1928* (Dublin: Gill and Macmillan)

Gaughan, Anthony (1977), *Austin Stack: Portrait of a Separatist* (Dublin: Kingdom Books)

Giblin, Thomas, Kennedy, Kieran and McHugh, Deirdre (1988), *The Economic Development of Ireland in the Twentieth Century* (London: Routledge)

Girvin, Brian (1989), *Between the Two Worlds: Politics and Economy in Independent Ireland* (Dublin: Gill and Macmillan).

—— (2006), *The Emergency: Neutral Ireland 1939–45* (London: Macmillan)

Government of Northern Ireland (1969), *Disturbances in Northern Ireland* (Cameron Report) (Belfast: HMSO)

Grant, Adrian (2012), *Irish Socialist Republicanism, 1909–36* (Dublin: Four Courts Press)

Hanley, Brian (2002), *The IRA, 1926–1936* (Dublin: Four Courts Press)

——(2005) '"O Here to Adolph Hitler"? ... The IRA and the Nazis', *History Ireland*, 3 (13), pp. 31–53.

Hanley, Brian and Millar, Scott (2009), *The Lost Revolution: The Story of the Official IRA and the Workers' Party* (Dublin: Penguin Ireland)

Hogan, Gerard (1997), 'The Sinn Féin Funds judgement fifty years on', *Bar Review*, 2 (9), pp. 375–81.

Horgan, John (1998), 'Arms dump and the IRA, 1923–1932', *History Today*, 48 (2), pp. 11–17.

Joye, Labhras and Malone, Brenda (2006), 'The Roll of Honour of 1916', *History Ireland*, 2 (14), pp. 10–11.

Keane, Ronan (2004), 'Judges as lawmakers: the Irish experience', *Judicial Studies Institute Journal*, 4 (2), www.jsijournal.ie/html/volumes_4_2.htm (accessed 25 November 2014)

Kearney, Hugh F. (2007), *Ireland: Contested Ideas of Nationalism and History* (Cork: Cork University Press)

Kennedy, Michael (2000), *Division and Consensus: The Politics of Cross-border Relations in Ireland* (Dublin: Institute for Public Administration)

——(2011), 'Plato's cave'? Ireland's wartime neutrality reassessed', *History Ireland*, 19 (1), pp. 46–8.

Kennedy, Robert E. (1973), *The Irish, Emigration, Marriage and Fertility* (Berkeley: University of California Press)

Keogh, Dermot (1997), 'The diplomacy of "dignified calm": an analysis of Ireland's application for membership of the EEC, 1961–1963', www.ucc.ie/chronicon/keoghfra.htm (accessed 25 November 2014)

——(2005), *Twentieth-century Ireland: Revolution and State Building* (Dublin: Gill and Macmillan)

Keogh, D. and Haltzel, M. (eds) (1993), *Northern Ireland and the Politics of Reconciliation* (Cambridge and New York: Cambridge University Press)

Kirby, Peadar (2010), 'Civil society, social movements and the Irish state', *Irish Journal of Sociology*, 18 (2), pp. 1–21.

Kissane, Bill (2007), 'Eamon de Valera and the survival of democracy in inter-war Ireland', *Journal of Contemporary History*, 42 (2), pp. 213–26.

Knirck, Jason (2014), *Afterimage of the Revolution: Cumann na nGaedheal and Irish Politics, 1922–1932* (Madison: University of Wisconsin Press)

Laffan, Michael (1999), *The Resurrection of Ireland: The Sinn Féin Party, 1916–1923* (Cambridge: Cambridge University Press)

Lee, Joseph (1989), *Ireland, 1912–1985: Politics and Society* (Cambridge and New

York: Cambridge University Press)

Lyons, F. S. L. (1983), *Ireland since the Famine* (London: Fontana)

Lysaght, D. R. O'Connor (1993), *The Communists and the Irish Revolution* (Dublin: LiterÉire)

Macardle, Dorothy (1951) *The Irish Republic: A Documented Chronicle of the Anglo-Irish Conflict and the Partitioning of Ireland, with a Detailed Account of the Period 1916–1923* (Dublin: Irish Press Ltd)

Manning, Maurice (1971), *The Blueshirts* (Dublin: Gill and Macmillan)

Mansergh, Nicholas (1991), *The Unresolved Question: The Anglo-Irish Settlement and its Undoing, 1912–1972* (New Haven and London: Yale University Press)

McBride, Ian (2011), 'The shadow of the gunman: Irish historians and the IRA', *Journal of Contemporary History*, 46 (3), pp. 686–710.

McCarthy, Cal (2007), *Cumann na mBan and the Irish Revolution* (Cork: The Collins Press)

McCarthy, John Patrick (2006), *Ireland: A Reference Guide from the Renaissance to the Present* (New York: Facts on File)

McDermott, Eithne (1998), *Clann na Poblachta* (Cork: Cork University Press)

McGarry, Fearghal (1999), 'General O'Duffy, the National Corporate Party and the Irish Brigade', in Augusteijn, Joost (ed.), *Ireland in the 1930s: New Perspectives* (Dublin: Four Courts Press), pp. 117–42.

McInerney, Michael (1974), *Peadar O'Donnell, Irish Social Rebel* (Dublin: O'Brien Press)

McKee, Éamonn (1986), 'Church–state relations and the development of Irish health policy: the Mother-and-Child Scheme, 1944–53', *Irish Historical Studies*, 25 (98), pp. 159–94.

McMahon, Paul (2008), *British Spies and Irish Rebels: British Intelligence and Ireland, 1916–1945* (Rochester, NY: Boydell Press)

Mitchell, Arthur (1993), *Revolutionary Government in Ireland: Dáil Éireann, 1919–22* (Dublin: Gill and Macmillan)

Murphy, Brian P. (2005), *The Catholic Bulletin and Republican Ireland, 1898–1926: With Special Reference to J. J. O'Kelly ('Sceilg')* (Belfast: Athol Books)

Nolan, Brian (1995), *Ireland and the Minimum Income Guarantee* (Dublin: Combat Poverty Agency)

Nora, Pierre (1997), *Les Lieux de mémoire* (Paris: Gallimard)

Ó Beacháin, Donnacha (2003), 'From revolutionaries to politicians: deradicalization and the Irish experience', *Radical History Review*, 85, pp. 114–23.

—— (2009), 'Was Sinn Féin dying? A quantitative post-mortem of the party's decline and the emergence of Fianna Fáil', *Irish Political Studies*, 24 (3), pp. 385–98.

—— (2010a), *Destiny of the Soldiers: Fianna Fáil, Irish Republicanism and the IRA, 1926–1973* (Dublin: Gill and Macmillan)

—— (2010b), '"Slightly constitutional" politics: Fianna Fáil's tortuous entry to the Irish parliament, 1926–1927', *Parliamentary Politics*, 29 (3), pp. 376–94.

O'Brien, Conor Cruise (1972), *States of Ireland* (London: Hutchinson)

O'Brien, Marc (2001), *De Valera, Fianna Fáil and the Irish Press* (Dublin: Irish Academic Press)

Ó Broin, Eoin (2009), *Sinn Féin and the Politics of Left Republicanism* (London: Pluto Press)

O'Connor, Emmet (2004), *Reds and the Green: Ireland, Russia, and the Communist International, 1919–43* (Dublin: University College Dublin Press)

O'Donoghue, David (2011), 'New evidence on IRA/Nazi links', *History Ireland*, 19 (2), pp. 36–9.

Ó Drisceoil, Donal (2001), *Peadar O'Donnell* (Cork: Cork University Press)

—— (2006), 'Neither friend nor foe? Irish neutrality in the Second World War', *Contemporary European History*, 15 (2), pp. 245– 53.

—— (2011), 'When Dev defaulted: the land annuities dispute, 1926–38', *History Ireland*, 19 (3), May/June, pp. 42–5.

Ó Gráda, Cormac (1997), *A Rocky Road: The Irish Economy since the 1920s* (Manchester: Manchester University Press)

O'Halpin, Eunan (1999), *Defending Ireland: The Irish State and its Enemies since 1922* (Oxford: Oxford University Press)

O'Hegarty, P. S. (1924), *The Victory of Sinn Féin: How It Won It and How It Used It* (Dublin: Talbot Press)

Ó hÓgartaigh, Margaret (2006), *Kathleen Lynn: Patriot, Irishwoman, Doctor* (Dublin: Irish Academic Press)

Ó Longaigh, Seosamh (2006), *Emergency Law in Ireland 1922–1948* (Dublin: Four Courts Press)

O'Leary, Cornelius (1979), *Irish Elections 1918–1977* (Dublin: Gill and Macmillan)

O'Neill, Timothy M. (2008), 'Handing away the trump card? Peadar O'Donnell, Fianna Fáil and the non-payment of the Land Annuities Campaign', *New Hibernia Review*, 12 (1), pp. 19–40.

Patterson, Henry (2007), *Ireland since 1939: The Persistence of Conflict* (Dublin: Penguin Books)

Prager, Jeffrey (1986), *Building Democracy in Ireland: Political Order and Cultural Integration in a Newly Independent Nation* (Cambridge: Cambridge University Press)

Pyne, Peter (1969), 'The third Sinn Féin Party, 1923–1926', *The Economic and Social Review*, 1 (2), pp. 229–57.

Rafter, Kevin (1995), *The Clann: The Story of Clann na Poblachta* (Cork: Mercier)

—— (2005), *Sinn Féin 1905–2005: In the Shadow of Gunmen* (Dublin: Gill and Macmillan)

Rankin, K. J. (2006), 'The provenance and dissolution of the Irish Boundary

Commission', IBIS Working Papers, 79, University College Dublin, Institute for British-Irish Studies, www.ucd.ie/ibis/filestore/wp2006/79/79_kr.pdf (accessed 25 November 2014)

Regan, John (2001), *The Irish Counter-revolution, 1921–1936: Treatyite Politics and Settlement in Independent Ireland* (Dublin: Gill and Macmillan)

—— (2013), *Myth and the Irish State* (Salins: Irish Academic Press)

Renan, Ernest (1882), *What is a Nation?*, full text available at: http://ucparis.fr/files/9313/6549/9943/What_is_a_Nation.pdf (last accessed 12 November 2014)

RTÉ (1973), *The Staunchest Priest*, documentary on Fr Michael O'Flanagan, www.rte.ie/radio1/doconone/2011/0719/646834-documentary-podcast-father-michael-oflanagan-roscommon-republican-priest-story/ (last accessed 4 November 2014)

Rumpf, Erhard and Hepburn, Anthony C. (1977), *Nationalism and Socialism in Twentieth-century Ireland* (Liverpool: Liverpool University Press)

Ryan, Mark (1994), *War and Peace in Ireland: Britain and Sinn Féin in the New World Order* (London: Pluto Press)

Sloan, Geoffrey R. (1997), *The Geopolitics of Anglo-Irish Relations in the Twentieth Century* (London and Washington: Leicester University Press)

Staunton, Enda (1996), 'The Boundary Commission debacle 1925: aftermath and implications', *History Ireland*, 4 (2), pp. 42–5.

Treacy, Matt (2012), *The Communist Party of Ireland 1921–2011, vol. 1: 1921–69* (Dublin: Brocaire Books)

—— (2014), *The IRA 1956–1969: Rethinking the Republic* (Manchester: Manchester University Press)

Turpin, John (2007), 'Monumental commemoration of the fallen in Ireland, North and South, 1920–60', *New Hibernia Review*, 11 (4), pp. 107–19

Valiulis, Mariann Gialanella (1983), 'The 'Army Mutiny' of 1924 and the assertion of civilian authority in independent Ireland', *Irish Historical Studies*, 23 (92), pp. 354–66.

—— (1985), *Almost a Rebellion: The Irish Army Mutiny of 1924* (Cork: Tower)

—— (1992), *Portrait of a Revolutionary: General Richard Mulcahy and the Founding of the Irish Free State* (Dublin: Irish Academic Press)

Walsh, Pat (1994), *Irish Republicanism and Socialism: The Politics of the Republican Movement 1905 to 1994* (Belfast: Athol Books)

Ward, Alan J. (1993), 'A constitutional background to the Northern Ireland crisis', in Keogh, D. and Haltzel, M. (eds), *Northern Ireland and the Politics of Reconciliation* (Cambridge and New York: Cambridge University Press), pp. 39–40.

Younger, Carlton (1981), *Arthur Griffith* (Dublin: Gill and Macmillan)

Index